Everyday American English Dictionary

Editor
Richard A. Spears

Associate Editor
Linda Schinke-Llano

Consulting Editor
Betty Kirkpatrick

NTC Publishing Group
Lincolnwood, Illinois USA

Richard A. Spears, Ph. D. Specialist in lexicography; English language structure; phonetics; language standardization and codification; English as a second language; American culture.

Linda Schinke-Llano, Ph.D. Specialist in English as a second language, bilingual education, and second language acquisition.

Betty Kirkpatrick, M.A. Specialist in lexicography and English language reference books both for native speakers of English and for learners of English as a second language.

1997 Printing

Copyright © 1984 by NTC Publishing Group,
4255 West Touhy Avenue, Lincolnwood (Chicago), Illinois 60646-1975 U.S.A.
All rights reserved. No part of this book may be reproduced, stored
in a retrieval system, or transmitted in any form or by any means,
electronic, mechanical, photocopying, recording or otherwise,
without the prior permission of NTC Publishing Group.
Manufactured in the United States of America.
This work is partially based on the Chambers First
Learners' Dictionary published by W & R Chambers Ltd.

7 8 9 0 QB 19 18 17 16 15 14 13 12

About This Dictionary

English opens up the world to those who can speak and write it well. The *Everyday American English Dictionary* has been prepared for those who are learning the English language and who are making an effort to speak and write it well.

Dr. Richard A. Spears and Dr. Linda Schinke-Llano have brought together 5,500 words basic to the needs of those who are learning English. The entries in the dictionary deal with basic, everyday subjects of life such as food, clothing, sports, government, and school. All have been selected on the basis of word-frequency studies, as well as school and community "survival" word lists.

The *Everyday American English Dictionary* is a simplified dictionary. Its definitions are written in simple, controlled language, and many of the complicated features of full-size dictionaries have been omitted. Users of this reference will learn the basic methods of finding dictionary information with ease and confidence.

The *Everyday American English Dictionary* is the ideal dictionary for the student wishing to learn basic English and basic dictionary use at the same time. Used either as an educational tool or a portable dictionary, the *Everyday American English Dictionary* will serve as a valuable reference for students of English of all ages.

To The User

This dictionary is for people who are learning English. It contains the spellings, pronunciations, and meanings of approximately 5,500 common words most frequently used by beginning and intermediate students of the English language. The dictionary also has separate entries for all of the English pronouns, prepositions, irregular verbs, and contractions. Finally, you will find that many of the entry words have examples which help you better understand their meanings.

A special kind of spelling is used to indicate how to say the words in the dictionary. That special spelling is written between a [and a], like [si], "see." Remember that each special letter used to show pronunciation always illustrates the same sound. These special letters are not hard to learn. On the pages after this one is a chart you can look at to help you learn what the special letters mean.

Dictionary Terms and Abbreviations Used

adj =	adjective	n =	noun
adv =	adverb	pro =	pronoun
conj =	conjunction	prep =	preposition
cont =	contraction	pt =	past tense
Ex =	example	pp =	past participle
interj =	interjection	v =	verb

Your Guide to Pronunciation

[ɑ] shop, stop, top	[ey] date, late, rate	[ɪ] bit, hit, sit
[ɑw] cow, how, now	[ɛ] get, met, set	[i] feet, neat, street
[ɑy] buy, my, white	[ə] but, cut, nut	[k] can, caught, keep
[æ] bad, sat, track	[ɚ] bird, third, word	[l] lawn, leave, lie
[b] beet, bone, boot	[f] fan, feel, fit	[l̩] battle, bottle, puddle
[d] dead, dog, do	[g] get, girl, go	[m] mat, might, mouse
[dʒ] jail, joke, judge	[h] hat, hold, who	[m̩] enthusiasm, heroism, journalism
[ð] that, them, those	[hw] whale, wheel, while	[n] new, note, now

vi

[ņ]	button kitten written	[s]	sat sit sew	[U]	good look should

[ņ]	button	[s]	sat	[U]	good
	kitten		sit		look
	written		sew		should
[ŋ]	bring	[ʃ]	she	[v]	van
	sing		shell		vine
	thing		shoe		voice
[oy]	boy	[t]	tap	[w]	well
	spoil		toe		will
	toy		two		wind
[ow]	coat	[tʃ]	cheese	[y]	yellow
	wrote		chew		year
	vote		church		yes
[ɔ]	caught	[θ]	thin	[z]	zebra
	raw		think		zinc
	yawn		thought		zoo
[p]	Pete	[uw]	food	[ʒ]	measure
	pat		stew		pleasure
	pit		zoo		treasure
[r]	rat				
	round				
	run				

['] comes before the loudest syllable in words with two or more syllables.
() enclose sounds which are sometimes not pronounced.

To the Instructor

The *Everyday American English Dictionary* is an English-language dictionary especially designed for students of limited English proficiency ability. The most basic English words are listed as entries, and the definitions have been written for persons with a minimal knowledge of English using limited and controlled vocabulary. The complexities of full-size dictionaries, such as cross referencing and etymologies, have been omitted.

The *Everyday American English Dictionary* is written for people who are using English while they are learning it. Students at the beginning and intermediate levels of English will find the selection of entry words and the level of definitions far more useful than those found in full-size dictionaries.

Organization

Each entry in the *Everyday American English Dictionary* indicates spelling, pronunciation, part-of-speech, and meaning. Examples accompany difficult definitions. Irregular past tenses and past participles are found at their own entries as well as at the main verb entry. Function or "grammar" words, including pronouns, prepositions, and contractions, have separate entries. Entry words include basic, everyday English plus school and community "survival" words. The definitions are written with words which are either entries in this dictionary or words which most learners acquire early. The *Everyday American English Dictionary* can serve as a portable and handy reference for the meanings of approximately 5,500 common English words.

Word Choice

Entry words selected for the *Everyday American English Dictionary* provide users with the vocabulary necessary for situations encountered in daily life. The words have been selected on the basis of frequency of use in everyday situations.

Pronunciation

A learner's best source for pronunciation is a native speaker of English who does not exaggerate the pronunciation of words. A suggested pronunciation is provided for the learner who does not have access to a native speaker.

This dictionary uses the International Phonetic Alphabet (IPA) to indicate pronunciation. The phonetic transcriptions are given as a model of acceptable pronunciation. The pronunciations have been designed to lead the learner toward natural English while avoiding regional and pedantic pronunciations. The type of English represented here could be called "educated, spoken American English."

Table of Irregular Verbs

Verb	Past Tense	Past Participle
arise	arose	arisen
awake	awaked, awoke	awaked, awoke, awoken
be	was, were	been
bear	bore	born, borne
beat	beat	beat, beaten
become	became	become
begin	began	begun
bend	bent	bent
bid	bid	bid
bind	bound	bound
bite	bit	bitten
bleed	bled	bled
blow	blew	blown
break	broke	broken
breed	bred	bred

Verb	Past Tense	Past Participle
bring	brought	brought
build	built	built
burst	burst	burst
buy	bought	bought
catch	caught	caught
choose	chose	chosen
cling	clung	clung
come	came	come
cost	cost	cost
creep	crept	crept
cut	cut	cut
deal	dealt	dealt
dig	dug	dug
dive	dived, dove	dived
do	did	done
draw	drew	drawn
drink	drank	drunk
drive	drove	driven
eat	ate	eaten
fall	fell	fallen
feed	fed	fed
feel	felt	felt
fight	fought	fought
find	found	found
flee	fled	fled
fling	flung	flung
fly	flew	flown
forget	forgot	forgotten
forgive	forgave	forgiven
freeze	froze	frozen

Verb	Past Tense	Past Participle
get	got	got, gotten
give	gave	given
go	went	gone
grind	ground	ground
grow	grew	grown
hang	hanged, hung	hanged, hung
have	had	had
hear	heard	heard
hide	hid	hidden
hit	hit	hit
hold	held	held
hurt	hurt	hurt
keep	kept	kept
kneel	knelt	knelt
know	knew	known
lay	laid	laid
lead	led	led
leave	left	left
lend	lent	lent
let	let	let
lie	lay	lain
lose	lost	lost
make	made	made
mean	meant	meant
meet	met	met
mistake	mistook	mistaken
overcome	overcame	overcome
overtake	overtook	overtaken
overthrow	overthrew	overthrown

Verb	Past Tense	Past Participle
pay	paid	paid
put	put	put
quit	quit	quit
read	read	read
rid	rid	rid
ride	rode	ridden
ring	rang	rung
rise	rose	risen
run	ran	run
say	said	said
see	saw	seen
seek	sought	sought
sell	sold	sold
send	sent	sent
set	set	set
shake	shook	shaken
shed	shed	shed
shoot	shot	shot
show	showed	shown
shrink	shrank	shrunk
shut	shut	shut
sing	sang	sung
sink	sank	sunk
sit	sat	sat
slay	slew	slain
sleep	slept	slept
slide	slid	slid
sling	slung	slung
slink	slinked, slunk	slinked, slunk
slit	slit	slit
sow	sowed	sowed, sown
speak	spoke	spoken

Verb	Past Tense	Past Participle
speed	sped	sped
spend	spent	spent
spin	spun	spun
split	split	split
spread	spread	spread
spring	sprang	sprung
stand	stood	stood
steal	stole	stolen
stick	stuck	stuck
sting	stung	stung
stink	stank	stunk
stride	strode	stridden
strike	struck	struck, stricken
strive	strived, strove	strived, striven
swear	swore	sworn
sweep	swept	swept
swell	swelled	swelled, swollen
swim	swam	swum
swing	swung	swung
take	took	taken
teach	taught	taught
tear	tore	torn
tell	told	told
think	thought	thought
throw	threw	thrown
understand	understood	understood
undo	undid	undone
wake	waked, woke	waked, woke, woken
wear	wore	worn
weave	wove	woven
weep	wept	wept
win	won	won
wring	wrung	wrung
write	wrote	written

A

a [ə, ey] each; one; a word called an article which indicates one of a thing. *Ex* Please give me a pencil. A swim in the morning is very nice.

abandon [ə'bændən] *v* to go away forever from something or someone; to stop what you are doing before you have finished it.

abbreviation [əbrivi'eyʃṇ] *n* a short way of writing or printing a word, such as Dr. for doctor, Jan. for January.

abdomen ['æbdəmən] *n* the central part of the body which contains the stomach and other organs.

ability [ə'bɪləti] *n* strength, cleverness, or skill.

able ['eybḷ] *adj* having the strength, cleverness, or skill to do something.

abolish [ə'balɪʃ] *v* to get rid of something; to put an end to something.

about [ə'bawt] **1.** *prep* having to do with. *Ex* That book is about trains. **2.** *prep* near to; around. **3.** *adv* almost; approximately.

above [ə'bəv] **1.** *prep* higher than; over. **2.** *adv* to a higher place.

abroad [ə'brɔd] *adv* away in another country. *Ex* They spent the year abroad.

abrupt [ə'brəpt] *adj* sudden; hurried.

absence ['æbsṇ(t)s] *n* the state of not being present; the missing of a day of school.

1

absent ['æbsnt] *adj* missing; not present.

abundant [ə'bəndənt] *adj* more than enough; in great plenty.

accent ['æksɛnt] *n* the manner of pronouncing words. *Ex* People who live in different parts of the country have different accents.

accept [æk'sɛpt] *v* to agree to receive something; to agree to something.

accident ['æksədənt] **1.** *n* an event which occurs by chance. **2.** *n* an event which causes harm to a person or to property.

according to [ə'kordɪŋ tuw] *prep* as stated by; depending on.

account [ə'kɑwnt] *n* a record of money paid and received; an explanation.

accountant [ə'kɑwntn̩t] *n* a person who keeps records of money paid and received.

accurate ['ækyɚət] *adj* correct; exactly right.

accuse [ə'kyuwz] *v* to say that someone has done something wrong.

ache [eyk] *n* a dull pain that goes on and on.

acid ['æsəd] **1.** *n* a liquid which can eat metal or burn your skin. **2.** *adj* tasting sour or sharp.

acrobat ['ækrəbæt] *n* a person who does tricks high in the air. *Ex* Acrobats who walk on ropes can be seen at a circus.

acronym ['ækrənɪm] *n* a word made from the first letters of the words in a group of words. *Ex Radar* is an acronym for *radio detecting and ranging. Scuba* is an acronym for *self-contained underwater breathing apparatus.*

across [ə'krɔs] *prep* from one side to the other side of something.

act [ækt] **1.** *n* anything which is done or performed; part of a play. **2.** *n* a law. **3.** *v* to pretend you are someone other than yourself in a play or a film; to perform. **4.** *v* to behave in a particular way. *Ex* Please act your age!

action ['ækʃn̩] *n* something done; the doing of something; a series of acts performed.

active ['æktəv] *adj* doing something; busy or lively.

actor ['æktɚ] *n* a man or boy who acts in a play or a film.

actress ['æktrəs] *n* a woman or girl who acts in a play or a film.

actual ['æktʃəwəl] *adj* real; existing; not imaginary.

add [æd] *v* to put something together with something else. You add two and two to make four: 2 + 2 = 4.

addition [ə'dɪʃn̩] *n* something added; the act of adding.

address [ə'drɛs] **1.** *n* the directions for delivery written on a letter or package. *Ex* The address includes the number of the house or building, the street name or number, the city, state, and zip code. **2.** *v* to write an address on a letter or package. **3.** *v* to speak to a group of people.

adjective ['ædʒəktɪv] *n* a word which points out something specific about a noun. *Ex Long* is an adjective in *long road,* and *The road is long.*

adjourn [ə'dʒɚn] *v* to end a meeting.

admire [əd'mɑyr] *v* to think very well of something or someone.

admit [əd'mɪt] **1.** *v* to agree that something is so. **2.** *v* to allow someone to come in.

adolescent [ædə'lɛsn̩t] **1.** *n* a person who is almost an adult; a teenager. **2.** *adj* having to do with teenagers; in the manner of a teenager

adopt [ə'dɑpt] **1.** *v* to take over an idea and use it as your own. **2.** *v* to receive and raise the child of someone else.

advance [əd'væn(t)s] *v* to move forward.

adventure [əd'vɛntʃɚ] *n* an exciting or dangerous thing that you do or that happens to you.

adverb ['ædvɚb] *n* a word which points out something specific about a verb, an adjective, or another adverb. Adverbs tell how, how much, when, or where. *Ex Quickly* is an adverb in *The dog came quickly when called. Very* is an adverb in *The road is very long. Never* is an adverb in *You will never catch me.*

advertise ['ædvɚtayz] *v* to tell people about something through newspapers, radio, and television.

advertisement [ædvɚ'tayzmənt] *n* something said on radio, television, or in the paper which tells people about things to buy or about jobs.

affair [ə'fɛr] *n* a happening or an event.

affect [ə'fɛkt] *v* to do something that causes a change; to influence.

affection [ə'fɛkʃn̩] *n* fondness; great liking.

affirmative [ə'fɚmətɪv] *adj* indicating yes; indicating that something is so; the opposite of negative. *Ex The boy is here* is an affirmative sentence. *The boy is not here* is a negative sentence.

afford [ə'ford] *v* to have enough money for something you wish to buy or do.

afraid [ə'freyd] *adj* full of fear; frightened. *Ex* George is afraid of the dark.

after ['æftɚ] **1.** *prep* later; behind; following on. **2.** *adv* behind; afterward.

afternoon [æftɚ'nuwn] *n* the part of the day between noon and sunset.

afterward ['æftɚwɚd] *adv* at a later time.

again [ə'gɛn] *adv* once more; one more time.

against [ə'gɛn(t)st] *prep* in the opposite direction to; on the opposite side of; in contact with.

age [eydʒ] **1.** *n* the number of years something or someone has been alive, or has existed. **2.** *v* to become old.

agent ['eydʒn̩t] **1.** *n* a person or thing which does something or causes something to happen. **2.** *n* a person who is paid to look after someone else's business. **3.** *n* someone who finds out secrets or other information; a spy.

agree [ə'gri] *v* to consent to something; to accept someone else's thinking or opinion.

agreeable [ə'griəbl] *adj* friendly; pleasant; easy to get along with.

agreement [ə'grimənt] *n* the act of agreeing; holding the same opinion.

agriculture ['ægrɪkəltʃɚ] *n* farming; the science of farming.

ahead [ə'hɛd] *adv* in the future; toward the front.

aide [eyd] *n* an assistant; a helper.

aim [eym] *v* to point a gun or other weapon steadily at the target.

air [ɛr] *n* the mixture of gases that we breathe.

air conditioner ['ɛr kəndɪʃ(ə)nɚ] *n* an electric machine which cools the air in the rooms of homes and offices.

airplane ['ɛrpleyn] *n* a machine which carries people or cargo high in the air. *Ex* Airplanes are heavier than air, and they use propellers or jets to make them move through the air.

airport ['ɛrport] *n* the place where airplanes come in to land or take off.

aisle [ɑyl] *n* a pathway between rows of seats in a church, theater, or classroom.

alarm [ə'lɑrm] **1.** *n* sudden surprise or fear. **2.** *n* a loud bell or horn which is a warning of danger. A fire alarm warns that a fire has started in a building.

alarm clock [ə'lɑrm klɑk] *n* a clock which rings a bell or makes a loud sound when it is time to wake up.

album ['ælbəm] *n* a book of blank pages in which you can keep a collection of things like stamps or photographs.

alderman ['ɔldɚmən] *n* one of the people who is elected to make the laws for a city.

alert [ə'lɚt] *adj* wide awake; active; watchful.

algebra ['ældʒəbrə] *n* a branch of mathematics in which you use letters like "x" or "y" as well as numbers.

alibi ['æləbɑy] *n* an excuse; a statement which explains that an accused person was in another place when a crime took place.

alike [ə'lɑyk] **1.** *adj* similar to one another; nearly the same. **2.** *adv* in the same way; in the same manner.

alive [ə'lɑyv] *adj* living; not dead; existing.

all [ɔl] **1.** *adj* every one of; the full amount of. *Ex* She works all day. **2.** *adv* totally; completely. *Ex* It is all done. **3.** *pro* everything; everybody. *Ex* All are invited.

allege [ə'lɛdʒ] *v* to state a fact without giving proof; to accuse someone of something without giving proof.

allergy ['ælɚdʒi] *n* a bad reaction to a substance which is usually harmless. *Ex* Susan's baby sister has an allergy to orange juice.

alley ['æli] *n* a narrow passage between buildings in cities and towns.

alligator ['æləgeytɚ] *n* a large and dangerous reptile similar to a crocodile. *Ex* Alligators live in swamps and may grow as long as twenty feet.

allow [ə'law] *v* to let someone do something or let something happen.

all right [ɔl 'rayt] *adj* satisfactory; well; OK.

almanac ['ɔlmənæk] *n* a book that gives information about the weather and other things which may happen in the days, weeks, and months of one year.

almost ['ɔlmost] *adv* nearly, but not entirely.

alone [ə'lown] **1.** *adv* all by yourself. *Ex* I can't do it alone. **2.** *adj* with no one else; isolated. *Ex* I am all alone.

along [ə'lɔŋ] *prep* following the path of; in the course of.

aloud [ə'lawd] *adv* out loud; spoken; the opposite of silent.

alphabet ['ælfəbɛt] *n* all of the letters used in writing a language. They are arranged in a special order.

alphabetize ['ælfəbətayz] *v* to arrange words, names, or titles in the same order as the letters of the alphabet.

already [ɔl'rɛdi] *adv* sooner than expected.

also ['ɔlsow] *adv* as well as; too; in addition to.

altar ['ɔltɚ] *n* a kind of raised table inside a church.

alter ['ɔltɚ] *v* to make a change in something; to become different in some way.

..., *n* the act of altering; a change; the act of ... to a person.

...**n** [ɔl'ðow] *conj* even if; but; in spite of.

aluminum [ə'luwmənəm] *n* a lightweight, silver-colored metal.

always ['ɔlwɪz, 'ɔlweyz] *adv* at all times; forever.

am [æm] *v* the present tense form of the verb *to be* that goes with *I. Ex* I am a student. I am going to town.

amateur ['æmətʃɚ] **1.** *n* any person who plays a sport or does a job for pleasure and not for money. **2.** *n* a person who does something carelessly. **3.** *adj* careless; not good enough.

amaze [ə'meyz] *v* to surprise greatly.

ambition [æm'bɪʃn̩] *n* the desire to do very well; the desire to have power.

ambulance ['æmbyələn(t)s] *n* a special car or truck for taking people who are ill or hurt to the hospital.

among [ə'məŋ] *prep* in the midst of; surrounded by.

amount [ə'mɑwnt] *n* a quantity; the total of several things added together.

amphibian [æm'fɪbiən] *n* a class of animals which live and breathe in the water when young and breathe air when they are grown up. *Ex* Frogs and toads are amphibians.

ample ['æmpl̩] *adj* of a large size; plentiful.

amuse [ə'myuwz] *v* to make others smile or laugh by something you say or do.

an [ən, æn] one, each; a word called an article which indicates one of a thing. *Ex* Please give me an apple. An elephant is a very large animal.

analysis [ə'næləsəs] *n* a careful study of something.

anchor ['æŋkɚ] **1.** *n* a heavy metal hook which is attached to a ship or boat by a chain. *Ex* An anchor is put on the bottom of the sea where it digs in and holds the ship or boat in place. **2.** *v* to hold a ship or boat in place with an anchor; to fasten something securely.

ancient ['eyntʃənt] *adj* very, very old; in the distant past.

and [ənd, ænd] *conj* plus; in addition to; furthermore. *Ex* Apples and oranges are fruit. Please go home and eat your supper.

angle ['æŋgl̩] *n* the sharp turn where two straight lines meet at a point. *Ex* The letters L and V each show one angle. The letter W shows three. The letters C and O show no angles.

angry ['æŋgri] *adj* very cross; in a bad temper.

animal ['ænəməl] *n* any living creature which is not a plant. *Ex* Sometimes the word animal includes humans, and sometimes it does not.

ankle ['æŋkl̩] *n* the thin, bony part of the leg just above the foot; the part of the leg which joins the foot.

anniversary [ænəˈvɚsɚi] *n* a day which is remembered each year for something special which happened once in the past. *Ex* Married people celebrate wedding anniversaries.

announce [əˈnɑwn(t)s] *v* to make something known by telling everyone.

annoy [əˈnoy] *v* to make someone cross or angry.

annual ['ænyəwəl] *adj* happening one time a year; covering the period of one year; happening every year.

another [əˈnəðɚ] *adj* one more; a different one.

answer ['æn(t)sɚ] **1.** *n* a spoken or written reply to a question. **2.** *v* to give a reply to a question

ant [ænt] *n* a small insect which lives in colonies. *Ex* Some ants eat fat, and some eat sugar.

antarctic [ænt'ɑrktɪk] **1.** *n* the landmass surrounding the South Pole of the earth. **2.** *adj* having to do with the land surrounding the South Pole.

antenna [æn'tɛnə] **1.** *n* one of the two sensory organs on the head of an insect. The plural is antennas or antennae. *Ex* Ants have very active antennas. **2.** *n* a metal device which sends out or receives radio or television signals. The plural is antennas.

antique [æn'tik] **1.** *adj* very old; in existence for a very long time. **2.** *n* a piece of furniture or other object which is old and valuable.

anxiety [æŋ'zɑyəti] *n* worry; a feeling of fear about something you think might happen.

anxious ['æŋ(k)ʃəs] *adj* worried; fearful about something you think might happen.

any ['ɛni] *adj* one or some.

anything ['ɛniθɪŋ] *pro* a thing of any kind.

anyway ['ɛniwey] *adv* in any way; in any manner; in any case.

anywhere ['ɛnihwɛr] *adv* at, to, or in any place.

apart [ə'pɑrt] *adv* away from one another; separated; not together.

apartment [ə'pɑrtmənt] *n* a set of rooms used to live in; a flat.

ape [eyp] **1.** *n* a kind of large monkey with no tail. *Ex* Chimpanzees and gorillas are apes. **2.** *v* to copy someone's activities or motions awkwardly.

apex ['eypɛks] *n* the highest tip of something; the top point of a triangle.

apologize [əˈpɑlədʒɑyz] *v* to say that you are sorry for doing something.

apology [əˈpɑlədʒi] *n* a statement of regret; the act of saying that you are sorry.

apostrophe [əˈpɑstrəfi] **1.** *n* the mark (') placed in a word to show that a letter has been left out. Contractions, such as *can't, I'm, won't,* and *wasn't,* have apostrophes. **2.** *n* the mark (') used to show possession as in "the man's hat."

apparatus [æpəˈrætəs] *n* a collection of things to help a person do something; a set of tools and devices for doing something. *Ex* We have seven new sets of chemistry apparatus. Chemistry apparatus is found in a laboratory. Exercise apparatus is found in a gymnasium.

appeal [əˈpil] *v* to ask for help.

appear [əˈpir] *v* to come into sight.

appearance [əˈpirən(t)s] **1.** *n* the way someone or something looks to you. **2.** *n* the coming into sight of someone or something.

appetite [ˈæpətɑyt] *n* the desire to eat.

applaud [əˈplɔd] *v* to show that you like a performance by clapping your hands together.

apple [ˈæpl̩] *n* a round red, green, or yellow fruit which grows on a tree.

appliance [əˈplɑyən(t)s] *n* a tool or machine which helps do a special job. *Ex* Clothes washers and dryers, vacuum cleaners, and electric can-openers are home appliances.

application [æpləˈkeyʃn̩] **1.** *n* a written request for a job, membership in a club, or permission to go to a college. **2.** *n* the act of requesting a job, membership in a club, or permission to go to a college.

apply [əˈplɑy] **1.** *v* to request employment, membership, or college admission. **2.** *v* to use a rule; to make yourself work very hard; to put on medicine.

appoint [ə'poynt] *v* to choose someone for a job; to choose someone to do something special.

appointment [ə'poyntmənt] **1.** *n* a time chosen for a meeting; a plan for two or more people to meet. **2.** *n* a position or a job for which a person is chosen and not elected.

appreciate [ə'priʃieyt] **1.** *v* to admire; to recognize the value of. **2.** *v* to increase in value.

approach [ə'prowtʃ] *v* to go nearer to someone or something.

approximate [ə'praksəmət] *adj* nearly correct; very near to.

apricot ['æprɪkɑt] *n* a fruit which looks like a small, yellow peach.

apron ['eyprən] *n* a piece of cloth which is tied around someone to keep clothes clean. *Ex* Aprons are usually found in the ˙ıtchen.

aquarium [ə'kwɛrɪəm] **1.** *n* a container, usually a glass tank, where fish and other water animals are kept for people to look at. **2.** *n* a public building with many glass tanks containing fish on display.

arc [ɑrk] *n* a curved line which is part of a circle.

arch [ɑrtʃ] *n* a part of a house or a building which is curved over an opening. *Ex* Arches can be found over doorways and windows.

archery ['ɑrtʃɚi] *n* shooting at a target with a bow and arrow; the sport of shooting with a bow and arrow.

architect ['ɑrkətɛkt] *n* a person who designs a building and watches over its construction.

arctic ['ɑrktɪk] **1.** *n* the landmass surrounding the North Pole. **2.** *adj* very, very cold.

are [ɑr] *v* the form of the verb *to be* that goes with *you, we,* and *they. Ex* You are a student. We are students. They are students.

area ['ɛriə] *n* a region of a state, country, city, world, or other place; an amount of space on a table, the floor, the ground, or some other flat place.

area code ['ɛriə kowd] *n* the part of a telephone number which you dial to place a call to a city other than your own. *Ex* You must always dial a "1" before dialing the area code. The area code for New York City is 1 + 212.

arena [ə'rinə] *n* a large open place with seats around it. *Ex* Games and sports can be watched in an arena.

aren't [ɑrnt] *cont* are not.

argue ['ɑrgyuw] *v* to state reasons for or against something which is being discussed.

argument ['ɑrgyəmənt] *n* reasons for or against something which is being discussed; a discussion; a fight with words.

arise [ə'rɑyz] *v* to get up; to wake up and get out of bed. *pt* arose. *pp* arisen.

arisen [ə'rɪzn̩] *v* the past participle of arise.

arithmetic [ə'rɪθmətɪk] *n* the ways you work with numbers to get an answer. *Ex* Addition, subtraction, multiplication, and division are kinds of arithmetic.

arm [ɑrm] *n* the part of the body between the hand and the shoulder.

armchair ['ɑrmtʃɛr] *n* a chair which has places to rest your arms.

armistice ['ɑrməstəs] *n* a truce.

armpit ['ɑrmpɪt] *n* the hollow place under the top part of the arm.

army ['ɑrmi] *n* a large group of soldiers trained for war.

arose [ə'rowz] *v* the past tense of arise.

around [ə'rɑwnd] **1.** *adv* on all sides; somewhere near. **2.** *prep* on all sides of; circling; surrounding.

arouse [ə'rɑwz] *v* to wake someone up from sleep.

arrange [ə'reyndʒ] *v* to put into a special order.

arrest [ə'rɛst] **1.** *v* to make something come to end. **2.** *v* for a policeman to catch a criminal.

arrive [ə'rɑyv] *v* to reach the place which you have set out for.

arrow ['ɛrow] **1.** *n* a thin, straight stick made of wood with a sharp, pointed tip. *Ex* An arrow is shot with a bow. **2.** *n* a drawing of an arrow pointed at something important; a green light showing the shape of an arrow and telling you which way you may turn your car.

art [ɑrt] **1.** *n* drawing, painting, and sculpture. **2.** *n* an act which requires great skill. *Ex* Carving a turkey is an art.

article ['ɑrtɪkl] **1.** *n* a thing of a particular kind, such as an article of clothing. **2.** *n* a piece written in a newspaper or magazine. **3.** *n* a kind of word in the study of grammar. *Ex* A, an, and the are articles.

artist ['ɑrtɪst] **1.** *n* a person who paints, draws, or makes sculptures. **2.** *n* a person who does something with great skill.

ascend [ə'sɛnd] *v* to go up; to move upward.

ash [æʃ] *n* the powdery material left when something is completely burned up.

ashamed [ə'ʃeymd] *adj* feeling shame; feeling sorry and guilty because of doing something wrong.

aside [ə'sɑyd] *adv* to one side; apart; away.

ask [æsk] *v* to put a question to someone.

asleep [ə'slip] **1.** *adj* to be in the state of sleeping. *Ex* You are not asleep now. **2.** *adv* into a state of sleep. *Ex* Please do not fall asleep!

asphalt ['æsfɔlt] **1.** *n* a black substance like tar which is put down to make hard roads and playgrounds. **2.** *n* a playground or a road covered with asphalt.

aspirin ['æsprən] *n* a painkilling medicine which is made into white tablets; a white tablet of aspirin medicine.

assemble [ə'sɛmbl̩] **1.** *v* to meet together, as when the whole school is called together for an assembly. **2.** *v* to put something together; to gather things together.

assessor [ə'sɛsɚ] *n* a government official who decides how much property is worth for taxation.

assist [ə'sɪst] *v* to help.

assistant [ə'sɪstənt] *n* a helper.

association [əsowsi'eyʃn̩] *n* a group of people with the same goals who are organized into a club to work on those goals.

assorted [ə'sortəd] *adj* of many different kinds.

assure [ə'ʃɚ] *v* to make someone feel sure about something; to make someone feel safe or confident.

asterisk ['æstɚɪsk] *n* the sign (*) used in printing or writing. *Ex* An asterisk used after a word or sentence means to look at the bottom of the page for a message.

astrologer [ə'strɑlədʒɚ] *n* a fortune-teller who studies the stars.

astronaut ['æstrənɔt] *n* someone who travels in space; someone who pilots a spaceship, space capsule, or rocket; a spaceman.

astronomer [əˈstrɑnəmɚ] *n* a scientist who studies the stars and other bodies in the sky.

astronomy [əˈstrɑnəmi] *n* the scientific study of stars, comets, and planets and their moons.

at [æt] *prep* present on, in, or near; toward; to. *Ex* I will see you at school. I will be there at noon.

ate [eyt] *v* the past tense of eat.

athlete [ˈæθlit] *n* someone who is trained or skilled in sports or games; a person who is good at sports or games.

atlas [ˈætləs] *n* a book of maps or charts.

atmosphere [ˈætməsfir] *n* the air which surrounds the earth.

atom [ˈætəm] *n* an extremely small particle of anything. *Ex* Atoms cannot be seen.

attach [əˈtætʃ] *v* to fasten, join, or tie together.

attack [əˈtæk] **1.** *v* to make a move to hurt someone or something. **2.** *n* the start of a fight; the act of attacking.

attempt [əˈtɛmpt] **1.** *v* to try to do something; to make an effort to do something. **2.** *n* a try; an effort to do something.

attend [əˈtɛnd] *v* to be present at an event; to come to and be present at school.

attendance [əˈtɛndən(t)s] *n* being at the place where something is happening; the act of attending.

attendant [əˈtɛndənt] *n* a helper; a person who serves others in a public place.

attention [əˈtɛntʃn̩] **1.** *interj* a call which means that you should stop talking and listen carefully to what is being said. **2.** *n* a person's thinking about something; a person's concentration on something.

attic ['ætɪk] *n* a room just under the roof of a house. *Ex* Usually attics are unfinished, and they are used to store things.

attorney [ə'tɚni] *n* a person who handles someone else's legal business; a lawyer.

attract [ə'trækt] *v* to make someone want to come nearer; to cause something to come nearer.

attractive [ə'træktɪv] *adj* charming; lovely; having the quality of making people want to be near you.

auction ['ɔkʃn̩] *n* a public sale where things are sold to the people who offer the most money for them.

audience ['ɔdiən(t)s] *n* a group of people listening to or watching something like a movie or a concert.

auditorium [ɔdə'toriəm] *n* a large room where people sit to watch a performance or attend a meeting.

aunt [ænt] *n* the sister of your father or mother.

author ['ɔθɚ] *n* a person who has written something.

authority [ə'θorəti] **1.** *n* the power to control what other people do; the right to tell other people what to do. *Ex* The principal of a school has authority over the teachers and students. **2.** *n* a person who is in charge; the people who are in charge.

auto ['ɔtow] *n* a car. This is a short form of the word automobile.

autobiography [ɔtowbɑy'ɑgrəfi] *n* the story of a person's life written by the person and not by someone else.

automatic [ɔtə'mætɪk] *adj* able to work by itself. *Ex* An automatic door opens for you without touching it.

automobile ['ɔtəmowbil] *n* a car; a four-wheeled vehicle which you can drive from place to place.

autumn ['ɔtəm] *n* a season between summer and winter; fall.

avenue ['ævənuw] **1.** *n* a street or road; a wide street or road. **2.** *n* a path, road, or route.

aviation [eyvi'eyʃn̩] *n* the business of building, managing, and flying airplanes.

avoid [ə'voyd] *v* to keep out of the way of something; to keep away from someone.

await [ə'weyt] *v* to wait for; to look forward to.

awake [ə'weyk] **1.** *adj* alert; not sleeping. **2.** *v* to stop sleeping; to wake up; to cause someone to stop sleeping. *pt* awaked, awoke. *pp* awaked, awoke, awoken.

award [ə'word] **1.** *v* to give a prize to someone for winning or doing well. **2.** *n* a prize given to someone for winning or doing well.

aware [ə'wɛr] *adj* watchful; alert; knowledgeable.

away [ə'wey] **1.** *adv* from a place; a distance from a place. *Ex* We try to keep away from trouble. **2.** *adj* not at this place; absent. *Ex* He is away now.

awful ['ɔfl̩] *adj* very bad, ugly, or nasty.

awkward ['ɔkwɚd] **1.** *adj* clumsy; unable to move freely and easily. **2.** *adj* uncomfortable; inconvenient; embarrassing.

awoke [ə'wowk] *v* a past tense and past participle of awake.

awoken [ə'wowkn̩] *v* a past participle of awake.

axis ['æksɪs] *n* a real or imaginary line through the middle of an object, around which the object turns. *Ex* The axis of the earth passes through the North Pole and the South Pole.

axle ['æksl̩] *n* the rod in a vehicle to which the wheels are attached. *Ex* Carts, wagons, and bicycles have axles.

B

---

baby ['beybi] **1.** *n* a very young child who cannot walk yet. **2.** *adj* small; young; infantile. **3.** *v* to take care of as someone takes care of a baby; to treat as a baby.

baby carriage ['beybi kɛrɪdʒ] *n* a small carrier for a baby which is pushed along. It is also called a baby buggy.

bachelor ['bætʃ(ə)lɚ] *n* an unmarried man.

back [bæk] **1.** *n* the rear part of the body between the neck and the waist. *Ex* I have a pain in my back. **2.** *adv* to the rear; toward the rear. *Ex* He leaned back carefully. **3.** *adj* at or in the rear; rear. *Ex* She put it on the back porch. **4.** *v* to make something go backwards. *Ex* I will back the car out of the driveway.

backboard ['bækbord] *n* the board to which a basketball basket is attached. It keeps the ball from going out-of-bounds and helps it bounce into the basket.

background ['bæk(g)rawnd] **1.** *n* the part of a picture which is at the back; the curtain, picture, or wall at the rear of a stage where a play is being performed. **2.** *n* a statement of the events which led to the event which is being talked about.

backyard ['bæk'yɑrd] *n* the yard at the rear of a house.

bacon ['beykn̩] *n* meat from the side of a pig which has been salted and smoked to give it a special flavor. *Ex* Bacon is often eaten with eggs.

bacteria [bæk'tɪriə] *n* very tiny plants which live in water, soil, and other living bodies. The plural of bacterium.

bad [bæd] *adj* not good; wrong; spoiled.

badge [bædʒ] *n* a special sign or mark worn to show membership in a special group. *Ex* Police officers wear badges.

badly ['bædli] *adv* in a bad manner; poorly. *Ex* He did badly on the exam.

bag [bæg] **1.** *n* a sack made of paper, cloth, plastic, or leather. *Ex* Something that is purchased at a store will usually be placed in a bag. **2.** *v* to capture an animal; to capture or win something. *Ex* We went hunting yesterday and bagged four rabbits.

baggage ['bægɪdʒ] *n* bags used in traveling; luggage; suitcases. Baggage refers to one or more pieces. *Ex* Your baggage is under the seat.

bait [beyt] *n* food used to attract fish or other animals in order to catch them.

bake [beyk] *v* to cook something in an oven.

bakery ['beykri] *n* the place where bread and cakes are baked and sold.

balance ['bælən(t)s] **1.** *v* to hold something steady so that it does not tip over. **2.** *v* to check over financial records to make sure that all money is accounted for. **3.** *n* remainder; the amount remaining; the amount of money owed someone.

balcony ['bælkəni] *n* a platform, usually with railings or a low wall around it. It is built out from the side of a building.

bald [bold] *adj* without any hair on the top of the head.

bale [beyl] *n* a specially packed bundle of something, like cotton or hay.

ball [bol] **1.** *n* a completely round object used for playing games. **2.** *n* a very nice dancing party.

ballerina [bælə'rinə] *n* a female ballet dancer.

ballet [bæ'ley] *n* a kind of dancing which tells a story in movement and music without using words. *Ex* A ballet is performed on a stage in front of an audience.

balloon [bə'luwn] *n* a large cloth bag filled with gas which makes it rise high into the air; a small rubber bag which you can fill up with gas or blow up with your breath.

ballot ['bælət] *n* the paper on which a person's vote is recorded. *Ex* When you finish voting, please put your ballot in the ballot box.

ballpoint ['bɔlpoynt] *n* a type of ink pen which has a tiny metal ball on the end instead of a point. As the ball rolls on the paper, it spreads the ink. Ballpoint is short for the words ballpoint pen.

bamboo [bæm'buw] *n* a kind of very tall grass with stiff hollow stems. *Ex* Bamboo is used for making poles, walking canes, and furniture.

ban [bæn] **1.** *n* an order to put a stop to something; an order that something not be done. **2.** *v* to order that something not be done.

banana [bə'nænə] *n* a long fruit with thick, yellow skin.

band [bænd] **1.** *n* a group of people; a group of robbers. **2.** *n* a group of musicians who play brass and percussion instruments.

bandage ['bændɪdʒ] **1.** *n* a piece of cloth used to cover up a wound; a special strip of adhesive tape which is used to cover up a wound. **2.** *v* to cover up a wound with protective cloth or tape.

bang [bæŋ] **1.** *n* a loud and sudden noise. **2.** *v* to hit something very hard.

banister ['bænəstɚ] *n* a rail to hold on to at the side of a stairway.

banjo ['bændʒow] *n* a musical instrument which is played by plucking its strings.

bank [bæŋk] *n* a business firm which lends money or keeps it safe; a bank building.

banquet ['bæŋkwət] *n* a feast; a special dinner party.

bar [bɑr] **1.** *n* a long piece of hard material, usually metal or wood. **2.** *n* a counter where drinks can be bought.

barbecue ['bɑrbəkyuw] **1.** *n* an outdoor party where meat is cooked over an open fire. **2.** *v* to cook meat over an open fire.

barbed wire [bɑrbd 'wɑyr] *n* fence wire twisted so that sharp points stick out to the sides.

barber ['bɑrbɚ] *n* a person who cuts hair and shaves men.

bare [bɛr] *adj* without covering or decoration.

bargain ['bɑrgn̩] **1.** *n* something you buy at less than the usual price; a purchase made at a very good price. **2.** *v* to argue with the seller about the price of something you want to buy; to negotiate.

barge [bɑrdʒ] *n* a cargo boat which has a flat bottom.

bark [bɑrk] **1.** *n* the tough covering on a tree's trunk and branches. **2.** *n* the sharp noise made by dogs and some other animals. **3.** *v* for a dog to make its sharp noise of warning or anger.

barn [bɑrn] *n* a large farm building used to house animals and store crops.

barometer [bə'rɑmətɚ] *n* an instrument used to measure air pressure. *Ex* A barometer helps predict the weather.

barracks ['bɛrɪks] *n* the buildings where soldiers live.

barrel ['bɛrəl] *n* a container made of curved pieces of wood held together with hoops.

barrier ['bɛriɚ] *n* something, like a fence or a wall, that stops you from going further.

base [beys] *n* the bottom of anything; the part on which something stands or is built.

baseball ['beysbɔl] **1.** *n* a game where two teams take turns at using a bat to hit a ball. **2.** *n* the ball used in the game of baseball.

basement ['beysmənt] *n* the lowest room in a building, usually below the ground; the cellar.

bash [bæʃ] *v* to hit something so hard that it is smashed or dented.

bashful ['bæʃfl̩] *adj* timid; shy.

basin ['beysn̩] *n* a round bowl for holding water.

basket ['bæskət] **1.** *n* a container made of straw or thin pieces of wood. *Ex* Some baskets have handles for carrying. **2.** *n* the goal in the game of basketball.

basketball ['bæskətbɔl] **1.** *n* a game played by two teams who make goals by putting a ball through a hoop. The hoop and the net hanging from it are called the basket. **2.** *n* the ball used in the game of basketball.

bat [bæt] **1.** *n* a small, mouse-like animal that flies at night. **2.** *n* a special piece of wood used to hit the ball in the game of baseball. **3.** *v* to hit at something; to hit something with a bat; to hit a baseball with a bat.

bath [bæθ] **1.** *n* the act of washing yourself all over. **2.** *n* a shower or tub in which a person washes all over. **3.** *n* short for the word bathroom.

bathe [beyð] *v* to wash; to wash all over; to wash your entire body; to wash a baby all over; to clean part of the body.

bathing suit ['beyðɪŋ suwt] *n* the clothing which is worn when a person goes swimming.

bathroom ['bæθruwm] *n* a room with a bathtub or shower in it; the washroom.

baton [bə'tɑn] *n* a stick for beating time to music; a stick used to lead a band or orchestra.

batter ['bætɚ] **1.** *n* a mixture of flour and liquid used in cooking. **2.** *n* the player who hits the ball in the game of baseball.

battery ['bætɚi] *n* a container for storing electricity. *Ex* Batteries are used for electric power in things like flashlights and portable radios.

battle ['bætl̩] **1.** *n* a fight; an important fight in a war. **2.** *v* to fight something or someone very hard.

battleship ['bætl̩ʃɪp] *n* a large warship with heavy armor and big guns and rockets.

bay [bey] *n* a part of an ocean or a lake which makes a curve into the land. *Ex* Boats and ships can anchor safely in a bay.

bayonet [beyə'nɛt] *n* a long, sharp blade attached to a rifle, so that the rifle can be used as a spear.

be [bi] *v* to have identity with; to be the same as; to exist. Present tenses: am, are, is. *pt* was, were. *pp* been. *Ex* When will you be here?

beach [bitʃ] *n* a sandy strip of land next to an ocean or lake.

bead [bid] *n* a very small ball with a hole through it. *Ex* Many beads are threaded together to make a necklace.

beak [bik] *n* the hard, sharp part of a bird's mouth.

beaker ['bikɚ] *n* a tall glass or cup used for holding liquids in a laboratory.

beam [bim] **1.** *n* a long, thick piece of wood used to support something heavy like a floor. **2.** *n* a ray of light.

bean [bin] **1.** *n* a vegetable with large seeds that grow in pods. **2.** *n* the seed of the bean plant.

bear [bɛr] **1.** *n* a heavy animal with thick, shaggy fur and a very short tail. **2.** *v* to carry something; to put up with something; to endure something unpleasant. *pt* bore. *pp* born, borne. **3.** *v* to give birth to. *pt* bore. *pp* born.

beard [bird] *n* the hair which grows on a man's chin; all of the hair which grows on a man's face except the eyebrows.

beast [bist] *n* an animal, especially a large wild animal.

beat [bit] **1.** *v* to hit something or someone over and over again. **2.** *v* to keep regular time in music; to mark the tempo of music by moving a baton or the hand in rhythm. **3.** *v* to do better than another person or team in a game or race. *pt* beat. *pp* beat, beaten. **4.** *n* the rhythm in a piece of music.

beaten [ˈbitn̩] *v* a past participle of beat.

beautiful [ˈbyuwtəfl̩] *adj* lovely; very pretty. *Ex* Boys and men are said to be handsome, and girls and women are said to be beautiful.

beauty [ˈbyuwti] *n* great loveliness.

became [bɪˈkeym] *v* the past tense of become.

because [bɪˈkəz] *conj* for the reason that; due to

become [bɪˈkəm] **1.** *v* to grow to be; to develop into. **2.** *v* to suit someone; to look good on someone. *Ex* That dress becomes Margaret. *pt* became. *pp* become.

bed [bɛd] **1.** *n* a soft place for sleeping, usually with sheets, blankets, and pillows. **2.** *n* an area in a garden where flowers are grown. **3.** *n* the bottom of the sea.

bedroom [ˈbɛdruwm] *n* a room where there is a bed.

bedside [ˈbɛdsɑyd] *n* the space next to a bed.

bedspread ['bɛdsprɛd] *n* the top cover on a bed.

bee [bi] *n* an insect with four wings and a stinger. *Ex* Bees make honey and wax.

beef [bif] *n* the meat of a cow or a bull.

beehive ['bihɑyv] *n* the nest bees build to live in; a box provided for bees to build their nest in.

been [bɪn] *v* the past participle of be. *Ex* Where have you been?

beer [bir] *n* a strong drink made from malt. *Ex* Beer contains a small amount of alcohol.

beet [bit] *n* a vegetable with a dark red root.

beetle ['bitl̩] *n* a roundish insect with four wings. The two front wings are hard and protect the back wings when they are folded.

before [bɪ'for] **1.** *adv* ahead; at an earlier time. *Ex* He has done this before. **2.** *prep* in front of. *Ex* The prisoner stood before the judge.

beg [bɛg] *v* to ask earnestly or humbly for something. *Ex* She begged for forgiveness.

began [bɪ'gæn] *v* the past tense of begin.

beggar ['bɛgɚ] *n* someone who lives by asking for money and food from others.

begin [bɪ'gɪn] **1.** *v* to do the first part of something; to start. *Ex* The movie will begin on time. **2.** *v* to start doing something. *Ex* He is going to begin studying. *pt* began. *pp* begun.

beginning [bɪ'gɪnɪŋ] *n* the start of something.

begun [bɪ'gən] *v* the past participle of begin.

behave [bɪ'heyv] *v* to act in a particular way; to act in a good or bad way.

behavior [bɪ'heyvyɚ] *n* manners; how a person acts or behaves.

behind [bɪ'haynd] **1.** *prep* at the back of; to the rear of. *Ex* He stood behind the chair. **2.** *adv* at a former place; at an earlier time. *Ex* I left my books behind.

believe [bɪ'liv] **1.** *v* to have a strong religious faith. **2.** *v* to accept a statement as the truth.

bell [bɛl] *n* a cup-shaped metal object that makes a ringing noise when struck.

bellow ['bɛlow] *v* to yell or roar very loudly.

belly ['bɛli] *n* the underside of something; the rounded part of the body just above the waist; the stomach.

belong to [bə'lɔŋ tuw] *v* to be the property of; to be part of. *Ex* The book belongs to the teacher.

below [bɪ'low] **1.** *adv* in a lower place; to a lower place. *Ex* Please go below and check the cargo. **2.** *prep* at a lower level than. *Ex* Your ankles are below your elbows.

belt [bɛlt] *n* a strip of material, usually leather, which fastens around the waist.

bench [bɛntʃ] *n* a long seat, usually made of wood.

bend [bɛnd] **1.** *v* to make something crooked or curved. *pt* bent. *pp* bent. **2.** *n* a curve or turn in a river or a road.

beneath [bɪ'niθ] *prep* in a position lower than; below; directly under.

benefit ['bɛnəfɪt] **1.** *n* help; aid. **2.** *n* a payment of money during times of sickness, unemployment, or old age; a payment from an insurance company. **3.** *n* a performance given to raise money for charity. **4.** *n* something, such as

insurance or vacation time, which is part of the payment for
working for a company. **5.** *v* to receive something good or
worthwhile; to get profit or value from something. *Ex* How
does that benefit me?

bent [bɛnt] *v* the past tense and past participle of bend.

berry ['bɛri] *n* any small, round juicy fruit without a stone.

beside [bɪ'saɪd] *prep* near; next to.

besides [bɪ'saɪdz] **1.** *adv* also; in addition. *Ex* It is too big, and
besides, it is ugly. **2.** *prep* other than; in addition to. *Ex* I
don't want anything besides happiness.

best [bɛst] **1.** *adj* most good; as good as is possible. *Ex* This is
the best fruit I have ever eaten. **2.** *adv* in a manner which is as
good as possible. *Ex* I work best when I am hungry. **3.** *n* a
very good person or thing; a person or thing which is as good
as is possible. *Ex* I will try to do my best.

betray [bɪ'treɪ] **1.** *v* to give away or reveal a secret. **2.** *v* to let
someone down by breaking a promise.

better ['bɛtɚ] **1.** *adj* improving in health; getting over an
illness. **2.** *adj* more than good. *Ex* John is good, and Mary is
even better. **3.** *adj* more clever or skilled than someone else.
Ex Mary is better than John. **4.** *adv* in a more excellent
manner. *Ex* John runs well, but Mary runs better.

between [bɪ'twin] *prep* among; with one on each side.

beverage ['bɛv(ə)rɪdʒ] *n* a liquid for drinking, other than
water.

beware [bɪ'wɛr] *v* to be very careful about something that may
be dangerous, like a fierce dog or dangerous traffic.

bewilder [bɪ'wɪldɚ] *v* to puzzle a person; to confuse a person;
to make a person not sure of what to do.

beyond [bɪ'yɑnd] *prep* farther on; farther away.

Bible ['baybl̩] *n* the holy writings of Christians; the book containing the holy writings of Christianity; the book containing the holy writings of Judaism.

bibliography [bɪbli'agrəfi] *n* an alphabetical list of authors and the books or articles which they have written.

bicycle ['baysɪkl̩] **1.** *n* a two-wheeled vehicle with a seat, pedals, and handlebars. *Ex* The rider pushes pedals to make the bicycle move. **2.** *v* to travel by bicycle.

bid [bɪd] **1.** *v* to command or invite someone; to make an offer for something. *pt* bid. *pp* bid. **2.** *n* an offer of money for something; the act of bidding.

big [bɪg] *adj* large; important.

bike [bayk] *n* a bicycle; a motorcycle.

bikini [bə'kini] *n* a bathing suit made of two small parts for a woman or one small part for a man.

bilingual [bay'lɪŋgwl̩] **1.** *adj* knowing or using two languages; having to do with two languages. **2.** *n* a person who knows or uses two languages.

bill [bɪl] **1.** *n* a written note of how much money is due for work which has been done, or for something which has been bought. **2.** *n* the hard part of a bird's mouth. **3.** *n* the flat part of a hat or cap that points forward to keep the sun out of the eyes. **4.** *n* a piece of paper money, such as a dollar bill or a ten-dollar bill.

billboard ['bɪlbord] *n* a very large sign showing an advertisement.

billiards ['bɪlyɚdz] *n* a game played with hard balls and sticks called cues, on a table covered with thick, green cloth.

billion ['bɪlyən] *n* the name of the number 1,000,000,000.

bin [bɪn] *n* a large container for things like coal or rubbish.

bind [baynd] *v* to fasten or tie something together. *pt* bound. *pp* bound.

bingo ['bɪŋgow] *n* a game of lucky numbers which can be played by many people at once in a hall or at a theater.

binoculars [bə'nakyələɚz] *n* a device which allows you to see for great distances. *Ex* A pair of binoculars has a small telescope for each eye.

biography [bay'agrəfi] *n* the story of a person's life written by another person.

biology [bay'alədʒi] *n* the scientific study of living things.

bird [bɚd] *n* a winged animal covered with feathers.

bird cage ['bɚd keydʒ] *n* a small cage for a pet bird.

birth [bɚθ] *n* the act of coming into life; the act of being born.

birthdate ['bɚθdeyt] *n* the date of a person's birth.

birthday ['bɚθdey] *n* the day of the year when a person was born; the anniversary of the day a person was born.

biscuit ['bɪskət] *n* a small, quickly made kind of bread. *Ex* Dough is rolled out and cut into biscuits, which are then baked.

bisect ['baysɛkt] *v* to divide something into two equal parts.

bit [bɪt] **1.** *n* a small piece of something. **2.** *v* the past tense of bite.

bite [bayt] **1.** *v* to take a piece out of something with the teeth; to clamp the teeth into someone or something in order to cause pain. *Ex* That dog bit me. *pt* bit. *pp* bitten. **2.** *n* the act of biting. **3.** *n* a piece of food the right size for chewing and swallowing.

bitten ['bɪtn̩] *v* the past participle of bite.

bitter ['bɪtɚ] *adj* tasting sharp or sour; not sweet.

black [blæk] **1.** *adj* of the color of tar or coal. **2.** *adj* having to do with a person of the Negro race. **3.** *n* a person of the Negro race.

blackbird ['blækbɚd] *n* a black songbird with a yellow beak; any bird of the color black.

blackboard ['blækbord] *n* a hard surface, usually of black color, which can be written on with chalk; a chalkboard. *Ex* In the schoolroom blackboards are attached to the walls.

blacksmith ['blæksmɪθ] *n* a man who makes and mends iron things, and who puts iron shoes on horses.

blacktop ['blæktɑp] **1.** *n* a black material used for roads and playgrounds. **2.** *n* a playground or parking lot made of a hard, black material.

blade [bleyd] **1.** *n* one leaf of grass. **2.** *n* the metal cutting part of a knife, the part other than the handle.

blame [bleym] **1.** *v* to find fault with. **2.** *n* the responsibility for something wrong which has happened.

blank [blæŋk] **1.** *adj* without any writing or marks. **2.** *n* a line or form which is to be filled out; an application.

blanket ['blæŋkət] *n* a bed-cover which helps to keep you warm.

blast [blæst] **1.** *n* an explosion; a strong gust of air. **2.** *v* to use explosive materials like dynamite to make a hole or to loosen rock.

blaze [bleyz] **1.** *n* a brightly burning fire. **2.** *v* to burn brightly. *Ex* The fire in the fireplace was blazing brightly.

bleach [blitʃ] **1.** *v* to take the color out of something. **2.** *n* a liquid used to take the color out of something. *Ex* Bleach is used to help wash white clothes.

bleachers ['blitʃɚz] *n* rows of seats made of boards arranged so that people can watch games and contests. This word is used in the plural.

bleak [blik] *adj* cold and windy; grim; without cheer.

bled [blɛd] *v* the past tense and past participle of bleed.

bleed [blid] *v* to lose blood. *pt* bled. *pp* bled.

blend [blɛnd] **1.** *v* to mix together; to combine things. **2.** *n* a mixture.

blender ['blɛndɚ] *n* an electric appliance used to mix liquids.

blew [bluw] *v* the past tense of blow.

blind [blɑynd] *adj* not able to see.

blink [blɪŋk] *v* to open and shut your eyes very quickly.

blister ['blɪstɚ] *n* a swelling on the skin, like a small bubble, often filled with water or blood.

blizzard ['blɪzɚd] *n* a very windy snowstorm.

block [blɑk] **1.** *n* a big piece of something, like wood, metal, or stone. **2.** *n* an area of a town or city enclosed by four streets. **3.** *v* to be in the way of something.

blond [blɑnd] *adj* of light coloring; with very light-colored hair.

blood [blɤd] *n* the red liquid which is circulated inside the bodies of animals.

bloom [bluwm] **1.** *v* to come into flower. **2.** *n* a flower blossom.

blossom ['blɑsəm] **1.** *v* to come into flower. **2.** *n* a single flower.

blot [blɑt] **1.** *n* a spot or mark; a spot of ink. **2.** *v* to soak up a tiny puddle of a liquid; to soak up ink.

blouse [blɑws] *n* a loose garment covering the upper part of the body. It is worn by girls and women.

blow [blow] **1.** *v* to push air out of the mouth with the lungs. *pt* blew. *pp* blown. **2.** *n* a hard knock.

blown [blown] *v* the past participle of blow.

blue [bluw] **1.** *n* the color of the sky on a sunny day. **2.** *adj* of a blue color.

blunt [blənt] *adj* having a dull edge or point; the opposite of sharp.

blur [blɚ] **1.** *v* to make something look dim or not clear. **2.** *n* an unclear image.

blush [bləʃ] *v* to turn red in the face because of shame, shyness, or being upset by something.

board [bord] **1.** *n* a long, flat piece of wood. **2.** *n* a group of people appointed to oversee something. **3.** *v* to get on a ship, airplane, or railroad train.

boarder ['bordɚ] *n* someone who pays to sleep and eat in someone else's house.

boast [bowst] *v* to talk a lot about how good you are at things; to talk a lot about yourself and your possessions.

boat [bowt] *n* a small ship; a vessel that floats on water.

bobbin ['babn̩] *n* a spool for holding thread or yarn.

bobby pin ['babipɪn] *n* a U-shaped pin made of flat wire used to hold a woman's hair in place.

body ['badi] *n* the whole of a person or animal; the whole of things like lakes, ponds, and oceans.

bodyguard ['badigard] *n* a person who guards and protects someone.

boil [boyl] **1.** *v* to make water so hot that it bubbles and makes steam. **2.** *n* a sore swelling on the body.

boiler ['boylɚ] *n* a container for boiling water; an apparatus for making steam.

bold [bowld] *adj* brave; without fear.

boldface ['bowldfeys] *n* wide, dark printing. *Ex* **This sentence is in boldface.**

bolt [bowlt] **1.** *n* a metal fastening for doors and gates. **2.** *v* to run away.

bomb [bɑm] **1.** *n* an object which can be made to explode and cause great damage. **2.** *v* to destroy with bombs.

bomber ['bɑmɚ] **1.** *n* an airplane which carries bombs to drop. **2.** *n* a person who leaves bombs in public places.

bond [bɑnd] **1.** *n* something which unites people in a friendly way. **2.** *n* a guarantee of money to be paid. **3.** *n* (*usually plural*) ropes or bands used to tie or fasten things.

bone [bown] *n* one of the hard, white parts which are joined together to make the skeletons of humans and other animals.

bonfire ['bɑnfayr] *n* a large fire out-of-doors.

book [bʊk] **1.** *n* pages of print bound together in a cover. **2.** *v* to reserve a place or a ticket in advance. **3.** *v* to charge with a crime.

bookcase ['bʊkkeys] *n* a set of shelves for books.

bookkeeper ['bʊkkipɚ] *n* a person who keeps track of money spent and money earned.

boom [buwm] *n* a sudden sound which is very loud and low.

boomerang ['buwmɚæŋg] *n* a curved, wooden weapon that turns in the air and comes back to the person who throws it. *Ex* Boomerangs are from Australia.

boot [buwt] *n* a shoe that covers part of the leg as well as the foot.

border ['bordɚ] *n* the outside edge of something.

bore [bor] **1.** *v* to make a hole by twisting a special tool round and round. **2.** *v* to make someone tired by dull talk. **3.** *v* the past tense of bear.

born [born] **1.** *adj* having come to life. **2.** *v* a past participle of bear.

borne [born] *v* a past participle of bear.

borrow ['barow] *v* to take something which you intend to give back.

bosom ['buzm̩] *n* the chest; the breasts.

boss [bɔs] *n* a chief or leader.

botany ['batṇi] *n* the scientific study of plants.

both [bowθ] **1.** *adj* having to do with two things or people. *Ex* She greeted both students. **2.** *pro* each of two things or people. *Ex* She greeted both.

bother ['baðɚ] **1.** *v* to annoy or worry. **2.** *n* fuss; trouble; an annoyance.

bottle ['batl̩] *n* a container for liquids. *Ex* Bottles are usually made of glass.

bottom ['batm̩] *n* the lowest part of anything; the underside of anything.

bough [baw] *n* a branch of a tree.

bought [bɔt] *v* the past tense and past participle of buy.

boulder ['bowldɚ] *n* a very large rock or stone.

bounce [bɑwn(t)s] *v* to spring up after hitting the ground; to make a ball spring up after hitting the ground.

bound [bɑwnd] *v* the past tense and past participle of bind.

bouquet [bow'key] *n* a bunch of picked flowers.

bow 1. *n* [bow] a kind of knot used to tie ribbon or shoelaces. **2.** *n* [bow] a curved strip of wood with a string. A bow is used for shooting arrows. **3.** *v* [bɑw] to show respect by bending forward and lowering your head.

bowl [bowl] **1.** *n* a deep, round dish for holding liquids or food. **2.** *v* to roll a heavy ball down a special smooth floor in the sport of bowling.

bowling ['bowlɪŋ] *n* a sport where a heavy ball is rolled down a special smooth floor to hit objects at the end. The objects at the end are called bowling pins.

box [bɑks] **1.** *n* a stiff-sided container. **2.** *v* to strike at an opponent in the sport of boxing; to do the sport of boxing.

boy [boy] *n* a male child.

bracelet ['breyslət] *n* a pretty chain or band worn on the arm.

bracket ['brækət] *n* a piece of wood or metal that holds up a shelf.

brag [bræg] *v* to boast; to say many good things about yourself or your possessions.

braid [breyd] **1.** *v* to weave hair or strips of material into something like a rope. **2.** *n* a woven length of hair or material.

brain [breyn] *n* the part of the body inside the head. *Ex* The brain sends and receives messages and thoughts and controls the body.

brakes [breyks] *n* the parts of a vehicle which the driver operates to make the vehicle stop.

branch [bræntʃ] *n* an arm of a tree that grows out of its trunk.

brand [brænd] **1.** *n* a mark placed on cattle to show whom they belong to. **2.** *n* the name or identification of a kind of a product. *Ex* What brand of coffee do you prefer?

brass [bræs] *n* a yellowish metal made from melting copper and zinc together; an alloy of copper and zinc.

brave [breyv] *adj* unafraid; not running away from danger even when you are afraid.

brawn [brɔn] *n* strength; powerful muscles.

bread [brɛd] *n* a food made mostly from flour and baked into a loaf.

breadth [brɛdθ] *n* the wideness or broadness of something.

break [breyk] **1.** *v* to pull something apart; to damage or spoil something. *pt* broke. *pp* broken. **2.** *n* an opening, such as a break in the clouds or a break in a water pipe.

breakfast ['brɛkfəst] *n* the first meal of the day.

breast [brɛst] **1.** *n* the chest; the top front of the body. **2.** *n* one of the glands in a mammal which can produce milk.

breath [brɛθ] *n* the air that is taken in and forced out by the lungs.

breathe [brið] *v* to move air in and out of the body with the lungs.

bred [brɛd] *v* the past tense and past participle of breed.

breed [brid] **1.** *n* a species or kind of animal or plant. *Ex* I don't care for that breed of dog. **2.** *v* to mate and produce young; to keep plants or animals and mate them for the production of young. *pt* bred. *pp* bred.

breeze [briz] *n* a gentle wind.

brick [brɪk] *n* a block of baked clay used in building.

bride [braɪd] *n* a woman on her wedding day.

bridesmaid ['braɪdzmeɪd] *n* a woman who attends the bride on her wedding day.

bridge [brɪdʒ] **1.** *n* a roadway built over a road, river, or railway so that you can get across to the other side. **2.** *n* a complicated card game.

brief [brif] *adj* short; not long.

bright [braɪt] **1.** *adj* shining; giving out light. **2.** *adj* smart; clever.

brilliant ['brɪlyənt] **1.** *adj* very bright; dazzling. **2.** *adj* very clever; very smart.

brim [brɪm] *n* rim; the upper edge of something; the rim of a hat.

bring [brɪŋ] *v* to carry something with you as you come. *pt* brought. *pp* brought.

brisk [brɪsk] *adj* alert; lively.

bristle ['brɪsl̩] *n* a short, stiff hair as in a brush.

brittle ['brɪtl̩] *adj* easily broken.

broad [brɔd] *adj* wide; the opposite of narrow.

broadcast ['brɔdkæst] *v* to send out radio or television programs of news and entertainment.

broil [brɔyl] *v* to cook something by putting it near a very hot source of heat.

broke [browk] **1.** *adj* having no money. **2.** *v* the past tense of break.

broken ['browkn̩] *v* the past participle of break.

bronchitis [brɑŋ'kɑytəs] *n* an illness in the throat and chest that makes you cough a lot.

bronze [brɑnz] *n* a reddish-brown metal made by melting copper and tin together; an alloy of copper and tin.

brood [bruwd] **1.** *v* to sit quietly and think or worry about something. **2.** *n* a group of birds that all hatched in one nest at the same time.

brook [brʊk] *n* a small stream.

broom [bruwm] *n* a brush with a long handle. *Ex* A broom is used for cleaning floors.

broth [brɔθ] *n* a kind of thin soup; the liquid in which foods have been cooked.

brother ['brəðɚ] *n* a male child who has the same parents as another child.

brought [brɔt] *v* the past tense and past participle of bring.

brow [brɑw] *n* the forehead; the eyebrow.

brown [brɑwn] *n* the color of chocolate.

bruise [bruwz] *n* a dark-colored mark where the skin has been hit but not broken.

brunette [bruw'nɛt] **1.** *adj* brownish; with brownish hair. **2.** *n* a person having brown or dark brown hair; a white person with relatively dark coloring.

brush [brəʃ] **1.** *n* a bunch of hairs or bristles on a handle. *Ex* Brushes are used for doing your hair, cleaning, and painting. **2.** *v* to make something clean with a brush; to make the hair neat with a brush.

bubble ['bəbl̩] *n* a very thin ball of liquid containing gas or air.

bucket ['bəkət] *n* a container with a handle for holding or carrying liquids.

buckle ['bəkl] **1.** *n* a fastening on a belt or a strap. **2.** *v* to fasten your belt. **3.** *v* to be made to bend or wrinkle.

bud [bəd] *n* a flower or a leaf before it has fully opened.

budge [bədʒ] *v* to move; to move a little; to give way; to yield. *Ex* The door was stuck, and it would not budge.

budget ['bədʒət] *n* a statement of how much money is to be earned and spent.

bug [bəg] *n* a tiny insect.

build [bɪld] *v* to make or construct something. *pt* built. *pp* built.

builder ['bɪldə˞] *n* a person who constructs things; a person who builds buildings, especially houses.

building ['bɪldɪŋ] *n* a structure with walls, a floor, and a ceiling; a large structure with many levels.

built [bɪlt] *v* the past tense and past participle of build.

bulb [bəlb] **1.** *n* a small glass lamp which gives out light when electricity is applied to it. **2.** *n* the rounded root from which flowers such as tulips grow.

bulge [bəldʒ] **1.** *v* to swell out. **2.** *n* a lump; a swelling.

bulk [bəlk] *n* a large amount.

bull [bʊl] *n* the male of cattle, moose, or elephants.

bulldozer ['bʊldowzə˞] *n* a powerful tractor used for moving loads of earth, sand, or rubbish.

bullet ['bʊlət] *n* a small piece of metal which is shot from a gun.

bulletin board ['bʊlətn̩ bord] *n* a panel of cork or other soft material on which messages or notices are tacked.

bullfrog ['bʊlfrɔg] *n* a large frog with a very deep voice.

bully [ˈbuli] *n* someone who picks on smaller or weaker persons.

bumblebee [ˈbəmbl̩bi] *n* a large bee which makes a loud buzzing sound.

bump [bəmp] **1.** *n* a swelling; a raised lump. **2.** *v* to knock into something; to knock a part of the body into something. *Ex* Ouch! I bumped my head.

bumper [ˈbəmpɚ] *n* pieces of curved metal on the front and back of cars to protect them if they bump into something.

bun [bən] **1.** *n* a small, round cake or loaf of bread. **2.** *n* a small loaf of bread shaped to hold a hot dog or a hamburger.

bunch [bəntʃ] *n* a group of things.

bundle [ˈbəndl̩] *n* a number of things tied together, like a bundle of clothes or newspapers.

bungalow [ˈbəŋgəlow] *n* a house with no upstairs.

bunk [bəŋk] *n* a shelf-like bed attached to a wall.

buoy [ˈbuwi] *n* an object floating in the water and anchored to the bottom. *Ex* Buoys aid boats in following a safe passage and warn them of danger.

burden [ˈbɚdn̩] *n* a load that is very heavy to carry; worrisome thoughts that are difficult to bear.

bureau [ˈbyɚow] **1.** *n* a chest of drawers. **2.** *n* an office, especially a government office.

burglar [ˈbɚglɚ] *n* someone who breaks into buildings and steals things.

burial [ˈbɛriəl] *n* the burying of something, like a dead body, in the ground.

burn [bɚn] **1.** *v* to be on fire; to set something on fire so that it will burn up. **2.** *n* an injury to the skin from fire.

burrow ['bɝow] **1.** *n* a hole or tunnel in the ground which has been dug by wild animals. *Ex* Rabbits and foxes dig and live in burrows. **2.** *v* to dig a hole or tunnel.

burst [bɝst] **1.** *v* to explode; to rush forth; to pop like a balloon. *pt* burst. *pp* burst. **2.** *n* a sudden outbreak; an explosion.

bury ['bɛri] *v* to put an object deep into something, usually in the ground.

bus [bəs] **1.** *n* a large vehicle which carries many people. **2.** *v* to cause people to be carried by bus.

bush [buʃ] *n* a small tree with many branches growing close to the ground; a shrub.

business ['bɪznəs] *n* an occupation; commerce.

businessman ['bɪznəsmæn] *n* a man who works for or manages a business firm.

businesswoman ['bɪznəswumən] *n* a woman who works for or manages a business firm.

bus route ['bəs rawt] *n* the streets that a bus follows.

bus stop ['bəs stap] *n* one of the places that a bus will stop to take in or let out passengers.

bust [bəst] **1.** *n* a sculpture of someone's head, shoulders, and chest. **2.** *n* the breasts.

bustle ['bəsl̩] *v* to rush about busily.

busy ['bɪzi] *adj* with your time fully occupied; working hard.

but [bət] **1.** *prep* except. *Ex* Everyone but me got an apple. **2.** *conj* except that, unless, if not. *Ex* I would have come, but I wasn't invited.

butcher ['butʃɚ] **1.** *v* to kill a food animal and cut up the meat. **2.** *n* a person who cuts up meat for sale in a store.

butter ['bətɚ] **1.** *n* a kind of soft, yellow fat made from cream. **2.** *v* to spread butter on bread.

butterfly ['bətɚflɑy] *n* an insect with large, colored wings.

buttermilk ['bətɚmɪlk] *n* the milk left after butter has been made; a sour milk made by growing special bacteria in sweet milk.

butterscotch ['bətɚskɑtʃ] *n* a candy made from brown sugar and butter.

buttocks ['bətəks] *n* the two rounded parts of the body that you sit on.

button ['bətn̩] **1.** *n* a small, round fastener on clothing. **2.** *n* a small, round disk that you press to ring a bell or operate a radio. **3.** *v* to fasten clothing by putting buttons through buttonholes.

buttonhole ['bətn̩howl] *n* a narrow hole or slot in cloth for a button to fit into.

buy [bɑy] *v* to give money in exchange for something. *Ex* I am going to buy a new car. *pt* bought. *pp* bought.

buzz [bəz] **1.** *n* a humming sound like that made by bees or flies. **2.** *v* to cause an electric buzzer to buzz; to signal a person by the use of an electric buzzer.

buzzer ['bəzɚ] *n* an electric device which makes a loud humming sound when electricity is applied to it.

by [bɑy] **1.** *prep* near; near to. *Ex* There is a post office by our house. **2.** *prep* past. *Ex* The bus went right by him and didn't stop. **3.** *prep* as an act of. *Ex* The dinner was cooked by Rachel. **4.** *adv* past. *Ex* The bus went right by.

bye [bɑy] *interj* short for the word good-bye.

C

---

cab [kæb] **1.** *n* a taxi. **2.** *n* the place in a truck where the driver sits.

cabin ['kæbən] **1.** *n* a small house made of logs or other rough materials. **2.** *n* a room for passengers on a ship or an airplane.

cabinet ['kæb(ə)nət] **1.** *n* a cupboard for storing things. **2.** *n* a group of people chosen to advise the U.S. President.

cable ['keybl̩] *n* a very strong, thick rope made of wires twisted together.

cable television [keybl̩ 'tɛləvɪʒn̩] *n* a system of television where the programs are carried over wires rather than being sent out from an antenna.

cactus ['kæktəs] *n* a plant with thick leaves and stems. *Ex* Cactus usually grows in the desert. The plural is cactuses or cacti.

cadet [kə'dɛt] *n* a young man who is learning to be an officer in the army, navy, or air force.

cafe [kæ'fey] *n* a small restaurant; a place where you can buy a meal or a snack.

cafeteria [kæfə'tɪriə] *n* an eating place where you pick out your food at a counter and carry it to your table.

cage [keydʒ] *n* a box or room with bars where birds or animals are kept.

cake [keyk] **1.** *n* a sweet food made of flour, fat, eggs, and sugar and baked in an oven. **2.** *n* a flat lump of something, like a cake of soap.

calamity [kə'læməti] *n* something terrible that happens, like an earthquake or an airplane crash in which many people are killed or hurt.

calcium ['kælsiəm] *n* an important element which we need for strong bones and teeth. *Ex* There is much calcium in milk.

calculator ['kælkyəleytɚ] *n* a machine, usually electronic, which solves mathematical problems.

calculus ['kælkyələs] *n* a type of mathematics which uses special symbols.

calendar ['kæləndɚ] *n* a chart of all of the days and dates of each month in the year.

calf [kæf] **1.** *n* a young cow or bull. **2.** *n* the back part of the leg below the knee. The plural is calves.

call [kɔl] **1.** *n* a telephone call. **2.** *n* a stop at someone's house for a short time. **3.** *v* to cry out; for an animal or bird to make its sound. **4.** *v* to say someone's name aloud.

calm [kɑm] **1.** *adj* still; relaxed. **2.** *v* to comfort someone.

came [keym] *v* the past tense of come.

camel ['kæməl] *n* a big animal with a long neck and one or two humps on its back. *Ex* Camels carry people or things from place to place in some hot countries.

camera ['kæm(ə)rə] *n* a device for taking photographs.

camouflage ['kæməflɑʒ] *v* to disguise something so that the enemy cannot see it.

camp [kæmp] **1.** *v* to live outdoors in a tent. **2.** *n* a place where tents are set up for outdoor living.

campaign [kæm'peyn] **1.** *n* a series of actions which cause something important to happen; a battle. **2.** *v* to attempt to cause something to happen; to wage a battle.

campus ['kæmpəs] *n* the buildings and grounds of a college or other school. The plural is campuses.

can [kæn] **1.** *n* a metal container for foods or liquids. **2.** *v* to be physically or mentally fit to do something; to be able to. *Ex* She can paint beautiful pictures. *pt* could.

canal [kə'næl] *n* a very large ditch, dug across land and filled with water so that ships and boats can move along it.

canary [kə'nɛri] *n* a small, yellow bird kept as a pet because of its sweet song.

cancel ['kæn(t)sl̩] *v* to do away with; to call off.

candidate ['kændədeyt, 'kæn(d)ədət] *n* a person who is running for an office; a person who is being considered for an award.

candle ['kændl̩] *n* a rounded stick of wax with a string through the center. When the string is lit, the wax burns slowly and gives off light.

candlestick ['kændl̩stɪk] *n* a holder for a candle. *Ex* The end of the candle is stuck in the candlestick so that the candle stands up straight.

candy ['kændi] *n* sugar made into good-tasting things to eat.

cane [keyn] **1.** *n* the hard stem of a plant; a stick of bamboo. **2.** *n* a stick which is used to help a person walk.

cannon ['kænən] *n* a big, heavy gun on wheels; a big, heavy gun mounted on a ship.

cannot [kæn'nɑt] *v* not able to; not permitted to.

canoe [kə'nuw] *n* a light, narrow boat, usually pointed at both ends. *Ex* A paddle is used to make the canoe move through the water.

canopy ['kænəpi] *n* a covering hung over something, such as a bed, a throne, or a patio.

can't [kænt] *cont* can not.

canvas ['kænvəs] *n* a tough, strong cloth used for tents and sails and for painting pictures on.

canyon ['kænyən] *n* a deep, narrow valley, often with a stream or river running through it.

cap [kæp] *n* a soft, small hat, usually with a bill.

capacity [kə'pæsəti] *n* the greatest amount a container will hold.

cape [keyp] **1.** *n* a piece of clothing without sleeves that goes over the back and shoulders and fastens around the neck. **2.** *n* a piece of land sticking out into the sea.

capital ['kæpətl] **1.** *n* the large letters of the alphabet used at the beginnings of sentences. **2.** *n* the chief city in a state or country. **3.** *n* an amount of money used for investment.

capitol ['kæpətl] *n* a building in which a legislative body meets.

capsule ['kæpsl] **1.** *n* a tiny container for medicine something like a large pill. *Ex* When you swallow a capsule, it melts and lets the medicine out. **2.** *n* the closed cabin of a spacecraft.

captain ['kæptən] *n* the person in charge of a group of people like a group of soldiers, sailors, or a sports team.

captive ['kæptɪv] **1.** *n* someone who has been captured and held prisoner. **2.** *adj* held under control; held as a prisoner.

capture ['kæptʃɚ] *v* to catch something or someone and hold by force.

car [kɑr] *n* a motor vehicle used for driving from place to place.

caramel ['kɑrməl] *n* a kind of candy made by cooking sugar, butter, and cream together.

caravan ['kɛrəvæn] *n* a group of people traveling together for safety, usually in the desert, and usually with camels.

carbon paper ['kɑrbn̩ peypɚ] *n* very thin paper with a colored coating on one side. When a sheet of carbon paper is placed between two white sheets of paper, whatever is written or typed on the top sheet will appear on the bottom sheet.

carburetor ['kɑrbɚeytɚ] *n* the part of a car's engine which mixes gasoline with air so that the engine can burn the mixture.

card [kɑrd] **1.** *n* a square or rectangle of stiff paper. **2.** *n* a postcard on which short notes are written. Some postcards have brightly colored pictures on one side. **3.** *n* a greeting card on which is printed a design and a message for special occasions, such as Christmas or a wedding anniversary. **4.** *n* a playing card which is used in card games, such as bridge, poker, or gin rummy.

cardboard ['kɑrdbord] *n* a very thick and stiff kind of paper.

care [kɛr] **1.** *n* a worry; trouble. **2.** *v* to have concern; o provide comfort for someone; to like; to be fond.

career [kə'rir] **1.** *n* a person's progress through life; a period of existence. **2.** *n* a job or profession.

careful ['kɛrfl̩] *adj* giving special attention to what is being done.

careless ['kɛrləs] *adj* not taking care; not thinking about what is being done.

caretaker ['kɛrteykɚ] *n* a person who looks after a building or part of a building.

cargo ['kɑrgow] *n* the load of goods carried by a ship, truck, or airplane.

carol ['kɛrəl] *n* a song of joy; a special kind of song sung at Christmastime.

carpenter ['kɑrpəntɚ] *n* someone who makes things out of wood.

carpet ['kɑrpət] *n* a thick, soft woven covering for the floor.

carry ['kɛri] *v* to take something from place to place.

cart [kɑrt] **1.** *n* an open wagon with two or four wheels. *Ex* Carts are sometimes pulled by horses. **2.** *v* to carry or transport with a cart; to carry or haul something.

carton ['kɑrtn̩] *n* a box or similar container made from cardboard.

cartoon [kɑr'tuwn] *n* a funny drawing in a newspaper or a magazine; a short, funny film in which the scenes are drawn by hand.

cartridge ['kɑrtrɪdʒ] **1.** *n* a case for holding the gunpowder and bullet which is to be shot from a gun. **2.** *n* a case which holds a length of tape for a sound or television recorder.

carve [kɑrv] *v* to cut a piece of wood into a shape; to cut a piece of cooked meat or fowl into slices.

case [keys] **1.** *n* a kind of box to keep or carry things in. **2.** *n* a set of circumstances which needs to be examined; the circumstances surrounding a crime and the crime itself.

caseworker ['keyswɚkɚ] *n* a kind of public helper who works with the problems of a specific person.

cash [kæʃ] **1.** *n* money; coins and bills. **2.** *v* to receive cash for a check.

cashier [kæ'ʃir] *n* a person whose job is to receive and pay out money.

cassette [kə'sɛt] *n* a small, plastic case holding tape for a sound or television recorder.

cast [kæst] **1.** *v* to throw something outward with force. **2.** *v* to create something by pouring liquid metal or plaster into a mold. **3.** *n* the group of performers in a play or opera.

castle ['kæsḷ] *n* an old building with thick stone walls to resist enemy attacks.

cat [kæt] *n* a furry animal with sharp teeth and claws, often kept as a pet; a kind of mammal, including pet cats, lions, tigers, and panthers, which eats meat.

catalog ['kætḷɔg] *n* a list of things in a special order, such as a list of books in a library; a special book which lists things for sale.

catch [kætʃ] *v* to get hold of something; to capture something. *pt* caught. *pp* caught.

catcher ['kætʃɚ] *n* the baseball player who stands behind the batter and catches the balls that the batter does not hit. *Ex* The catcher throws the ball back to the pitcher.

caterpillar ['kætɚpɪlɚ] *n* a worm or a grub which turns into a moth or a butterfly.

cathedral [kə'θidrəl] *n* a very large and important church.

catsup ['kɛtʃəp] *n* a mildly seasoned sauce made from tomatoes.

cattle ['kætḷ] *n* cows, bulls, and oxen. The word is plural, and it has no singular form.

caught [kɔt] *v* the past tense and past participle of catch.

cause [kɔz] **1.** *v* to make something happen. **2.** *n* something or someone which causes a thing to happen.

caution ['kɔʃṇ] **1.** *n* a statement of warning; a reminder to be careful. *Ex* Pay attention to his words of caution. **2.** *n* carefulness. *Ex* Please use caution when crossing the street. **3.** *v* to advise someone to be careful; to warn someone. *Ex* The teacher cautioned me about crossing the street.

cave [keyv] *n* a big hole in rocks or in the side of a hill.

cavern ['kævɚn] *n* a large cave.

cease [sis] *v* to stop doing something; to stop.

ceiling ['silɪŋ] *n* the top of a room.

celebration [sɛlə'breyʃn̩] *n* a party or a festival on a special day like a birthday or a national holiday.

cell [sɛl] **1.** *n* a single room in a prison. **2.** *n* a very tiny part of a living being contained in a very thin wall.

cellar ['sɛlɚ] *n* an underground room where things like wine are stored; a basement.

Celsius ['sɛlsiəs] *adj* a type of heat measurement in degrees; centigrade. *Ex* Freezing is 0 degrees and boiling is 100 degrees Celsius.

cement [sɪ'mɛnt] **1.** *n* a grayish, powdered clay mixture that hardens when it is mixed with sand and water. *Ex* Cement is used to stick bricks and other building materials together. **2.** *n* a type of glue that is different from paste. **3.** *v* to stick things together with cement.

cemetery ['sɛmətɛri] *n* a place where people who have died are buried.

cent [sɛnt] *n* 1/100th of a dollar; a penny.

center ['sɛntɚ] *n* the middle part of anything.

centigrade ['sɛntəgreyd] *adj* a scale for measuring heat expressed in degrees. *Ex* The boiling point of water is 100 degrees centigrade, and the freezing point is 0 degrees centigrade.

centimeter ['sɛntəmitɚ] *n* 1/100th of a meter; a distance equal to 0.39 inches.

century ['sɛntʃɚi] *n* a hundred years.

cereal ['sɪriəl] *n* any kind of grain used as food; a food product made from grain and usually eaten for breakfast.

ceremony ['sɛrəmowni] *n* an important or special happening, like a wedding.

certain ['sɚtṇ] *adj* sure; without any doubt.

certainly ['sɚtṇli] *adv* without any doubt.

certificate [sɚ'tɪfəkət] *n* something written or printed which proves that something is true.

chain [tʃeyn] *n* metal rings joined together to make a long, strong thing like a rope.

chair [tʃɛr] *n* a single seat with a back to lean on.

chalk [tʃɔk] *n* a soft, white stone which can be made into sticks for writing on the blackboard.

chalkboard ['tʃɔkbord] *n* a hard surface which can be written or drawn on with chalk; a blackboard.

challenge ['tʃæləndʒ] **1.** *v* to invite someone to beat you at something, such as running or swimming. **2.** *n* something that makes a person wish to compete or to succeed.

champion ['tʃæmpiən] *n* someone who is better at a sport than other players; someone who wins often at a sport.

chance [tʃæn(t)s] *n* an opportunity.

change [tʃeyndʒ] **1.** *v* to make something different from what it was before. **2.** *n* the act of becoming different. **3.** *n* coins and bills returned to you when you make a purchase and pay for it with an amount of money larger than the selling price.

channel ['tʃænl] **1.** *n* a deep strip of water in a lake or harbor or between two areas of land. *Ex* Ships and large boats can go through channels without hitting bottom. **2.** *n* a kind of electrical pathway used for television signals.

chap [tʃæp] **1.** *n* a fellow. **2.** *v* for the skin, especially of the lips, to become sore and rough in cold, dry weather.

chapel ['tʃæpəl] *n* a small church or a separate part of a large church.

chapter ['tʃæptɚ] *n* a section of a book. *Ex* Chapters are usually numbered, chapter 1, chapter 2, and so forth.

character ['kɛrɪktɚ] **1.** *n* what a person is like. *Ex* A person's character may be good or bad, honest or dishonest, nice or nasty. **2.** *n* a person in a story or a play.

charcoal ['tʃɑrkowl] *n* a hard piece of burned wood. *Ex* Charcoal is used to cook with or to draw pictures with.

charge [tʃɑrdʒ] **1.** *v* to rush at something. **2.** *n* control; custody. *Ex* I am in charge of the books. **3.** *v* to use a credit card to buy something; to buy something and be billed for it later. *Ex* Do you want to pay cash or charge it? Cash or charge?

charity ['tʃɛrəti] *n* a feeling of kindness and affection toward other people; a gift of money, food, or shelter to someone in need.

charm [tʃɑrm] **1.** *v* to make people think you are nice and pleasant to know. **2.** *n* something that has magic powers or can bring good luck.

chart [tʃɑrt] *n* a map, usually of the sea; a table of information.

chase [tʃeys] **1.** *v* to run after something or someone. **2.** *n* the act of running after someone or something.

chassis ['tʃæsi] *n* the framework which forms the base of a car.

chat [tʃæt] **1.** *v* to talk with someone in a friendly way. **2.** *n* a friendly talk.

chatter ['tʃætɚ] **1.** *v* to talk a lot about things that are not important. **2.** *n* a lot of unimportant talk.

chauffeur ['ʃowfɚ] *n* a person who is paid to drive someone else's car.

cheap [tʃip] *adj* not expensive; not costing much money.

cheat [tʃit] *v* to do something which is not honest or right, like copying someone else's answers during a test.

check [tʃɛk] **1.** *v* to go back over something to make sure it is correct. **2.** *n* a pattern with small squares in it. **3.** *n* a note directing your bank to pay a sum of money to the person presenting the note.

check out ['tʃɛk 'awt] **1.** *v* to borrow something from a place which keeps a record of what is lent to whom. *Ex* Books are checked out from a library. **2.** *v* to take purchases to a counter in a store and pay for them just before you leave the store. **3.** *n* the place where you pay for purchases just before you leave a store. Often written *checkout*.

checkup ['tʃɛkəp] *n* a general physical examination of the body.

cheek [tʃik] *n* the soft side of your face below the eyes and on either side of the nose.

cheer [tʃir] **1.** *n* joy; happiness. **2.** *v* to shout and cry out in honor of someone or in honor of someone's accomplishments.

cheerful ['tʃirfl̩] *adj* happy; joyful.

cheese [tʃiz] *n* a food made from milk.

chemistry ['kɛməstri] *n* the scientific study of what things are made of.

cherry ['tʃɛri] *n* a sweet, round, red or yellow fruit with a stone in it.

chess [tʃɛs] *n* a game for two people, using pieces called chessmen, played on a board marked with black and white squares.

chest [tʃɛst] **1.** *n* a large, strong box with a lid. **2.** *n* the front part of the body between the neck and the waist.

chew [tʃuw] *v* to crush or grind with the teeth.

chewing gum ['tʃuwɪŋ gəm] *n* a substance, something like candy, that is chewed but not swallowed.

chick [tʃɪk] *n* a baby chicken; a baby bird.

chicken ['tʃɪkn̩] *n* a hen or a rooster.

chicken pox ['tʃɪkn̩ pɑks] *n* an illness where a person has a fever and spots on the body.

chief [tʃif] **1.** *n* a leader or ruler. **2.** *adj* the most important.

child [tʃɑyld] *n* a human being who is older than a baby but younger than an adolescent.

children ['tʃɪldrən] *n* boys and girls; the plural of child.

chilly ['tʃɪli] *adj* cool; cold; feeling cold.

chime [tʃɑym] *n* a musical sound made by a set of bells, usually in a clock.

chimney ['tʃɪmni] *n* a small tunnel from a fireplace to the roof to let smoke out.

chimpanzee [tʃɪmpæn'zi] *n* a clever and intelligent ape which is smaller than a gorilla. *Ex* Chimpanzees can be trained to perform many acts.

chin [tʃɪn] *n* the part of the face under the mouth.

china ['tʃɑynə] *n* cups and plates made from a kind of fine clay.

chip [tʃɪp] **1.** *v* to knock off a small piece of something like a cup or a vase. **2.** *n* a small piece of something which has been knocked off of something larger.

chipmunk ['tʃɪpməŋk] *n* a small, wild animal, like a squirrel with stripes.

chirp [tʃɚp] *n* a short, shrill sound made by some birds and insects.

chisel ['tʃɪzl̩] *n* a tool with a cutting edge at the end. A chisel is used for cutting stone or wood.

chocolate ['tʃɔklət] *n* a sweet, brown food or drink made from sugar and cocoa.

choice [tʃɔys] *n* the power to select something; the person or thing chosen. *Ex* Is your choice the red one or the white one? He is my choice for president.

choir [kwɑyr] *n* a group of people trained to sing together.

choke [tʃowk] **1.** *v* to find it very hard to breathe because there is something stuck in your throat or because there is smoke in your lungs. **2.** *v* to cut off the breathing of a person or an animal.

choose [tʃuwz] *v* to take one thing rather than another; to make a choice. *pt* chose. *pp* chosen.

chop [tʃɑp] **1.** *v* to cut something with hard blows. **2.** *n* a piece of meat, usually lamb or pork, on a bone.

chopsticks ['tʃɑpstɪks] *n* two thin sticks of wood or ivory used for eating food by people living in some Far Eastern countries.

chorus ['korəs] **1.** *n* the part of a song that comes after each verse. **2.** *n* the people on a stage in an opera or a concert who sing together.

chose [tʃowz] *v* the past tense of choose.

chosen ['tʃowzn̩] *v* the past participle of choose.

chrome [krowm] *n* a silvery-looking metal.

chuckle ['tʃəkl̩] *v* to laugh quietly.

chum [tʃəm] *n* a close friend.

church [tʃɚtʃ] *n* a building where people go to worship God. This usually refers to a Christian church.

churn [tʃɚn] **1.** *n* a simple machine for making butter. **2.** *v* to make butter in a churn.

cigar [sə'gɑr] *n* a stick of tobacco made of tobacco leaves rolled tightly together, for smoking.

cigarette [sɪgə'rɛt] *n* finely cut pieces of tobacco rolled in a thin paper, for smoking.

cinder ['sɪndɚ] *n* a piece of coal or wood that has been burned, but not burned away to ashes. *Ex* Cinders are often hard and rough.

cinema ['sɪnəmə] *n* a building where motion pictures are shown.

circle ['sɚkl] *n* a completely round ring.

circular ['sɚkyələ] *adj* in the shape of a circle.

circulate ['sɚkyəleyt] *v* to move around and come back to the starting point. *Ex* Blood circulates through the veins of our body. Library books circulate when they are checked out from the library and then returned to the library.

circulation [sɚkyə'leyʃn̩] **1.** *n* the movement of blood throughout the body. **2.** *n* the department of a library in charge of checking books in and out.

circumference [sɚ'kəmfrən(t)s] *n* the distance around a circle or any other round object.

circumstance ['sɚkəmstæn(t)s] *n* the time, place, and facts relating to an event.

circus ['sɚkəs] *n* a traveling show with acrobats, animals, and clowns.

citizen ['sɪtəzn̩] *n* a person who lives in a city, town, county, state, or nation.

citizenship ['sɪtəzn̩ʃɪp] *n* the condition of being a citizen of a country.

citrus ['sɪtrəs] *n* a kind of fruit. *Ex* Oranges, lemons, and grapefruit are citrus fruits.

city ['sɪti] *n* a very large town consisting of houses and other buildings.

city hall [sɪti 'hɔl] *n* the place where the business of a city is conducted.

civil ['sɪvl̩] **1.** *adj* having to do with people or the government, but not having to do with the armed forces. **2.** *adj* polite; courteous.

claim [kleym] **1.** *v* to demand or ask for something because you believe you should have it. **2.** *n* a right to have something; the demand for something which is due to you.

clam [klæm] *n* a type of shellfish. *Ex* The meat is inside, and the clam must be opened in order to get it out.

clang [klæŋ] *n* a loud, deep echoing noise, usually made by striking something metal, like a bell.

clap [klæp] *v* to slap the palms of the hands together to make a noise.

clash [klæʃ] **1.** *n* a loud noise made when things are banged together. **2.** *n* a disagreement; a battle. **3.** *v* for two or more things, especially colors, to look bad when placed close together. *Ex* Your orange sweater and purple skirt clash.

clasp [klæsp] **1.** *v* to hold something tightly. **2.** *n* the fastening for a brooch or other piece of jewelry.

class [klæs] **1.** *n* a group of children or older people learning something together. **2.** *n* any group of people or things sharing one or more features in common.

classical ['klæsɪkl̩] **1.** *adj* having to do with the ancient Greek or Roman cultures. **2.** *adj* having to do with music like symphonies, operas, and chamber music.

classified ['klæsɪfɑyd] *adj* having to do with newspaper advertisements which are divided into different types or classes.

classroom ['klæsruwm] *n* a room in a school where children learn things.

clatter ['klætɚ] *n* a rattling noise, as when dishes are being washed or stacked.

claw [klɔ] *n* one of the sharp, curved nails on the foot of an animal or bird.

clay [kley] *n* a soft, sticky material which can be modeled into things; a soft, sticky earth that can be baked to make bricks or pots.

clean [klin] **1.** *adj* without dirt or dust; free of anything dirty or unpleasant. **2.** *v* to remove the dirt or dust from something or someplace.

cleaner ['klinɚ] *n* a tool or chemical substance used to help clean something.

cleanse [klɛnz] *v* to make something clean.

clean up [klin 'əp] *v* to make something clean; to remove a mess or a problem. *Ex* Please clean this mess up. Please clean up this mess.

clear [klir] **1.** *adj* bright, or with nothing in the way, so that you can see things clearly. **2.** *v* to clean up; to remove everything. *Ex* Please clear the dirty dishes off the table. **3.** *v* to become sunny. *Ex* The sky is clearing.

clench [klɛntʃ] *v* to close your teeth or fist tightly on or around something. *Ex* He clenched his teeth on the X-ray film.

clerk [klɚk] **1.** *n* someone who does office work, such as answering letters and keeping accounts; a person who sells things in a store. **2.** *v* to work as a clerk in an office or a store.

clever ['klɛvɚ] *adj* quick to learn; able to do things very well.

click [klɪk] *n* a short, snapping sound.

cliff [klɪf] *n* a high, steep wall of rock, earth, or ice. *Ex* One must be careful not to fall off of a cliff.

climate ['klɑymət] *n* the kind of weather a country or region usually has. *Ex* Africa and India have hot climates.

climb [klɑym] *v* to move upward using your feet and sometimes your hands to hold on. *Ex* She climbed the stairs with ease. She climbed the cliff with difficulty.

cling [klɪŋ] *v* to hold on to something tightly. *pt* clung. *pp* clung.

clinic ['klɪnɪk] *n* a place where people go to see doctors or nurses.

clip [klɪp] **1.** *v* to cut or trim something with scissors. **2.** *n* a small, metal device for holding papers together.

cloakroom ['klowkruwm] *n* a place where people can leave hats and coats.

clock [klɑk] *n* a machine that tells you what time it is.

clockwise ['klɑkwɑyz] *adv* in the circular direction in which a clock's hands move as seen from the front of the clock; the opposite of counterclockwise.

clog [klɔg] *v* to block a passage, tube, or pipe to keep things from going through. *Ex* There was no water because the pipe was clogged.

close 1. *v* [klowz] to shut something. *Ex* Please close the door. **2.** *adv* [klows] near; nearby.

closet ['klɑzət] *n* a very small room in which clothing is hung.

cloth [klɔθ] *n* a woven material that clothes and coverings are made of.

clothes [klow(ð)z] *n* all of the things made of cloth that a person wears.

clothesline ['klow(ð)zlɑyn] *n* a rope stretched above the ground and used for hanging clothes on to dry.

clothespin ['klow(ð)zpɪn] *n* a wooden or plastic device used to fasten clothing onto a clothesline.

clothing ['klowðɪŋ] *n* clothes.

cloud [klɑwd] *n* one of the very large white bodies seen in the sky. *Ex* A cloud is made of millions of tiny water drops floating in the air.

cloudy ['klɑwdi] *adj* having to do with a day with so many clouds in the sky that little sunlight gets through.

clout [klɑwt] *n* a hard blow.

clover ['klowvɚ] *n* a plant with three rounded leaves at the end of each stem and small white or pink blossoms.

clown [klɑwn] *n* a circus performer who has a painted face and who does funny tricks.

club [kləb] **1.** *n* a heavy stick for hitting. **2.** *n* a group of people who meet together to do things or discuss things.

cluck [klək] *n* the soft, short sound a hen makes to her chicks.

clue [kluw] *n* something that helps you find the answer to a puzzle or a mystery.

clump [kləmp] *n* a number of plants or trees growing close together.

clumsy ['kləmzi] *adj* not graceful; not good at handling things.

clung [kləŋ] *v* the past tense and past participle of cling.

cluster ['kləstɚ] *n* a bunch; a group.

clutch [klətʃ] **1.** *v* to grab something and hold on to it tightly; to clench something. **2.** *n* a part of the machinery which makes it possible to control the power of an engine. **3.** *n* a pedal in some cars which is pushed down when the gears are shifted.

coach [kowtʃ] **1.** *n* a large bus used to carry people over long distances. **2.** *n* the standard class or second class of airplane travel. *Ex* Are you flying first-class or coach? **3.** *n* a person who trains sports teams and gives players advice during games. **4.** *v* to train the member of a sports team; to train a person in skills such as acting, singing, or debate.

coal [kowl] *n* a hard, black mineral used for fuel.

coarse [kors] *adj* rough; rude.

coast [kowst] **1.** *n* the border of land next to the sea. **2.** *v* to go downhill in a vehicle without applying power. *Ex* If I can pedal my bicycle to the top of the hill, I can coast for the rest of the way to school.

coat [kowt] *n* an item of warm outer clothing with sleeves.

coat hanger ['kowt hæŋɚ] *n* a device made of wire, wood, or plastic on which a coat or other clothing can be hung neatly. *Ex* The coat hanger is hung on a pole in a closet.

coat hook ['kowt hʊk] *n* a hook on which a coat or other clothing can be hung.

cobbler ['kɑblɚ] **1.** *n* a person who repairs shoes. **2.** *n* a type of fruit pie with a thick crust.

cobweb ['kɑbwɛb] *n* the net of very fine threads made by a spider; a net of fine threads and dust which looks like the net made by a spider.

cockroach ['kɑkrowtʃ] *n* an insect pest which crawls about in houses. It is also called a roach.

cocoa ['kowkow] *n* a brown powder made from cocoa beans. *Ex* Cocoa is used to make chocolate candy or hot chocolate.

coconut ['kowkənət] *n* a very large nut with white meat and a white liquid inside; the meat of the coconut. *Ex* The coconut is the fruit of the palm tree.

cod [kɑd] *n* a large ocean fish caught for food.

code [kowd] *n* secret words or signals used to send messages.

coffee ['kɔfi] *n* a hot drink made from ground-up, roasted coffee beans.

coffin ['kɔfn̩] *n* a large metal or wooden box that a dead body is put into.

coil [koyl] **1.** *v* to wind something, such as a rope, in rings. **2.** *n* a length of something, such as wire or rope, wound in rings.

coin [koyn] *n* a piece of money made of metal.

coin return ['koyn rɪtɚn] **1.** *n* an opening in a vending machine or pay telephone where change is given back to you. **2.** *n* the button or lever which causes coins to be returned to you from a vending machine or a telephone.

coin slot ['koyn slɑt] *n* a slot on a vending machine or a pay telephone where money is put in.

cola ['kowlə] *n* a cold, sweet, and bubbly drink which comes in cans or bottles.

cold [kowld] **1.** *adj* not hot. *Ex* Fire is hot, and ice is cold. **2.** *n* an illness which affects the nose and throat.

cold-blooded ['kowld'blədəd] **1.** *adj* having to do with animals which do not have naturally warm bodies; having to do with reptiles and other lower animals. **2.** *adj* cruel; vicious.

coliseum [kɑlə'siəm] *n* a large arena or other structure used for public performances. Sometimes spelled colosseum.

collage [kə'lɑʒ] *n* a work of art made from many different things glued onto a surface.

collapse [kə'læps] *v* to fall to pieces; to fall down into a heap.

collar ['kɑlə·] *n* the part of a shirt, blouse, or coat which goes around the neck.

collect [kə'lɛkt] *v* to bring together; to gather together.

collection [kə'lɛkʃn̩] *n* the things that a person collects, such as stamps, seashells, or coins.

college ['kɑlɪdʒ] *n* a place where a person can continue schooling after high school.

collide [kə'lɑyd] *v* to come into sudden, hard contact with something. *Ex* The two cars collided.

colon ['kowlən] **1.** *n* the punctuation mark (:) used to direct attention to what follows it. **2.** *n* the lower part of the large intestine; the lower part of the bowels.

colonist ['kɑlənɪst] *n* a person who settles in a colony.

colony ['kɑləni] **1.** *n* a large population of insects, such as ants or termites. **2.** *n* a country or a region ruled by another country. *Ex* The United States used to be a colony of Great Britain. **3.** *n* a group of people living together and sharing common interests. *Ex* Artists and musicians sometimes live in colonies.

color ['kələ·] **1.** *n* a quality of light that makes things appear as red, yellow, blue, and so forth. **2.** *v* to use crayons or pencils to add colors to pictures or to draw pictures.

column ['kɑləm] **1.** *n* a pillar; a tall square or round support on a building. **2.** *n* a line of soldiers. **3.** *n* a list of numbers or words where there is one number or word on each line.

comb [kowm] **1.** *n* a piece of plastic or metal with teeth in it. *Ex* A comb is used to make a person's hair neat. **2.** *v* to use a comb to make the hair neat.

combination [kɑmbə'neyʃn̩] **1.** *n* a mixture; a combining. **2.** *n* the special letters or numbers that are needed to open a combination lock.

combination lock [kɑmbəneyʃn̩ 'lɑk] *n* a kind of lock which will open only when the proper set of letters or numbers has been set on its dial.

combine [kəm'bɑyn] *v* to mix together; to join together.

come [kəm] *v* to approach; to arrive; to move near. *Ex* Come to me. When do you think the train will come? *pt* came. *pp* come.

comedian [kə'midiən] *n* an actor who makes people laugh.

comedy ['kɑmədi] *n* a funny play or motion picture.

comfort ['kəmfɚt] **1.** *n* assistance; the state of being at ease. **2.** *v* to make a sad person feel better. *Ex* The nurse comforted the patient.

comfortable ['kəm(p)ftɚbl̩, 'kəm(p)fɚtəbl̩] *adj* feeling at ease, without pain or worries.

comic ['kɑmɪk] **1.** *adj* funny; having to do with a funny person. **2.** *n* a comedian. **3.** *n* a thin booklet of entertaining drawings, usually for young people.

comics ['kɑmɪks] *n* (*plural*) the section of a newspaper where the funny drawings are found.

comma ['kɑmə] *n* a punctuation mark (,) used as a separator within a sentence.

command [kə'mænd] *v* to tell someone what to do. *Ex* He commanded the soldiers to go to sleep.

commence [kə'mɛn(t)s] *v* to begin.

commencement [kə'mɛn(t)smənt] *n* the graduation ceremony at a school or college.

commercial [kə'mɚʃl] **1.** *adj* having to do with commerce; having to do with selling things. **2.** *n* an advertisement on radio or television.

commit [kə'mɪt] *v* to do something, usually something wrong, like a crime.

committee [kə'mɪti] *n* a small number of people who meet together to arrange things.

common ['kɑmən] *adj* ordinary; usual; everyday.

commotion [kə'mowʃn̩] *n* noise and fuss.

community [kə'myuwnəti] *n* a group of individuals living in one particular area; the area that a group of people live in.

companion [kəm'pænyən] *n* a friend; a friend who accompanies you.

company ['kəmpəni] **1.** *n* a business firm. **2.** *n* a group of people who are guests at a party.

comparative [kəm'pɛrətɪv] *n* a form of an adjective or adverb that shows more of something. *Ex* Better is the comparative of good. Redder is the comparative of red.

compare [kəm'pɛr] *v* to say how things are alike or different; to show whether one thing is better or worse than another.

compass ['kəmpəs] **1.** *n* an instrument which shows directions, such as north, south, east, and west. **2.** *n* a tool for drawing a circle or an arc.

compel [kəm'pɛl] *v* to force someone to do something.

compete [kəm'pit] *v* to be in a test or race with someone to see who is best. *Ex* The tall boy will compete with me in the archery contest.

competition [kɑmpə'tɪʃn̩] *n* a test of how much people know or how good they are at something.

complain [kəm'pleyn] *v* to tell about something that you think is wrong, or that is upsetting you.

complaint [kəm'pleynt] *n* a statement of protest; a charge against someone.

complete [kəm'plit] **1.** *adj* whole; total. **2.** *v* to finish something.

complicated ['kɑmpləkeytəd] *adj* not easy; not simple; difficult to do.

compliment ['kɑmpləmənt] *n* something nice said about a person.

composition [kɑmpə'zɪʃn̩] **1.** *n* things put together to make a whole. **2.** *n* a story or report written in school. **3.** *n* a piece of music.

comprehension [kɑmpri'hɛntʃn̩] *n* the ability to understand.

compress [kəm'prɛs] *v* to press things together; to put pressure on something.

computer [kəm'pyuwtɚ] *n* an electronic device which can be instructed to do mathematics and other things with numbers or words.

computer program [kəmpyuwtɚ 'prowgræm] *n* a set of instructions given to a computer.

conceal [kn̩'sil] *v* to hide something; to keep something secret.

conceited [kn̩'sitəd] *adj* thinking too highly of yourself.

concentrate ['kɑn(t)sn̩treyt] **1.** *v* to bring things together in one place. **2.** *v* to think hard about something.

concern [kn̩'sɚn] **1.** *v* to interest or trouble yourself with something. *Ex* I cannot concern myself with that problem. **2.** *n* a worry; something which must be remembered or watched over.

concert ['kɑnsɚt] *n* a performance of musical compositions.

conclude [kn̩'kluwd] *v* to end something; to finish something.

conclusion [kṇ'kluwʒṇ] *n* the end of something; the final part of something.

concrete ['kɑnkrit] *n* a mixture of cement, gravel, and water that dries as hard as stone.

condense [kṇ'dɛn(t)s] *v* to make something small or shorter by taking part of it away. *Ex* Milk is condensed by taking away part of the water in the milk. Books are condensed by taking out parts that are not very important to the story.

condition [kṇ'dɪʃṇ] *n* the state in which something or someone is.

condominium [kɑndə'mɪniəm] *n* an apartment or building which is owned by the people who live in it.

conduct 1. *n* ['kɑndəkt] behavior. **2.** *v* [kṇ'dəkt] to lead someone or something; to lead a chorus, orchestra, or band.

conductor [kṇ'dəktɚ] **1.** *n* the person who leads a chorus, orchestra, or band. **2.** *n* the person who supervises a bus or a train car.

cone [kown] **1.** *n* the fruit of pine and fir trees. **2.** *n* an object which is round at the bottom and pointed at the top.

conference ['kɑnf(ə)rən(t)s] *n* a meeting of two or more people to discuss something.

confess [kṇ'fɛs] *v* to say that you have done something wrong; to admit to having done something wrong. *Ex* The postmaster confessed making the error.

confetti [kṇ'fɛti] *n* tiny bits of colored paper thrown in the air at parades and celebrations.

confirm [kṇ'fɚm] *v* to give approval for something; to assure that something has been said or done.

confuse [kṇ'fyuwz] **1.** *v* to mix a person up. *Ex* Please don't confuse me with too many facts at one time. **2.** *v* to mistake one thing or person for another thing or person. *Ex* People always confuse me with my sister.

congratulate [kn'grætʃəleyt] *v* to tell a person you are glad about something good that has happened to him.

congregation [kaŋgrə'geyʃn̩] *n* a gathering; a gathering of people in a religious service.

congress ['kaŋgrəs] *n* a group of people elected to make laws; the United States House of Representatives and the United States Senate.

conjunction [kn̩'dʒəŋkʃn̩] *n* a word which joins together sentences, clauses, phrases, or words.

connect [kə'nɛkt] *v* to join or fasten two or more things together. *Ex* Please connect me with the telephone number I gave you. Please connect the microphone to the recorder.

connection [kə'nɛkʃn̩] *n* the place where two or more things are joined together; something which joins things together.

conquer ['kaŋkɚ] *v* to beat an opponent; to overcome someone or something.

conscious ['kantʃəs] *adj* knowing what is going on; able to hear and understand what is going on around you.

consent [kn̩'sɛnt] **1.** *v* to agree to something. *Ex* I consent to your going to Washington. **2.** *n* permission. *Ex* I give my consent for you to go to Washington.

consider [kn̩'sɪdɚ] *v* to think carefully about something.

considerable [kn̩'sɪdɚəbl̩] *adj* much; a lot of.

considerate [kn̩'sɪdɚət] *adj* kind to others; thoughtful.

consideration [kn̩sɪdɚ'eyʃn̩] *n* thoughtfulness; kindness.

consonant ['kansənənt] *n* a sound of language which is not a vowel sound. *Ex* The letters *p*, *t*, *k*, *v*, *f*, and *h* represent consonants.

constitution [kɑnstə'tuwʃn̩] **1.** *n* the nature of something; the structure and physical makeup of a person or thing. **2.** *n* a document stating a country's basic principles. The laws of that country are based on the stated principles.

construct [kn̩'strəkt] *v* to build or make something.

construction [kn̩'strəkʃn̩] *n* the act of building or constructing; the business of building.

contain [kn̩'teyn] *v* to hold something inside.

container [kn̩'teynɚ] *n* a can, box, or bottle which holds something.

contented [kn̩'tɛntəd] *adj* happy; pleased with the state of things.

contents ['kɑntɛnts] *n* what is contained in something. *Ex* A list of what is contained in a book is found in the table of contents.

continent ['kɑntənənt] *n* one of the seven major landmasses on the earth. The continents are Africa, Antarctica, Asia, Australia, Europe, North America, and South America.

continual [kn̩'tɪnyuwəl] *adj* frequent; constant, repeated.

continue [kn̩'tɪnyuw] *v* to keep on; to go on; to keep doing something.

continuous [kn̩'tɪnyuwəs] *adj* keeping on without stopping.

contract 1. *n* ['kɑntrækt] a written agreement; a formal agreement. **2.** *v* [kn̩'trækt] to become smaller.

contraction [kn̩'trækʃn̩] **1.** *n* the act of becoming smaller. **2.** *n* a word which has been made shorter by leaving out one or more letters.

contractor ['kɑntræktɚ] *n* a person whose job is to manage the construction of buildings.

contradict [kɑntrə'dɪkt] *v* to state the opposite; to claim the opposite.

contrast 1. *n* ['kɑntræst] the difference between two things, such as light and dark, heavy and light, or big and small. **2.** *n* ['kɑntræst] the control on a television set that makes the difference between the light and dark areas greater or smaller. **3.** *v* [kn̩'træst] to compare things as to their differences or as to their degree of difference.

control [kn̩'trowl] **1.** *v* to be in charge of something or someone. **2.** *n* a knob, lever, or button which operates some machine or device.

convenient [kn̩'vinyənt] *adj* easy to use or reach.

convent ['kɑnvɛnt] *n* a building for nuns to live in.

convention [kn̩'vɛntʃn̩] *n* a group of people gathered together to conduct business and make decisions. *Ex* Political parties hold conventions.

conversation [kɑnvɚ'seyʃn̩] *n* talk between two or more people.

convict 1. *n* ['kɑnvɪkt] a person, guilty of a crime, who has been sent to prison. **2.** *v* [kn̩'vɪkt] to find a person guilty of a crime.

convince [kn̩'vɪn(t)s] *v* to persuade someone that you are right; to persuade someone of a fact.

cook [kʊk] **1.** *v* to heat food and prepare it for eating. **2.** *v* to cook food for a living; to be able to cook food satisfactorily. **3.** *n* a person who cooks food; a person who cooks food well.

cookie ['kʊki] *n* a small, flat, sweet shape of dough, baked in an oven.

cool [kuwl] *adj* not quite cold.

copper ['kɑpɚ] *n* a reddish-brown metal.

copy ['kɑpi] **1.** *v* to make or do something exactly the same as something else. **2.** *n* something which is made exactly like something else.

copyright ['kɑpirɑyt] *n* the legal right to copy or sell music, writing, or art work.

coral ['korəl] **1.** *n* a deep pink color. **2.** *n* a hard, stony, pink or white material made from the shells of millions of tiny sea animals which live in a colony. *Ex* Coral is sometimes used in making jewelry.

cord [kord] *n* heavy string.

corduroy ['kordɚoy] *n* a heavy cloth with many tiny parallel ridges. Trousers made of corduroy are called corduroys.

core [kor] *n* the middle part of something; the part where the seeds are in an apple or a pear.

cork [kork] **1.** *n* a very soft wooden material from a special tree. **2.** *n* a cork or rubber stopper put in the opening of a bottle to keep liquid from spilling out.

corkscrew ['korkskruw] *n* a tool used to pull corks out of bottles.

corn [korn] **1.** *n* the hard seeds of the corn or maize plant. **2.** *n* a lump on the toe which hurts when a tight shoe is worn.

corncob ['kornkɑb] *n* a cylinder of plant material on which corn kernels or seeds grow.

corner ['kornɚ] *n* the place where two walls meet; the place where two roads or streets meet.

cornflakes ['kornfleyks] *n* a breakfast cereal made from corn. This is the plural. *Ex* Cornflakes are eaten cold with milk and sugar.

corporation [korpə'reyʃn̩] *n* a large business firm.

correct [kə'rɛkt] **1.** *adj* right; true; with no mistakes. **2.** *v* to make right. **3.** *v* to grade papers, marking things which are wrong.

corridor ['korədɚ] *n* a hallway; a long, narrow passage with rooms leading off it.

cost [kɔst] **1.** *n* what you have to pay for something; the price of something. *Ex* The cost of a house is very great. **2.** *v* to require a particular amount of money in payment. *Ex* This hat costs twelve dollars. *pt* cost. *pp* cost.

costly ['kɔstli] *adj* expensive; costing a lot.

costume ['kastuwm] **1.** *n* the clothes worn by an actor on stage. **2.** *n* the style of clothes worn at different times in history.

cot [kat] *n* a small bed; a collapsible or portable bed.

cottage ['katɪdʒ] *n* a small house in the country or in the woods.

cotton ['katn̩] *n* thread or cloth made from the cotton plant.

couch [kawtʃ] *n* a long, soft seat where more than one person can sit.

cough [kɔf] **1.** *n* the loud noise made when a person has a sore throat or bronchitis. **2.** *v* to make a loud noise like a bark when sick with a sore throat or bronchitis.

could [kʊd] *v* the past tense of can.

couldn't ['kʊdn̩t] *cont* could not.

council ['kawn(t)sl̩] *n* a group of people in charge of something like a town, city, or other organization.

count [kawnt] **1.** *v* to name the numbers in their proper order. *Ex* Please count from one to one hundred. **2.** *v* to find out and say how many of something there are. *Ex* He is counting the sailboats on the lake.

countdown ['kɑwntdɑwn] *n* the counting backwards of seconds of time as is done before a rocket is fired.

counter ['kɑwntɚ] *n* a kind of long table in a shop or a cafe; a drainboard.

counterclockwise [kɑwntɚ'klɑkwɑyz] *adv* in a direction opposite to the way the hands of a clock move; the opposite of clockwise.

country ['kəntri] **1.** *n* a nation; an independent state. **2.** *n* the land areas which are not towns or cities, and in which few people live. *Ex* Farms are located in the country.

county ['kɑwnti] *n* a local unit of government in a state. *Ex* Almost every state in the United States is divided up into a number of counties.

couple ['kəpl̩] *n* two of anything; a pair.

coupon ['k(y)uwpɑn] *n* a printed piece of paper which can be exchanged for something else.

courage ['kɚɪdʒ] *n* bravery; without fear even when there is danger.

course [kors] **1.** *n* the direction in which anything goes. **2.** *n* a number of lessons on one special subject.

court [kort] *n* a judge, lawyers, and, sometimes, a jury; a session in a courtroom where a case is to be heard; the judge who speaks for the legal system in a courtroom.

courtroom ['kortruwm] *n* the place where judges, juries, and lawyers work; the place where accused criminals have trials and where lawsuits are tried.

courtyard ['kortyɑrd] *n* an enclosed space near a building or surrounded by a building.

cousin ['kəzn̩] *n* the child of your uncle or aunt.

cover ['kəvɚ] **1.** *v* to put one thing over another so as to hide it. *Ex* Please cover the food so that flies won't get on it. **2.** *n* a lid; a blanket; something used to cover something else.

cow [kɑw] *n* the female of cattle. *Ex* Cows give milk, but bulls do not.

coward ['kɑwɚd] *n* someone who is not brave.

cowboy ['kɑwbɔy] *n* a man on a ranch who looks after cattle.

crab [kræb] *n* a water animal with a hard shell and large claws. *Ex* Some crabs are good to eat.

crack [kræk] **1.** *v* to cause something to break but not fall apart. *Ex* She cracked the egg on the side of the bowl. **2.** *n* a split or large opening in something. *Ex* There is a crack in this cup. **3.** *n* a sharp, sudden noise. *Ex* I was wakened by a crack of thunder.

cracker ['krækɚ] *n* a thin, crisp biscuit or cookie, sometimes salted.

cradle ['kreydl̩] **1.** *n* a baby's bed with rockers instead of legs. **2.** *n* a frame or structure for holding something. *Ex* A boat may rest on a cradle when it is out of water. **3.** *v* to hold something carefully. *Ex* He cradled the kitten next to his chest.

craftsman ['kræftsmən] *n* a man who is good at making things with his hands.

crafty ['kræfti] *adj* clever; sly.

crane [kreyn] **1.** *n* a machine for lifting heavy things. **2.** *n* a kind of a long-legged bird.

crash [kræʃ] **1.** *n* a loud, smashing noise. **2.** *v* to bump into something noisily. *Ex* The train crashed into the car.

crate [kreyt] **1.** *n* a container for packing vegetables, eggs, fruit, or bottles. *Ex* Crates are made of thin pieces of wood fastened together. **2.** *v* to package something in a crate; to build a crate around something. *Ex* They had to crate the car for shipment on a boat.

crawl [krɔl] **1.** *v* to move forward on the hands and knees. **2.** *n* a stroke used in swimming.

crayon ['kreyɑn] *n* a soft stick of colored wax used to color pictures.

crazy ['kreyzi] *adj* silly; out of your mind.

cream [krim] *n* the rich, fatty part of milk. *Ex* Butter is made from cream.

crease [kris] *n* a mark or a ridge made by folding or doubling something like paper or cloth.

create [kri'eyt] *v* to make something; to bring something into being.

creator [kri'eytɚ] *n* a maker; a producer.

creature ['kritʃɚ] *n* a living thing, such as a bird, insect, or other animal.

credit ['krɛdət] *n* money that is due a person; permission to charge purchases.

credit card ['krɛdət kɑrd] *n* a plastic card you carry with you so that you can buy things and have them charged to you. *Ex* When you use a credit card you must pay for your purchases later.

creep [krip] *v* to move slowly and quietly, sometimes on the hands and knees. *pt* crept. *pp* crept.

crept [krɛpt] *v* the past tense and past participle of creep.

crescent ['krɛsn̩t] *n* anything shaped like the new moon; a curved shape, wide in the middle and pointed at both ends.

crew [kruw] *n* the people who work on a ship or on an airplane.

crib [krɪb] *n* a small bed with bars to keep a young child from falling out.

cricket ['krɪkət] *n* a brown or black insect, something like a grasshopper, which makes a chirping noise.

crime [kraym] *n* something wrong that can be punished by law.

crinkle ['krɪŋkl] *v* to wrinkle something by squeezing it tightly

cripple ['krɪpl] **1.** *v* to damage the arms and legs of someone. *Ex* He was crippled by a horrible accident. **2.** *n* a person whose arms or legs have been damaged in some way.

crisp [krɪsp] *adj* hard and dry; easily broken, like a potato chip.

critic ['krɪtɪk] *n* a person who makes a judgment of value; a person who determines the worth of something that someone else has done.

criticize ['krɪtəsayz] *v* to state what is right or wrong with someone or something.

croak [krowk] **1.** *n* a deep, hoarse noise, like the sound a large frog makes. **2.** *v* to make the sound a frog makes.

crocodile ['krakədayl] *n* a very large and dangerous, scaly reptile which lives in or near water in hot countries. *Ex* The crocodile is something like an alligator.

crook [krʊk] **1.** *n* a long, hooked stick carried by shepherds. **2.** *n* a person who is not honest.

crooked ['krʊkəd] **1.** *adj* not straight; bent; curved. **2.** *adj* not honest.

crop [krap] *n* grain, fruit, or vegetables grown for food.

cross [krɔs] **1.** *n* anything shaped like X or +. **2.** *adj* angry or grouchy.

crow [krow] **1.** *n* a large, black bird with a harsh, croaking voice. **2.** *v* to make the sound a rooster makes.

crowd [krɑwd] *n* a lot of people all together in one place.

crown [krɑwn] *n* a special headdress worn by a king or queen. *Ex* Crowns are made of precious metal and may have jewels attached.

cruel ['kruwl] *adj* very unkind.

cruise [kruwz] **1.** *v* to travel in a boat, airplane, or car at an even speed, usually for a long distance. **2.** *n* a pleasure trip in a boat.

crumb [krəm] *n* a very small piece of bread, cake, or cracker.

crumble ['krəmbl̩] *v* to break into small pieces; to break something into small pieces; to make something into crumbs.

crumple ['krəmpl̩] *v* to crush something into wrinkles. *Ex* He crumpled up the paper and threw it into the wastebasket.

crunch [krəntʃ] *v* to make a loud noise when you are chewing something hard and crisp like an apple or a cracker.

crush [krəʃ] *v* to press something together; to squash something. *Ex* She crushed the bug with her foot.

crust [krəst] *n* the hard outer covering of something like a loaf of bread or a pie.

crutch [krətʃ] *n* a special stick with a padded top piece that fits under the armpit. *Ex* People with broken legs use crutches to help them to walk.

cry [krɑy] **1.** *v* to weep; to weep and make tears. **2.** *v* to shout for joy or in anger. **3.** *n* a shout.

crystal ['krɪstl̩] *n* a hard mineral that is transparent.

cub [kəb] *n* a young bear, fox, or lion.

cube [kyuwb] *n* a shape having six sides of equal measurement, like a cube of sugar.

cuddle ['kədl̩] *v* to hug with affection.

cue [kyuw] **1.** *n* a signal to begin. **2.** *n* a stick used in the game of billiards.

cuff [kəf] *n* the end of a sleeve at the wrist.

culture ['kəltʃɚ] **1.** *n* a civilization; the beliefs and customs of a group of people. **2.** *n* an appreciation of the fine arts, science, and the humanities.

cunning ['kənɪŋ] *adj* crafty; clever in an unpleasant way.

cup [kəp] *n* a small, bowl-shaped container with a handle, used for drinking.

cupboard ['kəbɚd] *n* a set of shelves with doors. *Ex* Cups and dishes are stored in a kitchen cupboard.

curb [kɚb] *n* the raised edge at each side of the street.

cure [kyuwr] **1.** *v* to help make a sick person well again; to heal. **2.** *n* something used to help a person get well, usually a medicine or a treatment. *Ex* That cure did not make me well.

curious ['kyɚiəs] **1.** *adj* wanting to know or find out. **2.** *adj* odd; strange.

curl [kɚl] **1.** *v* to twist into curves or rings. *Ex* Wet weather makes my hair curl. **2.** *n* a ring of hair; a coil of hair.

curler ['kɚlɚ] *n* a roller or a pin which girls and women put into their hair to make it curly.

curly ['kɚli] *adj* not straight; going around in curves; with curls.

current ['kɚənt] **1.** *n* a flow of air, water, or electricity. **2.** *adj* at present; right now.

curtain ['kɚtṇ] *n* a piece of cloth hanging down to cover a window or a stage in a theater.

curve [kɚv] *n* a line shaped like part of a circle.

cushion ['kuʃṇ] *n* a soft pillow covered with material, usually on a couch or chair.

custodian [kəs'towdiən] *n* a person who guards and maintains property or important papers; a janitor.

custom ['kəstəm] *n* what is usually done; habit.

customer ['kəstəmɚ] *n* someone who wants to buy something, usually in a store.

customs ['kəstəmz] *n* the government office which collects money from people who bring goods into a country. The word is in the plural, and there is no singular word with this meaning.

cut [kət] **1.** *n* a wound. **2.** *v* to make pieces of something small by using scissors or a knife. *pt* cut. *pp* cut.

cycle ['saykḷ] **1.** *n* a bicycle; a motorcycle. **2.** *n* a repetition, such as a cycle of seasons or pulses of electricity.

cyclone ['sayklown] *n* a very bad storm in which a strong wind goes round and round.

cylinder ['sɪləndɚ] *n* a hollow, rounded piece of metal often used in machinery.

cymbal ['sɪmbḷ] *n* a large, round metal disk used as a musical instrument. *Ex* Two cymbals are struck together to make a crashing sound in an orchestra.

D

dab [dæb] **1.** *v* to touch something lightly. **2.** *n* a little bit of something, such as a bit of food or a patch of paint.

daffodil ['dæfədɪl] *n* a yellow spring flower shaped something like a trumpet.

dagger ['dægɚ] *n* a short sword.

daily ['deyli] **1.** *adv* every day; once every day. **2.** *adj* occurring every day; occurring once every day.

dainty ['deynti] *adj* pretty; delicate.

dairy ['dɛri] *n* a place where milk, butter, and cheese are processed and stored.

dam [dæm] *n* a special kind of wall which stops or slows down the flow of water. *Ex* Dams are built in rivers, streams, and canals.

damage ['dæmɪdʒ] **1.** *v* to harm or injure something. **2.** *n* harm or injury.

damp [dæmp] *adj* slightly wet.

dance [dæn(t)s] **1.** *v* to move in time to music. **2.** *n* a specific kind of bodily movement done in time with music. **3.** *n* a party or gathering where dancing is done.

dandruff ['dændrəf] *n* bits of the scalp which lift off and appear as white or grayish bits in the hair.

danger ['deyndʒɚ] *n* risk; the opposite of safety.

dangerous ['deyndʒɚəs] *adj* not safe.

dare [dɛr] **1.** *v* to have the courage to do something. *Ex* I wouldn't dare swim so far. **2.** *v* to challenge a person to do something. *Ex* I dare you to jump over that rock. **3.** *n* a challenge; an act of urging or tempting someone to do something. *Ex* He was silly to take the dare.

daring ['dɛrɪŋ] *adj* full of courage; brave.

dark [dɑrk] *adj* without light.

darling ['dɑrlɪŋ] *n* someone dearly loved.

darn [dɑrn] *v* to mend a hole by sewing over it with thread or yarn.

dart [dɑrt] **1.** *n* a kind of small arrow thrown by hand. *Ex* Darts are thrown at a target in a game called darts. **2.** *v* to run or move very quickly from one point to another.

dash [dæʃ] **1.** *v* to rush suddenly; to dart. **2.** *n* a short straight line in writing, like this—. *Ex* A dash is longer than a hyphen.

data ['deytə, 'dætə] *n* facts and figures; information. This word is plural. The singular form is datum.

date [deyt] **1.** *n* a time when something happens; an appointment; a certain day, month, or year. **2.** *n* the person with whom an appointment is made to go to a movie, party, or some other entertainment. **3.** *n* a sweet, sticky fruit with a large seed in it.

daughter ['dɔtɚ] *n* a female child of a father and mother.

dawn [dɔn] *n* the first light of day; the time of the first light of day.

day [dey] *n* the time between sunrise and sunset; a period of time lasting 24 hours.

day-care ['deykɛr] *adj* having to do with the care of preschool children during the day, especially when the parents work.

dazed ['deyzd] *adj* confused or bewildered.

dazzle ['dæzl] *v* to confuse someone with a bright light; to confuse or overpower someone with anything brilliant or overwhelming. *Ex* The speaker dazzled the crowd with his brilliant remarks.

dead [dɛd] *adj* without life.

dead end [dɛd 'ɛnd] *n* the end of a street where there is no place to go but back; a course of thought or action leading nowhere further.

deaf [dɛf] *adj* not able to hear; not able to hear well.

deal [dil] **1.** *n* an amount, usually large. *Ex* We spent a great deal of money on a new car. **2.** *v* to do business with someone; to manage or handle someone or something. *Ex* I am sure that I can deal with this problem. **3.** *v* to pass out cards to players in a card game. *Ex* Who is dealing the cards this time? *pt* dealt. *pp* dealt.

dealt [dɛlt] *v* the past tense and past participle of deal.

dear [dir] **1.** *adj* much loved; precious. *Ex* She is a very dear friend. **2.** *n* a person who is well liked or loved. *Ex* She is such a dear.

death [dɛθ] *n* the end of life.

debate [dɪ'beyt] **1.** *n* a formal discussion of an important question. **2.** *v* to discuss and argue an important subject.

debit ['dɛbət] *n* a charge against an account; an amount of money owed to an account.

debt [dɛt] *n* that which is owed to a person or an account.

decade ['dɛkeyd] *n* a period of ten years.

decay [dɪ'key] **1.** *v* to decrease gradually; to rot away; to spoil. **2.** *n* a decrease; a falling apart; a rotting away.

deceive [dɪ'siv] *v* to make someone believe something that is not true; to cheat. *Ex* Do not try to deceive me with your lies.

decent ['disn̩t] *adj* proper; considered polite by most people.

decide [dɪ'saɪd] *v* to make up your mind about something; to settle something; to choose a solution.

decimal ['dɛs(ə)ml̩] **1.** *adj* numbered by tens. **2.** *n* short for decimal point or decimal fraction.

decimal point ['dɛs(ə)ml̩ poynt] *n* a period standing after a whole number and before the tenths (hundredths, thousandths, and so on) of a whole number. *Ex* The number 10.2 has a decimal point between 0 and 2.

decision [dɪ'sɪʒn̩] *n* something which is to be decided; something which has been decided.

deck [dɛk] **1.** *n* the floor of a boat or a ship. **2.** *n* a stack of something, usually cards which are used in card games.

declarative [dɪ'klɛrətɪv] *adj* having to do with a sentence which makes a statement.

declare [dɪ'klɛr] *v* to say something clearly; to make something known.

decorate ['dɛkɚeyt] *v* to make something look pretty; to put ornaments on something; to paint a room or put new draperies in a room.

decrease [dɪ'kris] *v* to grow smaller in number or size.

deduct [dɪ'dəkt] *v* to take away an amount from the total. *Ex* They deducted ten dollars from my pay because I broke a vase.

deed [did] *n* the doing of something; something which has been done.

deep [dip] **1.** *adv* to or into a great distance downward. *Ex* The fish swam deep into the water. **2.** *adj* of a great length downward. *Ex* That is a very deep hole.

deer [dɪr] *n* a wild animal with four legs. *Ex* The male deer has large, branched horns on his head.

defeat [dɪ'fit] **1.** *v* to beat someone at a game; to conquer a person or a problem. *Ex* The other team defeated us. **2.** *n* the loss of a game or contest; failure. *Ex* We were sorry about our defeat in the soccer game.

defecate ['dɛfəkeyt] *v* to empty the bowels.

defend [dɪ'fɛnd] *v* to try to keep someone or yourself from being beaten; to guard someone or something against attack.

definite ['dɛfənət] *adj* certain; without doubt.

defy [dɪ'fɑy] *v* to refuse to obey a person or a rule. *Ex* Do not defy my orders. Do not defy me.

degree [dɪ'gri] *n* a unit of measurement. Temperature is measured in degrees, either centigrade or Fahrenheit. Longitude and latitude are measured in degrees.

delay [dɪ'ley] **1.** *v* to put something off until a later time. *Ex* We will have to delay the game until the rain stops. **2.** *n* a period of time during which something is stopped. *Ex* We will have a ten-minute delay until the playing field dries.

delegate **1.** *n* ['dɛləgeyt, 'dɛləgət] a person elected or appointed to represent other people at a convention or a conference. **2.** *v* ['dɛləgeyt] to appoint a person to represent a group of people; to grant authority to a person; to assign a task to a person.

deli ['dɛli] *n* a delicatessen. Short for delicatessen.

deliberate **1.** *adj* [dɪ'lɪbəˑət] not by accident; done on purpose. **2.** *v* [dɪ'lɪbəˑeyt] to think about something; to discuss the good and bad points of an idea.

delicate ['dɛlɪkət] *adj* fragile; easily broken or damaged.

delicatessen [dɛlɪkə'tɛsn̩] *n* a shop that sells food ready to eat, such as cooked meats or special cheeses and salads.

delicious [dɪˈlɪʃəs] *adj* very good to taste and eat.

delight [dɪˈlɑyt] **1.** *n* great pleasure or joy. **2.** *v* to make someone very happy.

deliver [dɪˈlɪvɚ] **1.** *v* to hand something over to someone else. **2.** *v* to rescue or set free. **3.** *v* to give birth to a baby.

delivery [dɪˈlɪvɚi] **1.** *n* the act of bringing or taking something to a place. **2.** *n* the act of giving birth to a baby.

demand [dɪˈmænd] **1.** *v* to ask for something in a commanding way, without saying please. **2.** *n* a claim for something due; an act of asking in a commanding way.

democracy [dɪˈmɑkrəsi] *n* a system of government where the people have a voice in the things that a government does.

Democrat [ˈdɛməkræt] *n* a member of the Democratic political party of the United States.

demon [ˈdimən] *n* an evil spirit or devil.

den [dɛn] **1.** *n* a cave or shelter where some kinds of wild animals live. **2.** *n* a comfortable room in a house; a study; a family room.

denominator [dɪˈnɑməneytɚ] *n* the part of a fraction which is below or to the right of the line in a fraction. *Ex* In the fraction 2/5, 5 is the denominator.

dense [dɛn(t)s] *adj* thick; difficult to make your way through, like a dense forest.

dent [dɛnt] *n* a bent place in something, usually caused by a blow.

dental [ˈdɛntl̩] *adj* having to do with the teeth.

dentist [ˈdɛntɪst] *n* someone who takes care of people's teeth as a profession.

deny [dɪ'nɑy] *v* to say that something which has been said is not true.

deodorant [di'owdɚənt] *n* a substance which takes away or covers up bad odors.

depart [dɪ'pɑrt] *v* to go away; to leave a place.

department [dɪ'pɑrtmənt] *n* a part or section of a shop, office, or factory.

depend [dɪ'pɛnd] *v* to count on someone or something; to rely on someone or something.

deposit [dɪ'pɑzət] **1.** *v* to put something down and leave it. *Ex* Please deposit this package on the table. **2.** *n* an amount of money put into a bank account. **3.** *n* a small amount of money left in partial payment for something.

depot ['dipow] *n* a train or bus station.

depression [dɪ'prɛʃn̩] **1.** *n* a hollow or pressed-in place. **2.** *n* an economic condition where there is much unemployment and very little business activity. **3.** *n* a state of mind where one feels very sad and unwanted.

depth [dɛpθ] *n* how deep something is.

descend [dɪ'sɛnd] *v* to go down something; to go down.

describe [dɪ'skrɑyb] *v* to say what something or someone is like.

desert 1. *n* ['dɛzɚt] an area of land where very little can grow because there is no water. **2.** *v* [dɪ'zɚt] to run away from something that you are supposed to do; to run away from one's duty.

deserve [dɪ'zɚv] *v* to be worthy of something; to be owed something because of something done well. *Ex* She deserves an award for bravery.

design [dɪ'zɑyn] **1.** *v* to draw a pattern; to make a plan or drawing. **2.** *n* a pattern or a plan.

desire [dɪ'zɑyr] **1.** *v* to want something very much. **2.** *n* a wish; a request.

desk [dɛsk] *n* a table used for reading or writing. *Ex* Many desks have drawers to keep things in.

despair [dɪ'spɛr] **1.** *n* sorrow; great sadness. **2.** *v* to give up hope.

despise [dɪ'spɑyz] *v* to dislike something or someone very much.

dessert [dɪ'zɚt] *n* something sweet, such as cake, pie, or ice cream, served after the main part of the meal.

destroy [dɪ'stroy] *v* to kill something; to ruin something completely.

detail [dɪ'teyl] *n* a small part; a small fact.

detective [dɪ'tɛktɪv] *n* a person who works in secret to find information which may help lead to a criminal.

detention [dɪ'tɛntʃn̩] **1.** *n* the act of holding back; being held by the police. **2.** *n* a notice that you are to stay after school as punishment.

detergent [dɪ'tɚdʒn̩t] *n* a substance which, like soap, helps get things clean.

determine [dɪ'tɚmən] *v* to decide something; to make a choice between two or more things. *Ex* Have you determined which shoes you will wear to school?

detest [dɪ'tɛst] *v* to hate something or someone very much.

detour ['dituwɚ] *n* a temporary path or route around an obstacle. *Ex* We had to make a detour because the bridge had washed out.

develop [dɪ'vɛləp] **1.** v to grow older gradually, as a puppy grows into a dog. **2.** v to show the symptoms of something; to cause something to increase. *Ex* I am developing a cold. **3.** v to cause photographic film to reveal images; to make pictures from photographic film.

device [dɪ'vays] n a piece of equipment; a tool; a gadget.

devil ['dɛvl] n an evil spirit; the supreme evil spirit, Satan; a wicked or cruel person.

dew [duw] n drops of moisture which cover the ground in the very early morning.

diagonal [day'ægənl] **1.** n a line drawn from one corner of something to the opposite corner. **2.** *adj* slanting.

diagram ['dayəgræm] **1.** n a plan or drawing to show what a thing is, or how it works. **2.** v to draw a plan; to make a line drawing of something. **3.** v to make a drawing showing the structure of a sentence.

dial [dayl] n the flat round part of something with numbers on it, like a clock, combination lock, or telephone.

dialect ['dayəlɛkt] n a special way of speaking a language in one part of a country.

dialog ['dayəlɔg] n a conversation between two people.

diameter [day'æmətɚ] n the length of a straight line drawn from one side of a circle to the other, passing through the center.

diamond ['day(ə)mənd] n a very hard, colorless precious stone which sparkles.

diaper ['daypɚ] n the cloth which is folded into a pants-like shape for a very young baby.

diary ['day(ə)ri] n a book in which you write down what you do every day.

dice [dɑys] *n* a pair of small cubes with a different number of spots on each side. They are used in various games. The word is plural. The singular is die.

dictation [dɪk'teyʃn̩] *n* the act of writing down words or sentences as they are spoken. *Ex* Some secretaries take dictation.

dictionary ['dɪkʃənɛri] *n* a book which tells you the meanings of words and how to spell them.

did [dɪd] *v* the past tense of do.

didn't ['dɪdn̩t] *cont* did not.

die [dɑy] **1.** *v* to stop living; to come to an end. **2.** *n* one of a pair of dice.

diesel engine [disl̩ 'ɛndʒn̩] *n* a powerful engine which burns a special kind of oil.

differ ['dɪfɚ] **1.** *v* to be unlike. *Ex* This one differs from that one. **2.** *v* to disagree; to be of different opinions. *Ex* I don't mind if you differ, but please don't shout.

difference ['dɪfrən(t)s] *n* that which makes something unlike something else. *Ex* This is bigger than that; the difference is size.

different ['dɪfrənt] *adj* not the same.

difficult ['dɪfəkəlt] *adj* hard to do; hard to deal with; hard to understand.

difficulty ['dɪfəkəlti] *n* trouble; disagreement; something which is difficult.

dig [dɪg] *v* to make a hole in the ground. *Ex* John dug a hole for the tree he was planting. *pt* dug. *pp* dug.

digest [dɪ'dʒɛst] *v* for the body to process food and turn it into energy and waste matter.

dignified ['dɪgnəfɑyd] *adj* acting in a serious manner.

dim [dɪm] *adj* with very little light; not bright.

dime [dɑym] *n* a U.S. coin worth ten cents.

dimple ['dɪmpl] *n* a little hollow, usually in your cheek or chin.

dine [dɑyn] *v* to eat dinner.

dingy ['dɪndʒi] *adj* dull; looking dirty.

dining room ['dɑynɪŋ ruwm] *n* a room where meals are eaten.

dinner ['dɪnɚ] *n* the main meal of the day.

dinosaur ['dɑynəsor] *n* a very large reptile that lived millions of years ago.

dip [dɪp] **1.** *v* to put a thing into and take it out of something quickly. *Ex* He dipped his spoon into his soup. **2.** *n* a swim. *Ex* Come on, let's go for a dip.

diploma [dɪ'plowmə] *n* a written statement or certificate showing that a person has met the necessary educational requirements.

direct [dɪ'rɛkt] **1.** *adj* straight; in the quickest or shortest way. **2.** *v* to lead someone; to show someone the way.

direction [dɪ'rɛkʃn̩] *n* the way in which something goes, such as up, down, left, right, north, south, and so on.

director [dɪ'rɛktɚ] *n* the leader; the person in charge.

dirt [dɚt] *n* soil; earth.

dirty ['dɚti] *adj* not clean; in need of washing.

disagree [dɪsə'gri] *v* to have a different opinion about something.

disappear [dɪsə'pɪr] *v* to go away suddenly; to vanish.

disappoint [dɪsə'poynt] *v* to make someone sad because of a failure. *Ex* They disappointed me by not winning. If I don't buy my mother a birthday present, she will be disappointed.

disaster [dɪ'zæstɚ] *n* a calamity; a great misfortune.

disciple [dɪ'saypl̩] *n* a follower or a pupil.

discount ['dɪskawnt] *n* a special price lower than the regular price.

discourage [dɪ'skɚɪdʒ] *v* to take away a person's desire to do something. *Ex* Please discourage the children from writing on the wall.

discover [dɪ'skəvɚ] *v* to find out something; to see something for the first time.

discovery [dɪ'skəvɚi] *n* something which has been found out.

discuss [dɪ'skəs] *v* to talk about something.

discussion [dɪ'skəʃn̩] *n* an argument or talk with other people.

disease [dɪ'ziz] *n* an illness; a sickness.

disgrace [dɪs'greys] **1.** *n* shame. **2.** *v* to bring shame on someone.

disguise [dɪs'gayz] **1.** *v* to change the appearance of someone or something so that recognition is not possible. **2.** *n* the materials used to disguise a person, such as clothing, a wig, or a mustache.

disgust [dɪs'gəst] *n* a feeling of dislike so strong that it makes you feel sick.

disgusting [dɪs'gəstɪŋ] *adj* sickening; horrible.

dish [dɪʃ] *n* a plate for food.

dishonest [dɪs'anəst] *adj* untrustworthy; not honest; the opposite of honest.

disk [dɪsk] *n* a thin, flat, circular object like a phonograph record. Also spelled disc.

dislike [dɪs'lɑyk] *v* to hate something or someone; not to like something or someone.

dismay [dɪs'mey] *n* fear; a feeling of being upset and sad.

dismiss [dɪs'mɪs] *v* to send someone away; to tell someone to leave.

dissect [dɪ'sɛkt] *v* to separate something into small pieces in order to study them better. *Ex* I dissected a frog in biology class.

distance ['dɪstən(t)s] *n* the length of the space between two places.

distant ['dɪstənt] *adj* faraway.

distinct [dɪ'stɪŋkt] *adj* separate; clearly seen or heard.

distinguish [dɪs'tɪŋgwɪʃ] *v* to notice that two or more things are different from one another; to pick out one thing from the midst of others. *Ex* Can you distinguish the sound of a harp in the orchestra?

distress [dɪs'trɛs] *n* the feeling of great pain, sorrow, or worry.

distribute [dɪs'trɪbyuwt] *v* to supply and deliver something. *Ex* Please distribute these papers to the class.

district ['dɪstrɪkt] *n* a part of a town or country.

disturb [dɪs'tɚb] *v* to interrupt someone; to bother someone.

disturbance [dɪs'tɚbən(t)s] *n* a noisy interruption, as when people upset a meeting by shouting out.

ditch [dɪtʃ] *n* a very long, narrow trench which is dug in the ground to drain water away.

ditto machine ['dɪtow məʃin] *n* a machine which makes copies of information you have typed on special paper.

dittos ['dɪtowz] *n* sheets of paper, such as lessons or a test, which have been copied on a ditto machine.

dive [dɑyv] *v* to plunge headfirst into the water or down through the air. *pt* dived, dove. *pp* dived.

diver ['dɑyvɚ] *n* someone who goes down into very deep water or down through the air; a person who dives.

divide [dɪ'vɑyd] *v* to separate into parts.

dividend ['dɪvədɛnd] **1.** *n* a number which is to be divided by another number. **2.** *n* a division or share of something.

division [dɪ'vɪʒn̩] *n* the part of arithmetic in which one number is separated into as many equal groups as another number.

division sign [dɪ'vɪʒn̩ sɑyn] *n* the sign ($\div$) which indicates that you are supposed to divide. *Ex* $10 \div 5 = 2$.

divisor [dɪ'vɑyzɚ] *n* in mathematics, the number which is divided into another number.

divorce [dɪ'vors] *n* the legal ending of a marriage.

dizzy ['dɪzi] *adj* giddy; feeling that your head is spinning around.

do [duw] *v* to perform an act. *Ex* What are you doing? I am doing the washing. Present tenses: do, does. *pt* did. *pp* done.

dock [dɑk] **1.** *n* the place where ships and boats are unloaded or repaired. **2.** *v* to bring a ship or boat to rest at a pier.

doctor ['dɑktɚ] **1.** *n* someone who helps people get better when they are ill. **2.** *v* to try to help a person get better; to treat a person medically.

dodge [dɑdʒ] **1.** *v* to avoid hitting something by jumping quickly to one side. **2.** *v* to avoid answering a question.

does [dəz] *v* the form of the verb *do* which is used with *he, she,* and *it. Ex* He does the laundry once a week.

doesn't ['dəzn̩t] *cont* does not.

dog [dɔg] *n* a four-legged animal which is often kept as a pet.

doll [dɑl] *n* a toy made to look like a human being.

dollar ['dɑlɚ] *n* a unit of money in the United States. *Ex* A dollar equals one hundred pennies or cents, four quarters, ten dimes, or twenty nickels.

dollar sign ['dɑlɚ sɑyn] *n* the sign ($) indicating dollars.

dome [dowm] *n* a curved roof shaped like half of a ball.

domino ['dɑmənow] *n* a small, oblong piece of wood painted black with white dots. *Ex* Dominos are used to play a game.

done [dən] *v* the past participle of do.

don't [downt] *cont* do not.

doodle ['duwdl̩] *v* to draw or scribble while thinking about something else.

door [dor] *n* a kind of barrier which has to be opened to go in or out of a building or room. *Ex* In a house a door is usually made of wood and is fitted with a handle.

doorman ['dormæn] *n* a man whose job is to open doors at the entrance of an important building.

doorstep ['dorstɛp] *n* the step just outside a doorway.

doorway ['dorwey] *n* the opening or frame into which a door is fitted.

dormitory ['dormətori] *n* a large room with lots of beds.

dose [dows] *n* the exact amount of medicine that should be taken at one time.

dot [dɑt] *n* a small, round mark.

double ['dəbḷ] **1.** *adj* twice as great; twice as much. *Ex* Please give me a double serving. **2.** *v* to grow to twice the size; to cause something to become twice as big.

double feature [dəbḷ 'fitʃɚ] *n* a special movie where two films are shown.

doubt [dɑwt] **1.** *v* to distrust something or someone. *Ex* He doubts my honesty. **2.** *n* a lack of trust. *Ex* Her mind is filled with doubt.

doubtful ['dɑwtfḷ] *adj* not quite believing; not being sure.

dough [dow] *n* a thick, floury mixture which is baked into bread or cakes.

doughnut ['downət] *n* a circular cake made of dough which has been fried in oil.

dove 1. *n* [dəv] a pretty bird, something like a pigeon. **2.** [dowv] *v* a past tense of dive.

down [dɑwn] **1.** *adv* to or at a lower place. *Ex* Please put that book down. **2.** *prep* toward a lower part of something. *Ex* The bucket fell down the well.

downstairs [dɑwn'stɛrz] **1.** *adv* to a lower floor; at a lower floor. *Ex* He carried it downstairs. **2.** *adj* located on or in the lower floor. *Ex* He is in the downstairs bathroom. **3.** *n* the lowest floor; a basement. *Ex* Does this house have a downstairs?

downtown [dɑwn'tɑwn] **1.** *adv* to or at the center of the city. *Ex* Please take this downtown with you. **2.** *adj* located in the center of the city. *Ex* Please come and see me at my downtown office. **3.** *n* a well developed center of the city. *Ex* This city doesn't even have a downtown!

doze [dowz] *v* to close the eyes because sleep is needed; to sleep lightly for a very short time.

dozen ['dəzn̩] *n* a set of twelve of anything.

draft [dræft] *n* a gust of cold air; an annoying breeze.

drag [dræg] **1.** *v* to pull something along the ground. **2.** *v* to be pulled along the ground.

dragon ['drægən] *n* a huge, imaginary animal which has a long tail and which breathes fire. *Ex* Dragons are found in fairy tales.

drain [dreyn] **1.** *v* to take away or release water or some other liquid; to free a container from its liquid contents. **2.** *n* an opening in a sink, bathtub, or floor which leads liquids to the sewer pipe.

drainboard ['dreynbord] *n* the counter on one or both sides of a sink.

drama ['dramə] **1.** *n* a play, especially a serious play. **2.** *n* a school subject where plays and acting are studied.

drank [dræŋk] *v* the past tense of drink.

drapery ['dreypri] *n* heavy curtains over a window.

draw [drɔ] **1.** *v* to pull something. *Ex* The horse is drawing the wagon. **2.** *v* to make a picture with pencils or crayons. *Ex* She is drawing a picture of a horse drawing a wagon. *pt* drew. *pp* drawn.

drawer [drɔr] *n* a kind of box that fits into a piece of furniture. *Ex* Drawers can be pulled out or pushed in.

drawing ['drɔɪŋ] **1.** *n* a picture which has been drawn with a pencil or a crayon. **2.** *n* a school subject in which you are taught to draw.

drawn [drɔn] *v* the past participle of draw.

dread [drɛd] **1.** *v* to fear something. **2.** *n* a great fear.

dreadful ['drɛdfl̩] *adj* causing great fear; terrible; awful.

dream [drim] **1.** *n* the thoughts that go on in your mind after you are asleep. **2.** *v* to have thoughts and pictures in your mind when you are asleep.

drench [drɛntʃ] *v* to soak something.

dress [drɛs] **1.** *n* a garment worn by girls and women. **2.** *v* to put clothes on yourself or someone else.

dressmaker ['drɛsmeykɚ] *n* a person who makes clothes for girls, women, and small children.

drew [druw] *v* the past tense of draw.

dribble ['drɪbḷ] **1.** *v* to let food or liquid run out of the mouth and down onto the chin. **2.** *v* to bounce a basketball with one hand in the game of basketball.

drift [drɪft] *v* to be floated or blown along. *Ex* The boat drifted down the river.

drill [drɪl] **1.** *v* to make a hole in something with a special tool. *Ex* I must drill a hole for this wire to pass through. **2.** *n* a tool used to make holes. *Ex* He drilled the hole with an electric drill. **3.** *n* a kind of practice; an exercise.

drink [drɪŋk] **1.** *v* to swallow water, milk, juice, or some other liquid. *pt* drank. *pp* drunk. **2.** *n* a serving of a liquid which is to be drunk.

drinking fountain ['drɪŋkɪŋ fɑwntṇ] *n* a special stand with a faucet from which a person can get a drink of water.

drip [drɪp] **1.** *v* to drop in little drips. *Ex* The faucet is dripping. The water is dripping from the faucet. **2.** *n* a drop of water; the sound of dripping.

drive [drɑyv] **1.** *v* to make something move along. *pt* drove. *pp* driven. **2.** *n* a trip in a car. *Ex* Let's go out for a drive.

driven ['drɪvṇ] *v* the past participle of drive.

driver ['drɑyvɚ] *n* a person who drives something, especially a car.

driveway ['drɑyvwey] *n* a paved road for cars which leads to a house or other building. *Ex* A driveway is not a public road.

drizzle ['drɪzl̩] *n* light rain.

droop [druwp] *v* to bend or flop over.

drop [drɑp] **1.** *v* to let something fall. **2.** *n* a tiny bead of water or some other liquid.

drove [drowv] *v* the past tense of drive.

drown [drɑwn] *v* to die under water because there is no air to breathe.

drowsy ['drɑwzi] *adj* sleepy.

drug [drəg] **1.** *n* a medicine or chemical substance used in treating illness. **2.** *n* a dangerous or illegal substance used for pleasure.

druggist ['drəgəst] *n* the person in a drugstore who sells medicine and fills prescriptions.

drugstore ['drəgstor] *n* a store where medicines are sold along with many other small items, such as books, combs, pencils, magazines, and so forth.

drum [drəm] *n* a hollow instrument that one beats to make music. *Ex* Andy plays drums in the school band.

drumstick ['drəmstɪk] **1.** *n* the stick that is used to beat a drum. **2.** *n* the leg of a chicken or a turkey when served as food.

drunk [drəŋk] **1.** *adj* sleepy or silly from drinking too much alcohol. **2.** *v* the past participle of drink.

dry [drɑy] **1.** *adj* not wet; without water. **2.** *v* to cause something to become dry.

dry cleaners [drɑy 'klinɚz] *n* a business which cleans clothing in a special way which uses no water.

dryer ['drɑyɚ] *n* a machine which dries things with electric or gas heat.

duck [dək] **1.** *n* a large, web-footed bird which swims on top of the water. **2.** *v* to dip under water for a moment; to lower the head to get it out of the way of something.

due [duw] *adj* owing; not paid.

dug [dəg] *v* the past tense and past participle of dig.

dull [dəl] *adj* uninteresting; not lively; not sharp.

dumb [dəm] **1.** *adj* not able to speak. **2.** *adj* stupid.

dummy ['dəmi] **1.** *n* a model made to look like a person; something used in place of a real thing used. **2.** *n* a stupid person.

dump [dəmp] **1.** *v* to throw something down; to get rid of something. **2.** *n* a place where rubbish is thrown.

dunce [dən(t)s] *n* a fool; someone who is slow to learn things.

dung [dəŋ] *n* waste matter from the bowels of an animal; manure.

dungeon ['dənd͡ʒn̩] *n* a dark prison cell, usually under the ground.

duplex ['duwplɛks] *n* a double house; a building which contains two dwellings, side by side.

during ['dʊrɪŋ] *prep* throughout; while something is happening. *Ex* Please don't talk during class.

dusk [dəsk] *n* the part of the evening just before the sky gets really dark.

dust [dəst] **1.** *n* tiny bits of powdery dirt. **2.** *v* to remove the bits of dirt from furniture or from all of the rooms of a house.

dustpan ['dəstpæn] *n* a pan or scoop into which dust is swept with a broom.

duty ['duwti] *n* what a person ought to do; what a person has to do.

dwarf [dworf] **1.** *n* an animal, plant, or person that is much smaller than most others of the same kind. **2.** *adj* small; smaller than usual.

dye [day] **1.** *n* a powder or liquid used to change the color of cloth or liquid. **2.** *v* to change the color of something, usually cloth or other material.

dynamite ['daynəmayt] *n* a powerful, explosive substance.

E

each [itʃ] **1.** *adj* every. **2.** *pro* every person or thing in a group; every one.

eager ['igɚ] *adj* wanting very much to do something.

eagle ['igḷ] *n* a large bird of prey, with claws and a sharp beak.

ear [ɪr] **1.** *n* one of the two organs of hearing. *Ex* Animals and people have two ears. **2.** *n* a spike or stick of corn.

earache ['ɪreyk] *n* a pain inside the ear.

early ['ɚli] **1.** *adv* before the appointed time. *Ex* He arrived early. **2.** *adj* near the beginning. *Ex* His early arrival surprised us.

earn [ɚn] *v* to get something, usually money, in return for working; to deserve something. *Ex* She earns ten dollars an hour. She has earned our respect.

earnest ['ɚnəst] *adj* serious; sincere.

earring ['ɪrɪŋ] *n* a piece of jewelry which is worn on the ear.

earth [ɚθ] **1.** *n* the planet we live on; the world. **2.** *n* the ground in a garden or field.

earthquake ['ɚθkweyk] *n* a violent shaking of the earth's surface.

ease [iz] *n* freedom from pain or worry; rest from work.

easel ['izḷ] *n* a special stand which holds a picture which is being painted by an artist.

easily ['izəli] *adv* with no difficulty.

east [ist] *n* the direction in which the sun rises; the opposite of west.

Easter ['istɚ] *n* a holiday which commemorates the time when Christians believe Jesus rose from the dead.

easy ['izi] *adj* not difficult; not hard to do or understand.

eat [it] *v* to chew and swallow food. *pt* ate. *pp* eaten.

eaten ['itn̩] *v* the past participle of eat.

eaves [ivz] *n* the edges of the roof sticking out over the tops of the walls.

echo ['ɛkow] *n* the sound that comes back to you, as when you shout in a tunnel or a cave.

eclipse [ɪ'klɪps] *n* a cutting off of the light from the sun when the moon comes between the sun and the earth; a cutting off of the sun's light on the moon when the earth comes between the sun and the moon.

economics [ɛkə'nɑmɪks] *n* the study of the relationship of money, workers, and goods in a country.

edge [ɛdʒ] **1.** *n* the cutting side of a knife. **2.** *n* the end of something like a tabletop or a shelf.

editor ['ɛdətɚ] *n* a person who makes decisions about material which is to be printed.

educate ['ɛdʒəkeyt] *v* to help someone to learn; to teach someone something.

education [ɛdʒə'keyʃn̩] *n* helping people learn, usually in schools or colleges.

eel [il] *n* a very long fish that looks like a snake.

effect [ə'fɛkt] *n* the result of something. *Ex* The effect of cold weather is to make you shiver.

effort ['ɛfɚt] *n* a hard try; a using of power. *Ex* Please make an effort to get your paper in on time. It takes much effort to move a piano.

egg [ɛg] *n* an oval object with a thin shell which holds a baby bird, fish, or reptile.

either ['iðɚ] **1.** *adj* each; both. *Ex* There is a house at either end of the street. **2.** *adj* one; one of two. *Ex* Please sit in either chair. **3.** *adv* a word that introduces a choice. *Ex* Either be polite or go home!

elaborate 1. *v* [ə'læbɚeyt] to work out in detail; to explain in detail. *Ex* Please elaborate on your plan. **2.** *adj* [ə'læbrət] detailed; complicated; complex. *Ex* The artist has painted an elaborate picture.

elastic [ə'læstɪk] **1.** *n* cloth made with rubber so that it will stretch. **2.** *adj* stretchy; flexible.

elbow ['ɛlbow] *n* the joint in the middle of the arm; the bony point on the joint in the middle of the arm.

elder ['ɛldɚ] *adj* older. *Ex* His elder sister is going to college next fall.

elect [ɪ'lɛkt] *v* to select a person for a job by a majority vote. *Ex* The voters elected John to be mayor

election [ɪ'lɛkʃn̩] *n* the act of electing; a time set aside for selecting public officials by voting.

electric [ɪ'lɛktrɪk] *adj* using electricity; operated by electricity.

electricity [ɪlɛk'trɪsəti] *n* an invisible force which is used to make light and heat. It also makes power for engines and machinery.

electron [ɪ'lɛktrɑn] *n* a tiny part of an atom which bears a negative charge.

electronic [ɪlɛk'trɑnɪk] *adj* having to do with electric or radio devices.

element ['ɛləmənt] *n* a basic part of something; one of the basic chemical materials of which all matter is made.

elephant ['ɛləfn̩t] *n* a very large animal with a long nose called a trunk. *Ex* Elephants live naturally in Africa and India.

elevator ['ɛləveytɚ] *n* a device like a small room which carries people up or down in a building.

elf [ɛlf] *n* a tiny, mischievous fairy.

elite [ɪ'lit] *n* a group of people with special power or privileges.

else [ɛls] **1.** *adv* in a different way; in a different place; at a different time. *Ex* He must put it there and nowhere else. **2.** *adj* other; different. *Ex* It must have been somebody else.

elsewhere ['ɛlshwɛr] *adv* in another place; to another place. *Ex* He must have put it elsewhere.

embarrass [ɛm'bɛrəs] *v* to make someone feel shy by teasing or by making difficulties for them.

embroider [ɛm'broydɚ] *v* to make pretty designs on material by using needles and thread.

emerald ['ɛmrəld] *n* a bright green precious stone.

emergency [ɪ'mɚdʒn̩(t)si] *n* a dangerous or urgent situation.

emperor ['ɛmpɚɚ] *n* the male ruler of an empire.

empire ['ɛmpayr] *n* a group of countries which is ruled by one king or queen, called an emperor or empress.

employ [ɛm'ploy] *v* to give work to someone, usually for payment.

employee [ɛm'ployi] *n* a person who is employed by an employer; a person who works for another person.

employer [ɛm'plɔyɚ] *n* a person who hires workers and pays them for their work.

employment [ɛm'plɔymənt] *n* working, a job.

empty ['ɛmpti] *adj* without anything inside.

enamel [ə'næml̩] *n* a hard, shiny paint

enclose [ɛn'klowz] *v* to put something in an envelope or package; to surround or shut in by a fence or a wall.

encourage [ɛn'kɚɪdʒ] *v* to help someone to keep on trying; to try to give courage to someone.

encyclopedia [ɛnsɑyklə'pidiə] *n* a book or set of books which tells something about every subject.

end [ɛnd] **1.** *n* the last part; the finish. **2.** *v* to bring something to a finish; to come to a finish.

endure [ɛn'd(y)uwr] *v* to bear trouble or pain with courage and patience.

enemy ['ɛnəmi] *n* someone who fights against you or your country.

energy ['ɛnɚdʒi] *n* force; power.

engaged [ɛn'geydʒd] *adj* bound by a promise, as when a man and a woman are engaged to be married to each other.

engine ['ɛndʒn̩] *n* a machine which makes things work. *Ex* Airplanes, cars, and trains are all moved by engines.

engineer [ɛndʒə'nir] **1.** *n* someone who makes or looks after machines. **2.** *n* someone who plans and builds dams, roads, railroads, and bridges. **3.** *n* a person whose job is to drive a train.

engineering [ɛndʒə'nirɪŋ] *n* the planning of buildings, roads, bridges, and so forth.

English [ˌɪŋglɪʃ] *n* the language spoken by people in the United Kingdom, the United States of America, Australia, New Zealand, and parts of Canada, Africa, and India.

enjoy [ɛnˈdʒoy] *v* to take pleasure in something.

enormous [ɪˈnorməs] *adj* very large; huge.

enough [ɪˈnəf] *adj* as much as is needed and no more.

enroll [ɛnˈrowl] *v* to put a name on a list; to register for school.

enrollment [ɛnˈrowlmənt] **1.** *n* the act of enrolling or registering. **2.** *n* the total number of people, usually students, who are enrolled.

enter [ˈɛntɚ] *v* to go into or come into a place.

entertain [ɛntɚˈteyn] **1.** *v* to amuse someone. **2.** *v* to have someone as your guest.

entertainment [ɛntɚˈteynmənt] *n* a show or concert that entertains or amuses.

enthusiasm [ɛnˈθuwziæzm̩] *n* eagerness; great interest in something.

entire [ɛnˈtayr] *adj* complete; whole.

entitle [ɛnˈtaytl̩] *v* to enable someone to do or get something. *Ex* This ticket entitles you to see the movie one time.

entrance [ˈɛntrən(t)s] *n* a doorway or a way into a place.

entry [ˈɛntri] *n* the act of entering; an entrance.

envelope [ˈɛnvəlowp] *n* a folded piece of paper in which you put a letter which is to be mailed.

envy [ˈɛnvi] **1.** *v* to feel a bit jealous of someone's possessions. *Ex* John envies Martha because she has a car. **2.** *n* a wish to have something that belongs to someone else. *Ex* John was overcome with his envy of Martha's car.

epidemic [ɛpə'dɛmɪk] *n* a disease which affects many people all at the same time.

episode ['ɛpəsowd] *n* an event in a story; a complete short story which is part of a longer story

equal ['ikwəl] *adj* of the same size, quantity, or value as something else.

equal sign ['ikwəl sɑyn] *n* the sign = which shows that two things are equal, as in 2 + 2 = 4.

equation [ɪ'kweyʒn̩] *n* a statement that two things are the same. *Ex* 10 + 1 = 11 is an equation.

equator [ɪ'kweytɚ] *n* an imaginary line around the middle of the earth's surface.

equipment [ɪ'kwɪpmənt] *n* all of the things needed to do a job, play a game, or go on an expedition.

eraser [ɪ'reysɚ] *n* a small object made of rubber which is used to wipe away pencil marks; a block of material used to wipe away chalk marks from a chalkboard.

erect [ɪ'rɛkt] *adj* upright; standing straight.

erode [ɪ'rowd] *v* to wear down the earth; to wash away the soil.

erosion [ɪ'rowʒn̩] *n* the wearing down of the land by wind and water.

errand ['ɛrənd] *n* a short journey to take a message or to deliver or pick up something.

error ['ɛrɚ] *n* a mistake; something that has been done incorrectly.

erupt [ɪ'rəpt] *v* to burst forth; to explode. *Ex* The volcano erupted and killed many cattle.

escalator ['ɛskəleytɚ] *n* a moving staircase.

escape [ə'skeyp] *v* to get free, usually from something unpleasant.

especially [ə'spɛʃ(ə)li] *adv* most of all; of greatest importance.

essay ['ɛsey] *n* a piece of written work in which the writer's opinions can be told.

estate [ə'steyt] **1.** *n* a large house located on a large piece of land. **2.** *n* the money and property left behind when a person dies.

estimate 1. *v* ['ɛstəmeyt] to guess the size, quantity, or value of something. **2.** *n* ['ɛstəmət] a guess at the size, quantity, or value of something.

etc. [ɛt'sɛtɚə] and so on; and other similar things. An abbreviation of *et cetera*.

ethnic ['ɛθnɪk] *adj* having to do with human races or groups of people from different countries and the customs they have.

eve [iv] *n* an evening before a special day, such as Christmas Eve or New Year's Eve.

even ['ivn̩] **1.** *adj* level; smooth. **2.** *adj* having to do with any number that can be divided exactly by two.

evening ['ivnɪŋ] *n* the time between afternoon and night.

event [ɪ'vɛnt] *n* something that happens; an episode.

ever ['ɛvɚ] *adv* always; for all time.

evergreen ['ɛvɚgrin] *n* a shrub or tree that keeps its leaves and stays green all through the year.

every ['ɛvri] *adj* each; each one.

everybody ['ɛvribɑdi] *pro* each person.

everyday ['ɛvridey] **1.** *adv* daily. **2.** *adj* common; usual; ordinary.

everyone ['ɛvriwən] *pro* each person; everybody.

everything ['ɛvriθɪŋ] *pro* all things.

everywhere ['ɛvrihwɛr] *pro* all places.

evidence ['ɛvədən(t)s] *n* facts that lead to a proof; information given in court which proves or disproves something.

evil ['ivl̩] **1.** *adj* very bad; wicked; not good. **2.** *n* badness; wickedness.

exactly [ɛg'zæk(t)li] *adv* in a correct manner; with no mistakes. *Ex* She did it exactly right.

exaggerate [ɛg'zædʒɚeyt] *v* to say that something is bigger or more important than it really is. *Ex* He exaggerated the size of the fish that he caught.

exam [ɛg'zæm] *n* a test. Short for examination.

examination [ɛgzæmɪ'neyʃn̩] *n* a test; a number of questions that you have to answer, usually in writing, to show how much you know about something.

examine [ɛg'zæmɪn] **1.** *v* to look at something very closely and carefully. *Ex* The jeweler examined the diamond slowly. **2.** *v* to give a test to someone about something. *Ex* The teacher examined the student on the parts of speech.

example [ɛg'zæmpl̩] **1.** *n* a sample; a single one of many. **2.** *n* a pattern to be copied, such as when you follow someone's good example.

excellent ['ɛksələnt] *adj* very, very good.

except [ɛk'sɛpt] *prep* leaving out something; apart from something. *Ex* Everyone can go except Martha.

exchange [ɛks'tʃeyndʒ] *v* to give one thing in return for another. *Ex* Please exchange the white shoes for red shoes.

exciting [ɛk'saytɪŋ] *adj* having to do with something which you feel strongly about; having to do with something which excites you. *Ex* We saw a very exciting movie last night. You can feel excited if something nice is going to happen.

exclaim [ɛk'skleym] *v* to say something suddenly and loudly.

exclamation [ɛksklə'meyʃn̩] *n* something which is shouted out.

exclamation point [ɛksklə'meyʃn̩ poynt] *n* a punctuation mark (!) which is placed after a written exclamation. *Ex Help!* is an exclamation.

excuse 1. *n* [ɛk'skuws] a reason for not doing something. *Ex* He gave a poor excuse for his behavior. **2.** *v* [ɛk'skuwz] to forgive the bad behavior of someone. *Ex* Please excuse John's rudeness. **3.** *v* [ɛk'skuwz] to permit someone to leave; to permit someone to be absent. *Ex* Please excuse me, I must leave now.

excused [ɛk'skuwzd] *adj* forgiven; pardoned. *Ex* John has an excused absence.

executive [ɛg'zɛkyətɪv] *n* a person who controls or directs a business firm.

exercise ['ɛksɚˌsayz] **1.** *n* the training of your body or mind. **2.** *v* to make your body or mind work; to train your body or mind to work; to do exercises; to practice movements of the body to make it strong.

exhaust [ɛg'zɔst] **1.** *n* gases which come out of a gasoline or diesel engine. **2.** *n* the pipe which lets out the gases from a gasoline or diesel engine. **3.** *v* to use something up; to tire someone or something out completely. *Ex* Running hard exhausts me.

exhausted [ɛg'zɔstəd] *adj* completely worn-out.

exhibit [ɛg'zɪbət] **1.** *n* a showing of art or other things or projects. **2.** *v* to show something; to put something on display.

exhibition [ɛksə'bɪʃn̩] *n* a public show of things, such as works of art, flowers, or furniture.

exist [ɛg'zɪst] *v* to be; to continue to live.

exit ['ɛgzɪt] *n* the way out of a place.

expand [ɛk'spænd] *v* to grow bigger; to swell.

expect [ɛk'spɛkt] *v* to look forward to something; to think that something will happen. *Ex* I expect the doorbell to ring at any moment.

expedition [ɛkspə'dɪʃn̩] *n* a journey to explore a place or to search for something, such as plants and animals.

expense [ɛk'spɛn(t)s] *n* cost; payment of money; the costs of doing business.

expensive [ɛk'spɛn(t)sɪv] *adj* costly; costing a lot of money.

experience [ɛk'spɪriən(t)s] *n* knowledge of something because you have seen it or done it.

experiment [ɛk'spɛrəmənt] *n* something tried out to see what will happen; a test to find out something.

expert ['ɛkspɚt] *n* someone who knows a lot about a particular subject.

explain [ɛk'spleyn] *v* to give the meaning of something; to make something clear. *Ex* Please explain this question to me.

explanation [ɛksplə'neyʃn̩] *n* anything said or written that helps you to understand clearly the reason for something.

explode [ɛk'splowd] *v* to cause something to blow up or burst with a loud bang; to burst or blow up with a loud bang. *Ex* A stick of dynamite exploded near the building.

explore [ɛk'splor] *v* to travel to places to try to find out about them. *Ex* I leave tomorrow to explore the Amazon.

explosion [ɛk'splowʒn̩] *n* a sudden burst with a loud noise; the act of blowing up or exploding.

express [ɛk'sprɛs] **1.** *v* to put thoughts into words, music, or pictures; to mean. *Ex* The word *will* expresses the future tense. **2.** *adj* very fast. **3.** *n* a very fast train; an express train.

expression [ɛk'sprɛʃn̩] **1.** *n* the look on faces when people are happy, sad, or worried. *Ex* Miguel has a very sad expression. **2.** *n* a way of saying things which tells people more than words alone. *Ex* Martha speaks with much expression. **3.** *n* a word or phrase; a peculiar word or phrase. *Ex* Please don't use that expression when I am around.

expressway [ɛk'sprɛswey] *n* a special highway where cars, trucks, and buses can move very fast.

extend [ɛk'stɛnd] *v* to stretch something out; to make something longer; to stretch out; to become longer.

extent [ɛk'stɛnt] *n* the length, size, or area of anything.

extra ['ɛkstrə] *adj* more than necessary or expected.

extracurricular [ɛkstrəkə'rɪkyələ˞] *adj* outside of school classes; in addition to schoolwork. *Ex* John is doing too many extracurricular activities.

extraordinary [ɛk'strordn̩ɛri] *adj* very unusual; not ordinary; surprising.

extreme [ɛk'strim] *adj* farthest. *Ex* Please put it on the extreme right-hand side.

eye [ɑy] *n* one of the two organs of sight; one of the two things which people and animals see with.

eyebrow ['ɑybrɑw] *n* the line of hairs over each eye.

eyelash [ˈɑylæʃ] *n* one of the little hairs that grow along the edge of the eyelid.

eyelid [ˈɑylɪd] *n* the piece of skin that covers the eye. It opens and closes.

eyepiece [ˈɑypis] *n* the glass part of a telescope or microscope which you look through.

F

fable ['feybḷ] *n* a short story, usually about animals, which teaches you a lesson.

face [feys] *n* the front of the head; the front of some objects, such as a mountain or a clock.

fact [fækt] *n* a thing that everyone knows is true and not imaginary; true information.

factor ['fæktɚ] **1.** *n* a number which divides evenly into another number. *Ex* Four is a factor of eight, but five is not. **2.** *n* a piece of information which must be known when explaining something.

factory ['fæktri] *n* a building where things are made in large quantities, usually by machines.

fade [feyd] *v* to lose color or freshness.

Fahrenheit ['fɛrənhɑyt] *n* a measurement of heat stated in degrees. The freezing point of water is 32 degrees Fahrenheit, and the boiling point is 212 degrees Fahrenheit.

fail [feyl] *v* not to be able to do something you try to do; to be unsuccessful.

failure ['feylyɚ] *n* an act of failing; an attempt which does not succeed.

faint [feynt] **1.** *adj* weak. *Ex* I can only hear a faint whisper on the telephone. **2.** *adj* dizzy; about to become unconscious. *Ex* I feel faint. **3.** *v* to pass out; to lose consciousness.

fair [fɛr] **1.** *adj* light in coloring. *Ex* Martha has very fair skin. **2.** *adj* just; right or good. **3.** *n* an event with contests, entertainment, and things like merry-go-rounds to ride.

fairy ['fɛri] *n* a very small, imaginary person who can do magic.

fairy tale ['fɛri teyl] *n* a story about fairies; a story about something which is not true.

faith [feyθ] **1.** *n* what a person believes in; a person's religious beliefs. **2.** *n* a trust that what is said is true.

faithful ['feyθfl] *adj* keeping your promises; believing.

fake [feyk] **1.** *adj* false; imitation. *Ex* You are wearing a fake diamond ring. **2.** *n* something that looks valuable but is not; a cheap copy of something. *Ex* That diamond is a fake.

fall [fɔl] **1.** *v* to drop through the air. *pt* fell. *pp* fallen. **2.** *n* the season between summer and winter; autumn.

fallen ['fɔlən] *v* the past participle of fall.

false [fɔls] *adj* wrong; not real or true; untrustworthy.

familiar [fə'mɪlyɚ] *adj* well known or close to you. *Ex* Oh, it's good to see a familiar face.

family ['fæmli] *n* a mother and father and their children; related people living in the same house or apartment.

family name [fæmli 'neym] *n* your last name; the name that goes after a title, such as Mr. or Mrs.

famine ['fæmən] *n* great scarcity of food; starvation.

famished ['fæmɪʃt] *adj* very hungry; starving.

famous ['feyməs] *adj* well-known.

fan [fæn] **1.** *n* something which makes the air move. *Ex* Some fans are run by electricity. **2.** *n* someone who is very fond of a certain sport, hobby, or famous person.

fancy ['fæn(t)si] *adj* decorated; highly ornamented.

fang [fæŋ] *n* a long, pointed tooth.

far [fɑr] *adv* a long way away.

farce [fɑrs] **1.** *n* a kind of a play where funny, but unlikely things happen. **2.** *n* a situation in real life where strange or impossible things happen.

fare [fɛr] *n* the price you pay for traveling on a public vehicle, such as a bus.

farewell [fɛr'wɛl] *n* a good-bye.

farm [fɑrm] **1.** *n* a place where a farmer keeps animals and grows food. **2.** *v* to run a farm.

farmer ['fɑrmɚ] *n* a person who runs a farm.

farmyard ['fɑrmyɑrd] *n* an area of land with barns, cowsheds, and other farm buildings.

farsighted ['fɑrsaytəd] **1.** *adj* able to see best at great distances. *Ex* People who are farsighted sometimes need glasses to see objects close by. **2.** *adj* having good foresight; being able to plan ahead.

farther ['fɑrðɚ] **1.** *adj* more distant. *Ex* Please take hold of the farther end. **2.** *adv* at a greater distance away. *Ex* Please move farther on.

fascinating ['fæsəneytɪŋ] *adj* very attractive; very charming; very interesting.

fast [fæst] **1.** *adj* very quick. *Ex* He is a fast runner. **2.** *adv* very quickly. *Ex* He will get there fast.

fasten ['fæsn̩] *v* to join together. *Ex* Please fasten the parts together.

fat [fæt] **1.** *adj* big and round. *Ex* Look at that fat cow! **2.** *n* the whitish, greasy part of meat. *Ex* She cut the fat off of the meat.

fatal ['feytl̩] *adj* causing death; disastrous. *Ex* The club struck a fatal blow.

father ['faðɚ] *n* a man who has children in his family.

faucet ['fɔsət] *n* a device near a sink which lets a person turn the water on and off.

fault [fɔlt] *n* a mistake; anything which spoils something which is otherwise good.

favor ['feyvɚ] *n* an act of kindness which is done for someone.

favorite ['feyvrət] **1.** *n* a person or thing which is liked better than any other. *Ex* Vanilla ice cream is my favorite. **2.** *adj* liked better than any other. *Ex* Vanilla is my favorite flavor.

fawn [fɔn] *n* a young deer.

fear [fir] **1.** *n* a feeling of alarm when you think you are in danger. *Ex* Mary was overcome by fear. **2.** *v* to have feelings of alarm about something. *Ex* John fears snakes.

fearful ['firfl] **1.** *adj* afraid. *Ex* Mary is fearful of tall buildings. **2.** *adj* terrible; awful. *Ex* We were awakened by a fearful noise.

fearless ['firləs] *adj* without fear; brave.

feast [fist] *n* a large, special meal with lots of good things to eat and drink. *Ex* Thanksgiving is an American feast.

feat [fit] *n* an act of great skill or strength.

feather ['fɛðɚ] *n* one of the light shafts of material which covers birds.

feature ['fitʃɚ] **1.** *n* a special or memorable part of something; one of the parts of the face which go together with other parts to help identify that face. *Ex* Petals are some of the important features of plants. **2.** *n* the main movie shown at a double feature; an item advertised as on sale.

fed [fɛd] *v* the past tense and past participle of feed.

Yesewzer

(301) 558 7578

federal ['fɛd(ə)rəl] *adj* having to do with the United States government in Washington, D.C.

fee [fi] *n* a charge for a service; the price of a service. *Ex* Dr. Jones' fee was too high, so I went to another doctor.

feeble ['fibḷ] *adj* very weak; not strong.

feed [fid] **1.** *v* to give food to a person or an animal. *pt* fed. *pp* fed. **2.** *n* the food given to an animal.

feel [fil] **1.** *v* to find out what something is like by touching it; to come into contact with something. **2.** *v* to be aware of; to experience. *Ex* He felt sick. *pt* felt. *pp* felt.

feelings ['filɪŋz] *n* emotions.

feet [fit] *n* the plural of foot.

fell [fɛl] *v* the past tense of fall.

fellow ['fɛlow] *n* a man; a companion.

felt [fɛlt] **1.** *v* the past tense and past participle of feel. **2.** *n* a thick material used for hats.

female ['fimeyl] **1.** *n* a human or animal that can become a mother. *Ex* Girls and women are females. **2.** *adj* having to do with girls and women or animals which can become mothers.

feminine ['fɛmənən] *adj* having to do with girls or women.

fence [fɛn(t)s] *n* something put around a field, yard, or garden to keep animals and people in or out.

fender ['fɛndɚ] *n* metal parts of the body of a car which cover the wheels.

fern [fɚn] *n* a plant which has lacy, feathery leaves but no flowers.

ferry ['fɛri] *n* a boat used to take people or cars across water where there is no bridge.

fertile ['fɝtḷ] *adj* able to produce seeds or plants abundantly; able to produce offspring. *Ex* The soil is fertile in Iowa. Our old cat is no longer fertile.

fertilizer ['fɝtḷayzɚ] *n* a substance which is placed on the soil around plants to help them grow.

festival ['fɛstəvḷ] *n* a joyful celebration with dancing, music, and sometimes food.

fever ['fivɚ] *n* an illness which makes your body very hot and makes you feel weak and thirsty.

few [fyuw] **1.** *adj* not many. **2.** *pro* not many people. *Ex* Few ever really learn calculus well.

fib [fɪb] **1.** *n* a small lie; something which is not quite true. **2.** *v* to tell a small lie.

fiber ['faybɚ] *n* a thread or a thread-like thing.

fiction ['fɪkʃn̩] *n* a made-up story or book about people and happenings that are not really true.

fiddle ['fɪdḷ] **1.** *n* a violin. **2.** *v* to play about with something in a careless sort of way. *Ex* Please don't fiddle with the light switch.

fidget ['fɪdʒət] *v* to wiggle or move about in a restless way. *Ex* People fidget when they are nervous.

field [fild] *n* an open piece of land, often surrounded by hedges.

fierce [firs] *adj* angry; wild.

fiery ['fayri] *adj* like fire; flaming or burning.

fight [fayt] **1.** *v* to struggle against someone or something. *pt* fought. *pp* fought. **2.** *n* a struggle; a battle; an act of fighting.

figure ['fɪgyɚ] **1.** *n* the shape of something; the shape of a person's body. **2.** *n* a number. **3.** *v* to work out something. *Ex* I was able to figure out the answer.

file [fɑyl] **1.** *n* a metal tool with a rough surface, used to make things smooth. **2.** *n* a line of people following one behind the other. **3.** *n* written records; a packet of written records.

file cabinet ['fɑyl kæb(ə)nət] *n* a set of drawers used for storing written records. *Ex* Please put these files into the file cabinet.

fill [fɪl] *v* to put so much in a container that you cannot get any more in.

filling ['fɪlɪŋ] *n* a dental cavity which has been filled by a dentist; the substance placed into a dental cavity by a dentist.

film [fɪlm] **1.** *n* a strip of special plastic used in a camera to record images. **2.** *n* a movie; a moving picture.

filmstrip ['fɪlm strɪp] *n* a strip of transparent plastic with pictures on it. *Ex* When a filmstrip is used in a projector, the pictures will be projected onto a screen.

filter ['fɪltɚ] **1.** *n* a special strainer used to separate dirt and other solids from liquids. **2.** *v* to use a special strainer to remove dirt and other solids from liquids.

filthy ['fɪlθi] *adj* very dirty.

fin [fɪn] *n* one of the wing-like parts of a fish which help it to balance and swim.

final ['fɑynl̩] *adj* the very last; coming at the end.

finally ['fɑynl̩i] *adv* at last; at the end.

find [fɑynd] *v* to see something you are looking for; to discover something. *pt* found. *pp* found.

fine [fɑyn] **1.** *adj* very good; excellent. **2.** *adj* very small; detailed.

finger ['fɪŋgɚ] *n* one of the five long parts of the hand.

fingernail ['fɪŋgɚneyl] *n* the hard part of the finger, located at the end of the finger.

fingerprint ['fɪŋgɚprɪnt] *n* the pattern made when you press your finger or thumb on the surface of something.

finish ['fɪnɪʃ] **1.** *v* to complete something; to come to an end. **2.** *n* the end of something.

fir [fɚ] *n* a kind of evergreen with leaves like needles.

fire [fɑyr] *n* the flames, light, and heat made by something burning.

fire alarm ['fɑyr əlɑrm] *n* a loud siren or horn which tells people that a fire has started.

fire drill ['fɑyr drɪl] *n* an exercise where the people in a large building practice leaving the building because of a pretend fire.

fire engine ['fɑyr ɛndʒn̩] *n* a big truck which carries the firemen and their equipment to put out a fire.

fire extinguisher ['fɑyr ɛkstɪŋgwɪʃɚ] *n* a tank full of water or chemicals used to help put out a fire.

fire fighter ['fɑyr fɑytɚ] *n* a person whose job is to put out fires; a fireman.

fire hose ['fɑyr howz] *n* a long, strong tube on a fire engine or in a building which carries water to put out fires.

firehouse ['fɑyrhɑws] *n* the place where fire engines are kept and where firemen wait to be called to a fire.

fireman ['fɑyrmən] *n* a man whose job it is to put out fires.

fireplace ['fɑyrpleys] *n* a chamber or open place under the chimney where a fire burns.

fireworks ['fɑyrwɚks] *n* devices made of gunpowder packed in cardboard tubes. *Ex* Fireworks are set off after dark on special days.

firm [fɜ·m] **1.** *adj* solid; strong and not easily moved. **2.** *n* a company; a business.

first [fɜ·st] **1.** *adv* at the beginning; before anything else. *Ex* Please do this one first. **2.** *adj* having to do with the one at the beginning; before the second. *Ex* He was the first person there.

fish [fɪʃ] **1.** *n* a swimming animal which cannot live out of water. *Ex* Fish have fins and scales, and they are good to eat. **2.** *v* to attempt to hook or net a fish. *Ex* The old man is going to fish for tuna.

fisherman ['fɪʃɚmən] *n* a man who catches fish.

fishing-rod ['fɪʃɪŋrɑd] *n* a pole which holds the string used in fishing.

fist [fɪst] *n* a tightly closed hand.

fit [fɪt] **1.** *v* to be the right size and shape for something; to put something neatly into something; to shape something so that it can be put into something else neatly. *Ex* This shirt doesn't fit well. **2.** *adj* healthy. *Ex* My, you look fit!

fix [fɪks] *v* to mend something. *Ex* Please fix this broken chair.

fizz [fɪz] *v* to bubble and make a hissing sound.

flag [flæg] *n* a piece of cloth with a colored pattern. *Ex* Each country in the world has its own flag with its own pattern.

flake [fleyk] *n* a very small, thin piece of something, such as a snowflake.

flame [fleym] *n* the bright fire that leaps from something burning.

flannel ['flænl̩] *n* a soft, wooly material.

flannel board ['flænl̩ bord] *n* a panel covered with flannel. It is used to hold colored flannel shapes and figures which stick to it easily.

flap [flæp] **1.** *v* to move something up and down. *Ex* The bird is flapping its wings. **2.** *n* anything which hangs loose or is hinged.

flare [flɛr] **1.** *v* to burst into bright light, as when a piece of wood suddenly bursts into flame. **2.** *n* a warning signal which uses a bright flame to attract attention.

flash [flæʃ] *n* a sudden bright light that appears only for a moment. *Ex* A flash of lightning lit up the sky.

flashlight ['flæʃlayt] *n* a small electric light run by batteries. *Ex* You hold a flashlight in your hand and aim it wherever you want to see.

flask [flæsk] *n* a kind of bottle, usually made of metal or glass, for holding liquids. *Ex* Flasks can be found in a chemistry laboratory.

flat [flæt] **1.** *adj* smooth; without bumps and being the same height all over. **2.** *n* a home on one floor which is part of a larger building; an apartment.

flavor ['fleyvɚ] *n* what makes foods taste different from one another. *Ex* Ice cream comes in many flavors, like strawberry, vanilla, and chocolate.

flea [fli] *n* a tiny, jumping insect. *Ex* Fleas are pests when they live in the fur of pet dogs and cats.

fled [flɛd] *v* the past tense and past participle of flee.

flee [fli] *v* to run away, usually because of danger. *pt* fled. *pp* fled.

fleece [flis] *n* the coat of wool on a sheep.

fleet [flit] *n* a number of ships or vehicles that belong together.

flesh [flɛʃ] *n* the soft parts of the body; the muscles and the skin.

flew [fluw] *v* the past tense of fly.

flexible ['flɛksəbl̩] *adj* bendable; not stiff or rigid.

flicker ['flɪkɚ] *v* to burn brightly and then dimly so that the light is not steady. *Ex* The candle is flickering.

flight [flɑyt] *n* the act of flying through the air; a journey in an airplane.

flimsy ['flɪmzi] *adj* not strong or thick; easily broken.

fling [flɪŋ] *v* to throw something away from you. *pt* flung. *pp* flung.

flint [flɪnt] *n* a very hard kind of stone which gives off sparks when you strike it with steel.

float [flowt] *v* to rest on top of a liquid or on air. *Ex* A boat floats on the water.

flock [flɑk] *n* a large group of birds.

flood [fləd] **1.** *n* a great overflowing of water, usually over dry land. **2.** *v* to fill or overfill with water or some other liquid.

floor [flor] *n* the part of a room that people walk on.

flop [flɑp] **1.** *v* to let yourself fall down heavily. **2.** *v* to throw or slap something down. **3.** *n* a play or film which is a failure.

florist ['florɪst] *n* a person who sells flowers and plants for a living.

flour ['flawɚ] *n* a white powder made from grain. *Ex* Flour is used to make bread and cakes.

flow [flow] *v* to move along smoothly. *Ex* A river flows from its head to its mouth.

flower ['flawɚ] *n* the pretty, colored part of a plant.

flowerpot ['flawɚpɑt] *n* a plastic or clay pot in which flowers or other plants are planted.

flown [flown] *v* the past participle of fly.

flu [fluw] *n* an illness causing a fever and a sore throat. This word is short for influenza.

fluff [fləf] *n* a light, soft stuff that comes off woolen cloth and similar materials, such as blankets and carpets.

fluid ['fluwəd] *n* something that can flow, such as a liquid or a gas. *Ex* Both water and air are fluids.

flung [fləŋ] *v* the past tense and past participle of fling.

flutter ['flətɚ] *v* to flap about; to move the wings quickly. *Ex* The butterfly fluttered from flower to flower.

fly [flay] **1.** *v* to move through the air. *pt* flew. *pp* flown. **2.** *n* a small flying insect which bothers people and gets on food.

foam [fowm] *n* a lot of tiny, white bubbles, usually on the top of a liquid or soapy water; froth.

focus ['fowkəs] *v* to adjust a microscope or a telescope in order to see better; for the eyes to adjust in order to see better.

foe [fow] *n* an enemy.

fog [fɔg] *n* thick, cloudy air.

foggy ['fɔgi] *adj* with much fog in the air.

fold [fowld] **1.** *v* to double something over. **2.** *n* a crease; a doubling over.

folder ['fowldɚ] *n* a piece of heavy paper, folded over so that it can hold important papers. *Ex* Please put those folders on my desk.

foliage ['fowlɪ(ə)dʒ] *n* the leaves on trees and plants.

folk [fowk] *n* people. This refers to two or more people. Folks means the same thing.

follow ['fɑlow] *v* to come after someone or something.

folly ['fɑli] *n* silliness; a foolish action.

fond [fɑnd] *adj* loving; liking very much.

food [fuwd] *n* the things we eat to keep us alive.

fool [fuwl] **1.** *n* a silly person. **2.** *v* to trick someone; to deceive someone.

foolish ['fuwlɪʃ] *adj* silly; stupid; not wise.

foot [fʊt] **1.** *n* the part of the body you stand on. The plural is feet. *Ex* A shoe fits on a foot. You have two feet. **2.** *n* a measure of twelve inches.

football ['fʊtbɔl] **1.** *n* a game in which you try to score goals by crossing a special line while holding the ball. **2.** *n* the special ball used in the game of football. *Ex* A football is pointed at both ends instead of being round.

footpath ['fʊtpæθ] *n* a path or a part of the road where people can walk but vehicles are not allowed.

footprint ['fʊtprɪnt] *n* a mark someone's foot leaves in wet sand or soft earth.

footstep ['fʊtstɛp] *n* the sound made by a foot when a person is walking. *Ex* She was startled by the sound of footsteps.

forbid [for'bɪd] *v* to command or order someone not to do something.

force [fors] **1.** *n* power; strength. **2.** *v* to use power or strength to get something done. *Ex* She forced me to leave the room.

ford [ford] *n* a place in the river where the water is shallow enough that a person can walk or drive through it easily.

forearm ['forɑrm] *n* the part of the arm between the wrist and the elbow.

forecast ['forkæst] **1.** *v* to say that something will happen before it does; to predict something. **2.** *n* a statement of what will happen in the future; a prediction.

forehead ['forhɛd] *n* the part of the face above the eyes.

foreign ['forən] *adj* from another country; strange.

foreigner ['forənɚ] *n* a person from outside the country.

foreman ['formən] *n* a worker who supervises other workers.

forest ['forəst] *n* a large area of land where lots of trees grow close together.

forethought ['forθɔt] *n* a thought or plan for the future.

foreword ['forwɚd] *n* a preface; a short statement at the beginning of a book.

forfeit ['forfɪt] *v* to give up something because of something you have done.

forgave [for'geyv] *v* the past tense of forgive.

forge [fordʒ] **1.** *n* a blacksmith's workshop, with a furnace for heating the metal. **2.** *v* to copy someone else's handwriting or an important document for a dishonest purpose.

forgery ['fordʒɚi] *n* something written or painted which is not genuine; someone else's handwriting copied for a dishonest purpose; a fake.

forget [for'gɛt] *v* not to remember. *pt* forgot. *pp* forgotten.

forgive [for'gɪv] *v* to pardon someone; to stop being angry with someone who has done something wrong. *pt* forgave. *pp* forgiven.

forgiven [for'gɪvn̩] *v* the past participle of forgive.

forgot [for'gɑt] *v* the past tense of forget.

forgotten [for'gatn̩] *v* the past participle of forget.

fork [fork] *n* a tool used to pick up food.

form [form] **1.** *v* to put something into a special shape. *Ex* She formed a vase with the clay. **2.** *n* a shape. *Ex* That vase has a lovely form. **3.** *n* a paper asking questions which are to be answered. *Ex* Please fill out this form.

former ['formɚ] *n* the first of two things named. *Ex* Cola and milk are both good, but I prefer the former.

fort [fort] *n* a strong building made to keep enemies out.

forth [forθ] *adv* onwards; out.

fortress ['fortrəs] *n* a fort; a building which looks like a fort.

fortunate ['fortʃənət] *adj* lucky.

fortune ['fortʃn̩] *n* what comes by luck or chance; great riches or wealth.

forward ['forwɚd] *adv* towards the front.

fossil ['fasl̩] *n* the remains of an animal or a plant which has turned to stone after being buried for millions of years.

fought [fɔt] *v* the past tense and past participle of fight.

foul [fawl] **1.** *adj* dirty; horrible. **2.** *n* an act of breaking a rule in a game such as basketball. **3.** *v* to interfere with another player in a game such as basketball.

found [fawnd] *v* the past tense and past participle of find.

foundation [fawn'deyʃn̩] **1.** *n* the solid part of a building below ground level. **2.** *n* a basic amount of learning on which more learning can be based.

fountain ['fawntn̩] **1.** *n* water pushed up into the air continually in one or more streams. **2.** *n* a drinking fountain which lets you get a drink when you turn it on.

fountain pen ['fɑwntn̩ pɛn] *n* a pen which must be filled with ink before it can be used. *Ex* Fountain pens have metal points which must be cared for.

fowl [fɑwl] *n* a type of large bird, such as a chicken, duck, or turkey.

fox [fɑks] *n* a wild animal which has a long, bushy tail. *Ex* Foxes are clever, and they sometimes steal chickens.

fraction ['frækʃn̩] *n* a part of a whole number, such as 1/2 or 3/4.

fracture ['fræktʃɚ] **1.** *v* to crack or break something. **2.** *n* a crack or break in something.

fragile ['frædʒl̩] *adj* delicate; easily broken or damaged.

fragment ['frægmənt] *n* a bit or piece broken off of something.

frame [freym] *n* the wood or metal around something such as a window or a picture.

framework ['freymwɚk] *n* the outline or the main parts of something that the rest is built onto.

frank [fræŋk] *adj* sincere; open and honest.

frankfurter ['fræŋkfɚtɚ] *n* a sausage something like a wiener or a hot dog.

fraud [frɔd] *n* dishonesty; cheating.

freak [frik] *n* a person, plant, or animal whose appearance is not ordinary or normal, such as a white blackbird.

freckle ['frɛkl̩] *n* one of many small, dark spots on the skin. *Ex* Mary has red hair and lots of freckles.

free [fri] **1.** *adj* without payment; without a charge for. *Ex* I received a free sample in the mail. **2.** *adj* not a prisoner. *Ex* He was in jail for a week, but he is free now. **3.** *v* to release something or someone. *Ex* George freed the butterfly from the net.

freedom ['fridəm] *n* the state of being free; the state of being free from something such as control by a government.

freeze [friz] **1.** *v* to become hard because of the cold; to make something hard by making it very cold. *pt* froze. *pp* frozen. **2.** *n* a short and sudden period of weather where the temperature goes below 32 degrees Fahrenheit.

frequent ['frikwənt] *adj* happening often; usual; common. *Ex* Mary is a frequent visitor at our house.

fresh [frɛʃ] *adj* new; healthy; not tired.

fret [frɛt] *v* to be discontented; to worry; to cry or complain about something.

friction ['frɪkʃn̩] *n* a difficulty in moving two things because they are rubbing together.

friend [frɛnd] *n* someone you know well and like a lot.

friendly ['frɛndli] *adj* kind; showing friendship.

fright [frɑyt] *n* sudden fear; alarm.

frightened ['frɑytn̩d] *adj* afraid of something.

frightening ['frɑytnɪŋ] *adj* fearful; terrifying.

fringe [frɪndʒ] *n* an edging of loose threads, usually on clothing, lamp shades, or rugs.

frisky ['frɪski] *adj* lively; playful.

frizzy ['frɪzi] *adj* very tightly curled.

frog [frɔg] *n* a small animal that lives in or near water and can jump a long way. *Ex* Frogs are amphibians.

frolic ['frɑlɪk] **1.** *v* to have fun; to dance and play games. **2.** *n* a party; a session of dancing and games.

from [frəm] *prep* out of; due to. *Ex* He just came from the house. He just arrived from Poland. The fish will die from being in the air.

front [frənt] *n* the opposite of back; the most forward part of anything.

frontier [frən'tir] *n* a border between two countries; the front edge of advancing settlement; the new areas being settled in the United States during the 1800s.

front yard ['frənt 'yɑrd] *n* the small area of land in front of a house.

frost [frɔst] *n* a thin, icy covering on the ground when it is cold.

frosting ['frɔstɪŋ] *n* a sweet, sugary coating on a cake or other kind of pastry.

froth [frɔθ] *n* a lot of tiny, white bubbles, usually on top of liquid; foam.

frown [frɑwn] **1.** *v* to wrinkle the forehead when you are angry or displeased. **2.** *n* a cross or angry look on your face.

froze [frowz] *v* the past tense of freeze.

frozen ['frowzn̩] **1.** *adj* solid with ice; below zero degrees centigrade; below 32 degrees Fahrenheit. **2.** *v* the past participle of freeze.

fruit [fruwt] *n* a part of a bush or tree which can be eaten. *Ex* Apples, peaches, and oranges are fruits. Please give me a piece of fruit.

fruitful ['fruwtfl̩] **1.** *adj* producing much fruit. **2.** *adj* productive. *Ex* The meeting was very fruitful, and many new ideas resulted.

frustrated ['frəstreytəd] *adj* discouraged; disappointed; unhappy because you cannot have, be, or do something.

fry [fray] *v* to cook something in fat or oil.

frying pan ['frayıŋ pæn] *n* a pan in which food is fried; a skillet.

fuel ['fyuwl] *n* anything used to make heat, such as coal, gas, or wood.

full [fʊl] **1.** *adv* completely; all the way to the top. *Ex* Please fill my glass full. **2.** *adj* total; holding as much as possible. *Ex* My glass is full.

fully ['fʊli] *adv* completely; entirely.

fun [fən] *n* enjoyment; a very happy kind of pleasure.

funeral ['fyuwn(ə)rəl] *n* the ceremony of burying a dead person.

funnel ['fənl] *n* a tube that is very wide at the top so that you can pour liquid through it into a very small opening.

funny ['fəni] *adj* amusing; laughable.

fur [fɚ] *n* the soft hair on animals.

furnace ['fɚnəs] *n* a place where great heat is produced by a fire; the equipment which provides heat for a house or other building.

furnish ['fɚnıʃ] *v* to provide something; to provide furniture for a room or building. *Ex* They will furnish paper for us to write on. They haven't furnished the house, so there is nothing to sit on.

furniture ['fɚnıtʃɚ] *n* things like chairs, beds, and tables which are found in houses and other buildings.

further ['fɚðɚ] **1.** *adv* to a greater distance. *Ex* I must go further. **2.** *adj* more. *Ex* I will make no further comments.

fury ['fyɚi] *n* very great anger.

fuse [fyuwz] **1.** *n* a piece of string or material attached to something that will explode. *Ex* A fuse burns slowly to allow time for the person who lit it to get away. **2.** *n* a piece of wire used for safety in an electric system. The wire is mounted in a round holder.

fuss [fəs] **1.** *n* an argument; a complaint. **2.** *v* to cry or complain.

future ['fyuwtʃɚ] **1.** *n* the time to come; the days, months, and years ahead of us. **2.** *adj* in the time ahead.

fuzzy ['fəzi] **1.** *adj* covered with tiny hairs or fluff. **2.** *adj* not clearly or easily seen.

G

gadget ['gædʒət] *n* a small, cleverly designed tool or piece of apparatus. *Ex* Where is the gadget which fits in this hole?

gain [geyn] *v* to earn or win; to add to what you have already. *Ex* I'm trying not to gain weight.

gale [geyl] *n* a strong wind.

gallery ['gælɚi] **1.** *n* the upper floor of seats in a theater. **2.** *n* a room or building where works of art can be seen. *Ex* We visited the art gallery yesterday.

gallon ['gælən] *n* a measure of liquid equal to four quarts or eight pints. *Ex* Eighteen gallons of gas cost a lot of money.

gallop ['gæləp] **1.** *n* the fastest speed at which a horse can run. **2.** *v* for a horse to run very rapidly.

galoshes [gə'lɑʃəz] *n* a special kind of waterproof overshoes.

gamble ['gæmbl̩] *v* to play a game for money.

game [geym] *n* an activity which is done according to the rules; a sports contest.

gang [gæŋ] **1.** *n* a group of people working together. **2.** *n* a band of robbers or thieves.

gangster ['gæŋ(k)stɚ] *n* a member of a gang of robbers and thieves.

gap [gæp] *n* an opening or break in something.

garage [gə'rɑʒ] *n* a place where vehicles are kept or repaired.

garbage ['gɑrbɪdʒ] **1.** *n* trash; paper, cans, glass, and food scraps from the kitchen. **2.** *n* the place where garbage or trash is put; a garbage can. *Ex* Please throw the broken glass in the garbage.

garbage can ['gɑrbɪdʒ kæn] *n* a container for garbage

garden ['gɑrdn̩] *n* a piece of land where flowers, fruit, or vegetables are grown.

garment ['gɑrmənt] *n* any article of clothing.

garter ['gɑrtɚ] *n* a ring made of elastic which keeps a stocking from falling down.

gas [gæs] **1.** *n* air or something like air which can fill a space. **2.** *n* short for the word gasoline.

gash [gæʃ] *n* a long, deep cut or wound.

gasoline ['gæsəlin] *n* a liquid fuel used by cars, trucks, and other vehicles.

gasp [gæsp] **1.** *v* to take a quick, deep breath; to struggle for breath. **2.** *n* a quick, deep breath which is a sign of fright or shock.

gate [geyt] *n* a door in a fence or wall.

gather ['gæðɚ] *v* to collect; to pick up one by one.

gave [geyv] *v* the past tense of give.

gay [gey] *adj* happy and lively.

gaze [geyz] *v* to look at something steadily; to stare.

gear [gir] **1.** *n* the part of a car or bicycle which changes the speed. **2.** *n* possessions; equipment. *Ex* Don't forget your camping gear.

geese [gis] *n* the plural of goose.

gem [dʒɛm] *n* a precious stone; a jewel.

general ['dʒɛn(ə)rəl] **1.** *adj* usual; happening everywhere. **2.** *n* a commander in the army.

generous ['dʒɛnɚəs] *adj* kind in sharing or giving things to others.

gentle ['dʒɛntl̩] *adj* quiet; soft or soothing; careful. *Ex* You must be gentle with a baby.

gentleman ['dʒɛntl̩mən] *n* a kind and honorable man; a polite term for man.

genuine ['dʒɛnyəwən] *adj* real; true; not a fake or a copy. *Ex* This is a genuine diamond.

geography [dʒi'ɑgrəfi] *n* the study of the surface of the earth and the people and animals living there.

geometry [dʒi'ɑmətri] *n* the part of mathematics having to do with lines, angles, and shapes such as triangles and circles.

germ [dʒɚm] *n* a very tiny bit of animal or plant life that you can only see under a microscope. *Ex* Some germs cause diseases.

get [gɛt] **1.** *v* to receive; to go and bring back something. **2.** *v* to become; to achieve. *Ex* I hope you get well. *pt* got. *pp* got, gotten.

ghost [gowst] *n* the spirit of a dead person.

giant ['dʒayənt] **1.** *n* a very big, strong person, usually in fairy tales. **2.** *n* an animal, plant, or person that is much larger than others of the same kind. **3.** *adj* very large; larger than usual.

giddy ['gɪdi] *adj* having the feeling that things are going around and around; silly.

gift [gɪft] *n* something which is given as a present.

gigantic [dʒɑy'gæntɪk] *adj* enormous; giant-like.

giggle [ˈgɪgl̩] **1.** v to laugh in a silly way. **2.** n a small, silly laugh.

gill [gɪl] n an opening in a fish's skin for breathing. Ex Every fish has a pair of gills.

ginger [ˈdʒɪndʒɚ] n the root of a plant. Ex Ginger tastes spicy and makes your mouth feel hot.

gingerbread [ˈdʒɪndʒɚbrɛd] n a cake or cookie made with ginger.

giraffe [dʒəˈræf] n a tall animal with a very long neck. Ex Giraffes are found in Africa.

girl [gɚl] n a female child; a child who will grow up to be a woman.

give [gɪv] v to hand something over freely to someone else. pt gave. pp given.

given [ˈgɪvn̩] v the past participle of give.

glacier [ˈgleyʃɚ] n a mass of ice that moves very slowly down a mountainside.

glad [glæd] adj pleased; happy.

glance [glæn(t)s] **1.** v to look at something or someone quickly. **2.** n a quick look.

glare [glɛr] **1.** n a dazzling bright light. **2.** v to stare angrily at someone.

glass [glæs] **1.** n a hard material you can see through. Ex Windows are made of glass. **2.** n a drinking vessel made of a hard material you can see through.

glasses [ˈglæsəz] n two framed pieces of a special kind of glass. Ex If you cannot see well, glasses help you to see better.

gleam [glim] v to shine. Ex Old metal gleams when it is polished.

glide [glayd] *v* to move smoothly and easily; to flow gently.

glider ['glaydɚ] *n* a light airplane which can fly for some time without an engine after being launched.

glimmer ['glɪmɚ] *v* to shine faintly and unsteadily.

glimpse [glɪmps] *n* a very brief sight of something or someone.

glisten ['glɪsn̩] *v* to shine or gleam.

glitter ['glɪtɚ] *v* to sparkle; to reflect light brightly.

globe [glowb] *n* a round object like a ball or the world.

gloomy ['gluwmi] *adj* dark; dim; miserable; the opposite of cheerful.

glossary ['glɔsɚi] *n* a short list of words and their meanings.

glove [glʌv] *n* a covering for the hand. *Ex* A glove has a separate covering for each finger.

glow [glow] *v* to burn without flames; to give out a steady light.

glue [gluw] **1.** *n* a strong substance like paste used to stick things together. **2.** *v* to stick things together with a paste-like substance.

glum [gləm] *adj* silent and sad; gloomy.

glutton ['glətn̩] *n* a person who is greedy and eats too much.

gnarled [narld] *adj* twisted and lumpy like the trunk of a very old tree.

gnash [næʃ] *v* to grind the teeth together when very angry.

gnat [næt] *n* a small, flying insect which stings.

gnaw [nɔ] *v* to wear something away by scraping at it with teeth. *Ex* The dog was gnawing a bone.

go [gow] *v* to start off or move. *pt* went. *pp* gone.

goal [gowl] **1.** *n* a kind of target. *Ex* The basket in basketball is a goal. **2.** *n* a scoring of points in sports like basketball or football. *Ex* He made four goals in the last game.

goat [gowt] *n* an animal something like a sheep. *Ex* Goats usually have little horns and a short beard.

gobble ['gɑbḷ] *v* to swallow food quickly without chewing it.

goblin ['gɑblən] *n* an ugly and troublesome elf.

going to ['gowɪŋ tuw] *v* will. *Ex* He is going to buy groceries tomorrow. She is not going to come to my party.

gold [gowld] *n* a yellow, shiny metal which is worth a lot of money.

goldfish ['gowldfɪʃ] *n* a small fish kept as a pet. *Ex* Goldfish are usually a pretty reddish-gold color.

golf [gɔlf] *n* a game which is played with a small white ball and a set of long-handled clubs.

gone [gɔn] *v* the past participle of go.

gong [gɔŋ] *n* a round, metal disc which makes a deep ringing sound when you hit it.

good [gʊd] *adj* right or satisfactory; nice; kind.

good-bye [gʊd'bay] *n* a word said to someone who is just going away.

goodness ['gʊdnəs] *n* the act of being good or kind.

goods [gʊdz] *n* things bought and sold.

goose [guws] *n* a big bird like a duck with a long neck. The plural is geese.

gorgeous ['gordʒəs] *adj* splendid; magnificent; richly colored and beautiful.

gorilla [gə'rɪlə] *n* the largest kind of ape. *Ex* Gorillas live in Africa.

gossip ['gɑsəp] **1.** *n* chatter about other people, sometimes spiteful and unkind. **2.** *v* to say unkind things about other people.

got [gɑt] *v* the past tense and a past participle of get.

gotten ['gɑtn̩] *v* a past participle of get.

govern ['gəvɚn] *v* to rule or control.

government ['gəvɚ(n)mənt] *n* a group of people who have the power to make laws and decide what is best for the country.

governor ['gəvə(r)nɚ] *n* the elected head of one of the U.S. states; the chief executive of a state.

gown [gɑwn] *n* a woman's dress; a loose-fitting cloak or a robe.

grab [græb] *v* to take hold of something suddenly.

graceful ['greysfl̩] *adj* easy and smooth in movement; the opposite of clumsy.

gracious ['greyʃəs] *adj* kind; charming.

grade [greyd] **1.** *v* to decide how good something is; to correct homework. *Ex* The teacher grades papers at home and brings them back to school. **2.** *n* a number or letter showing how well a person has done in school. *Ex* She deserves only a grade of C. What grade did you get?

gradual ['grædʒəwəl] *adj* happening slowly, little by little.

graduate 1. *v* ['grædʒəweyt] to earn and receive a school diploma; to finish with schooling. **2.** *n* ['grædʒəwət] a person who has received a school diploma.

graduation [grædʒə'weyʃn̩] *n* the ceremony where school diplomas are awarded.

grain [greyn] *n* one of the seeds of plants, such as wheat or corn, which we eat.

gram [græm] *n* a metric unit of weight equal to 0.035 ounce.

grammar ['græmɚ] *n* the study of the way people put words together when they speak or write.

grand [grænd] *adj* important; large; splendid.

grandchild ['græn(d)tʃayld] *n* a child born of one of your children. *Ex* Mary's daughter is named Martha. Martha's daughter is named Ann. Ann is Mary's grandchild.

grandfather ['græn(d)faðɚ] *n* your father's father; your mother's father.

grandmother ['græn(d)məðɚ] *n* your father's mother; your mother's mother.

grandparent ['græn(d)pɛrənt] *n* your father's mother or father; your mother's mother or father.

granite ['grænət] *n* a very hard rock used for buildings.

grant [grænt] *v* to give; to allow as a favor.

grape [greyp] *n* a green, purple, or red fruit that grows in bunches on a vine.

grapefruit ['greypfruwt] *n* a round fruit like a large orange with a yellow skin and a sharp taste.

graph [græf] *n* a diagram that shows how a series of measurements change.

grasp [græsp] *v* to seize and hold tightly.

grass [græs] *n* a low green plant which has thin leaves and covers fields and lawns.

grasshopper ['græshɑpɚ] *n* a hopping, leaping insect. *Ex* A grasshopper's back legs are very big and strong.

grate [greyt] **1.** *n* a framework of iron for holding a fire in a fireplace. **2.** *v* to rub something, such as cheese, against a rough surface to make small particles.

grateful ['greytfḷ] *adj* giving thanks; thankful.

grave [greyv] **1.** *adj* very serious. **2.** *n* a hole in the ground where a dead person is buried.

gravel ['grævḷ] *n* lots of little rocks which can be used to make paths and driveways.

gravity ['grævəti] *n* the force which makes things fall downward and holds things onto the earth.

gravy ['greyvi] *n* the juice of cooked meat, sometimes mixed with flour to make it thicker.

gray [grey] **1.** *n* a neutral color between black and white. **2.** *adj* of a neutral color; between black and white.

graze [greyz] **1.** *v* to eat grass. *Ex* The cows are grazing in the field. **2.** *v* to scrape the skin. *Ex* I grazed my elbow on the wall.

grease [gris] *n* a thick, oily substance; softened animal fat.

greasy ['grisi] *adj* slippery with oil or grease.

great [greyt] *adj* large; big; important; famous.

greed [grid] *n* a great longing to have more of something even though you already have enough.

green [grin] **1.** *n* the color of grass in the springtime. **2.** *adj* of the same color as grass in the springtime.

greenhouse ['grinhɑws] *n* a house made of glass where plants can grow all year long.

greet [grit] *v* to welcome; to speak to someone when you meet.

greeting ['gritɪŋ] *n* a welcome; a kind wish often written on a birthday or Christmas card.

grew [gruw] *v* the past tense of grow.

grief [grif] *n* great sadness.

grieve [griv] *v* to be very sad about something; to be very unhappy.

grill [grɪl] **1.** *n* a thin grate on which meat is cooked over an open fire; a flat panel of metal on which meat is cooked. **2.** *v* to cook meat on a grill.

grim [grɪm] *adj* stern; unsmiling; looking unpleasant. *Ex* Mrs. Green looks very grim. This stormy weather looks grim.

grime [graym] *n* dirt that sticks on and is hard to get off.

grin [grɪn] *v* to smile broadly.

grind [graynd] **1.** *v* to crush something to a powder. **2.** *v* to rub together. *Ex* Please stop grinding your teeth together! *pt* ground. *pp* ground.

grip [grɪp] **1.** *v* to hold on to something tightly. *Ex* You must grip the bat tightly. **2.** *n* a tight hold on something. *Ex* Get a good grip on the bat before you swing it.

grit [grɪt] *n* a small piece of dirt or sand.

groan [grown] **1.** *n* a deep, unhappy sound of pain or sorrow. **2.** *v* to make a deep, sorrowful sound.

grocer ['growsɚ] *n* a person who runs a grocery store.

groceries ['growsriz] *n* the food and other things that you buy at a grocery store. *Ex* This week's groceries cost nearly fifty dollars.

grocery store ['growsri stor] *n* the place where food and things like cleaning supplies are sold; a supermarket. *Ex* You can't buy gasoline at a grocery store.

groove [gruwv] *n* a long, narrow cut hollowed out, usually in wood or metal.

grope [growp] *v* to feel for something with your hands because you cannot see well. *Ex* John groped his way across the dark room.

gross [grows] **1.** *adj* very big; very fat. **2.** *n* twelve dozen (144).

grouch [grɑwtʃ] **1.** *v* to complain and be unpleasant about something or everything. **2.** *n* a person who is always complaining.

ground [grɑwnd] **1.** *n* the earth we walk on. **2.** *v* the past tense and past participle of grind.

ground beef ['grɑwnd 'bif] *n* chopped beef; hamburger.

group [gruwp] *n* a number of people or things together in one place.

grove [growv] *n* a small group of trees; a small field planted with fruit trees.

grow [grow] *v* to get bigger; to raise plants or crops. *Ex* My younger brother is growing very fast. My uncle grows wheat on his farm. *pt* grew. *pp* grown.

growl [grɑwl] **1.** *v* to make a low rumbling noise deep down in the throat. *Ex* Dogs and lions growl when they are angry or afraid. **2.** *n* a deep, low noise made by an angry animal.

grown [grown] *v* the past participle of grow.

grown-up ['grownəp] **1.** *adj* adult; fully grown; not childish. *Ex* Frank acts like a grown-up man. **2.** *n* an adult; a fully grown person. *Ex* Grown-ups don't drink as much milk as children do.

grudge [grədʒ] *n* a feeling of unfriendliness or dislike for someone.

gruff [grəf] *adj* rough in manner; stern; grouchy.

grumble ['grəmbl̩] *v* to find fault and say you are not satisfied.

grumpy ['grəmpi] *adj* bad-tempered; grouchy.

grunt [grənt] **1.** *v* to make a noise like a pig. **2.** *n* the sound that a pig makes.

guarantee [gɛrən'ti] *n* a written statement that a product will be repaired or replaced if it is not good.

guard [gɑrd] **1.** *v* to look after something or someone. **2.** *n* a person whose job is to look after something, someplace, or someone.

guardian ['gɑrdiən] *n* a guard; a keeper; a person assigned to take care of a child.

guess [gɛs] *v* to answer a question without knowing for sure that it is the right answer.

guest [gɛst] *n* a visitor; someone you invite to your house; someone who is invited somewhere.

guidance ['gɑydn̩(t)s] *n* explaining or showing the way to someone.

guidance counselor ['gɑydn̩(t)s kawn(t)sələ˞] *n* a person whose job is to give advice about school and jobs.

guide [gɑyd] **1.** *v* to show someone the way. **2.** *n* a person who shows the way.

guilt [gɪlt] *n* a feeling of having done something wrong.

guilty [gɪlti] *adj* responsible for something wrong; not innocent; judged to be a criminal.

guinea pig ['gɪni pɪg] *n* a small, furry animal with short ears and tail, often kept as a pet.

guitar [gɪ'tɑr] *n* a musical instrument with strings which are plucked to make music.

gulf [gəlf] *n* a very large bay that cuts into the land.

gull [gəl] *n* a web-footed seabird, usually colored gray and white.

gulp [gəlp] **1.** *v* to take a quick, deep swallow of food or air. **2.** *n* a quick, deep swallow of food or air.

gum [gəm] *n* a sweet, rubbery substance which you chew but don't swallow.

gun [gən] *n* a machine which shoots bullets.

gunpowder ['gənpɑwdɚ] *n* a special powder which explodes when a flame is touched to it.

gush [gəʃ] *v* to rush out suddenly, as when water rushes out of a burst pipe.

gust [gəst] *n* a sudden bursting out of wind or laughter.

gutter ['gətɚ] *n* a long, metal channel at the edge of a roof for draining off rainwater; the place at the side of a road where rainwater runs off.

gym [dʒɪm] **1.** *n* a gymnasium. **2.** *n* a course or class in physical education; gym class.

gymnasium [dʒɪm'neyziəm] *n* a large room fitted with ropes, bars, and all kinds of equipment for exercise.

gym suit ['dʒɪm suwt] *n* the special clothing worn in a physical education class.

Gypsy ['dʒɪpsi] *n* someone who belongs to a race of people who originally came from India.

H

habit ['hæbət] *n* something you do regularly and often, almost without thinking about it, such as brushing your teeth.

had [hæd] *v* the past tense and past participle of have. *Ex* She had already gone. She has had two helpings already.

hadn't ['hædn̩t] *cont* had not.

had to ['hæd tuw] *v* was obliged to; was made to do something. *Ex* I had to go to town yesterday. She didn't want to go to school, but she had to.

hail [heyl] *n* frozen rain which falls as little lumps of ice.

hair [hɛr] *n* the soft covering which grows on the head.

hairbrush ['hɛrbrəʃ] *n* a special brush used for arranging the hair.

hairdo ['hɛrduw] *n* an arrangement of the hair, especially one which someone has been paid to do. Usually said of women's hair.

hairpin ['hɛrpɪn] *n* a U-shaped wire pin used to hold hair in place.

half [hæf] *n* one of two equal parts. *Ex* When you cut something in half, you divide it into two parts which are the same size.

hall [hɔl] **1.** *n* the space inside the entrance to a building; a corridor. **2.** *n* a large room, usually in a public building, used for meetings and special occasions.

hall pass ['hɔl pæs] *n* a piece of paper which gives you the right to be in the hallways of a school.

148

halo ['heylow] *n* a ring of light around the sun or moon; a ring of light around the heads of holy people in paintings.

halt [hɔlt] **1.** *v* to stop. *Ex* All of the traffic halted when the policeman blew his whistle. **2.** *n* a stop; an act of stopping. *Ex* The traffic came to a halt.

halve [hæv] *v* to divide into two equal parts. *Ex* Frank halved the apple, and we both had a piece of it.

ham [hæm] *n* meat from the thigh of a pig.

hamburger ['hæmbɚgɚ] **1.** *n* chopped or ground beef. **2.** *n* a sandwich made of cooked ground beef on a bun, usually with such things as pickles, onions, mustard, and ketchup.

hammer ['hæmɚ] **1.** *n* a heavy tool used to drive nails into wood or to hit and break things. **2.** *v* to drive a nail into something; to pound constantly.

hammock ['hæmək] *n* a swinging bed of netting or canvas hung up by ropes at each end.

hamper ['hæmpɚ] **1.** *n* a large basket; a picnic basket; a basket or container used to collect dirty clothes for the laundry. **2.** *v* to hinder; to keep someone from doing something.

hamster ['hæm(p)stɚ] *n* a small, furry animal, usually golden-brown, often kept as a pet.

hand [hænd] *n* the end of your arm which you use to hold things.

handbag ['hændbæg] *n* a small, light bag that can be carried in one hand; a woman's purse.

handful ['hændfl] *n* a small number or quantity; as much as one hand will hold.

handicap ['hændikæp] *n* something that makes doing things very difficult.

handicraft ['hændɪkræft] *n* work in which things are made by hand and not by machine.

handkerchief ['hæŋkətʃɪf] *n* a small piece of cloth for wiping the eyes or the nose.

handle ['hændl̩] **1.** *n* a part of something by which you can hold on. *Ex* Cups, pans, and windows have handles. **2.** *v* to hold things and feel them with your hands.

handlebar ['hændl̩bɑr] *n* the part of a bicycle that a person holds on to and steers with.

handsome ['hæn(t)səm] *adj* good-looking.

handy ['hændi] **1.** *adj* useful and clever with your hands. **2.** *adj* nearby; close at hand.

handyman ['hændimæn] *n* someone who can fix many different things and do many different chores.

hang [hæŋ] *v* to fasten something to a firm support so that it swings freely, but cannot fall. *pt* hung, hanged. *pp* hung, hanged.

hangar ['hæŋɚ] *n* a large shed for airplanes.

hanged [hæŋd] *v* a past tense and past participle of hang.

hanger ['hæŋɚ] *n* a shaped piece of wood or metal used to hang clothes on so that they don't get wrinkled.

haphazard [hæp'hæzɚd] *adj* not planned; happening by chance.

happen ['hæpən] *v* to take place.

happiness ['hæpinəs] *n* joy; gladness.

happy ['hæpi] *adj* full of joy.

harbor ['hɑrbɚ] *n* a sheltered place where ships stay before going out to sea.

hard [hɑrd] **1.** *adj* not soft; solid. *Ex* Stones are hard. **2.** *adj* difficult.

hardly ['hɑrdli] *adv* barely; only just.

hardware ['hɑrdwɛr] **1.** *n* tools, nails, screws, and metal parts for machines. **2.** *n* computers and the machines which are attached to them.

hardy ['hɑrdi] *adj* tough; brave.

harm [hɑrm] **1.** *v* to damage or hurt. **2.** *n* damage.

harmful ['hɑrmfḷ] *adj* doing harm or damage.

harmless ['hɑrmləs] *adj* doing no harm; the opposite of harmful.

harness ['hɑrnəs] *n* the straps and other equipment worn by a horse.

harp [hɑrp] *n* a big musical instrument shaped like a triangle with strings which are plucked to make music.

harsh [hɑrʃ] *adj* rough; unkind; unpleasant.

harvest ['hɑrvəst] **1.** *v* to gather in grain, fruits, and vegetables when they are grown. **2.** *n* the gathering of food after it is grown.

has [hæz] *v* the present tense form of the verb *have* which goes with *he, she,* and *it. Ex* Mark has seven books.

hasn't ['hæzṇt] *cont* has not.

haste [heyst] *n* hurry.

hasten ['heysṇ] *v* to hurry up.

has to ['hæstuw] a phrase meaning *must. Ex* Sam has to go to the doctor today.

hat [hæt] *n* a covering for the head.

hatch [hætʃ] *v* to break out of the eggshell, as when baby birds are hatched.

hatchet ['hætʃət] *n* a small axe.

hate [heyt] *v* to dislike someone or something very much.

haughty ['hɔti] *adj* full of pride.

haul [hɔl] *v* to drag along; to pull.

haunt [hɔnt] *v* for a ghost or evil spirit to visit a place often.

haunted ['hɔntəd] *adj* dwelled in or visited by ghosts.

have [hæv] *v* to own; to hold. Present tenses: has, have. *pt* had. *pp* had. *Ex* I have two books. Martha has two books.

haven't ['hævn̩t] *cont* have not.

hawk [hɔk] *n* a bird of prey that hunts small birds and animals.

hay [hey] *n* dried grass used for feeding animals.

hay fever ['hey fivɚ] *n* an illness which causes sneezing and a runny nose. *Ex* Hay fever is caused by pollen in the air.

haze [heyz] *n* mist; a very thin cloud.

he [hi] **1.** *pro* a male person or animal. *Ex* He will put his hat on the peg. **2.** *pro* any person which has been talked about without referring to the sex of that person. *Ex* If someone comes in, he will have to sit here.

head [hɛd] **1.** *n* the part of the body above the neck. **2.** *n* the person who is in charge; a chief or leader. **3.** *n* the source of a river; the beginning of a river.

headache ['hɛdeyk] *n* a continuous, dull pain somewhere in the head.

headline ['hɛdlɑyn] *n* the very large print found at the top of a newspaper or magazine column.

headphones ['hɛdfownz] *n* a frame holding a pair of loud-speakers over the ears. *Ex* You can listen to things in private using headphones.

headset ['hɛdsɛt] *n* headphones; headphones with a micro-phone attached.

heal [hil] *v* to make someone well again.

health [hɛlθ] *n* how your body feels. *Ex* You have good health when you are not ill.

healthy ['hɛlθi] *adj* well in mind and body; free from illness.

heap [hip] **1.** *n* a pile, like a pile of dry leaves. **2.** *v* to make a pile; to pile up something. *Ex* He heaped the leaves into a pile.

hear [hir] *v* to use your ears to listen to sounds. *pt* heard. *pp* heard.

heard [hɚd] *v* the past tense and past participle of hear.

heart [hɑrt] *n* the part of the body which pumps the blood around.

heat [hit] **1.** *n* warmth; hotness. **2.** *v* to make something hot.

heater ['hitɚ] *n* a device which produces heat by burning fuel or electricity.

heave [hiv] *v* to haul or lift something up with a great effort.

heaven ['hɛvn̩] *n* the home of God; the sky above us.

heavy ['hɛvi] *adj* difficult to pick up and carry away; weighing a lot.

he'd [hid] *cont* he would; he had.

hedge [hɛdʒ] *n* a row of bushes growing close together in a line like a fence.

heel [hil] **1.** *n* the back end of the foot; the part of the foot which is directly under the leg when you are standing. **2.** *n* the back end of a shoe; the part of a shoe which holds up the heel of the foot.

height [hɑyt] *n* how tall something is.

heir [ɛr] *n* a person who will receive money or property when the present owner dies.

heiress ['ɛrəs] *n* a girl or woman who will receive money or property when the present owner dies.

held [hɛld] *v* the past tense and past participle of hold.

helicopter ['hɛləkɑptər] *n* a kind of aircraft without wings which can go straight up or down in the air as well as move along.

hell [hɛl] *n* a place of misery and punishment.

he'll [hil] *cont* he will.

helmet ['hɛlmət] *n* a covering, usually made of metal, which protects the head. *Ex* Football players wear helmets.

help [hɛlp] **1.** *v* to make something easier for a person to do. *Ex* Please help me wash the dishes. **2.** *n* aid; assistance. *Ex* Please give me some help with the dishes.

helpful ['hɛlpfl] *adj* being of help; giving assistance.

helping ['hɛlpɪŋ] *n* a serving of food; a portion of food.

helpless ['hɛlpləs] *adj* not being able to help yourself or others, often because of weakness.

helter-skelter [hɛltər'skɛltər] *adv* every which way; in all directions.

hem [hɛm] *n* an edge of cloth which is folded over and sewn to make it neat.

hemisphere ['hɛməsfir] *n* one half of the earth; one half of a sphere. *Ex* The United States is in the northern hemisphere.

hen [hɛn] *n* a mother bird; a mother chicken.

her [hɚ] **1.** *pro* belonging to a female. *Ex* Her car is in the driveway. **2.** *pro* the objective form of she. *Ex* I did it for her.

herb [ɚb] *n* a plant which is used for flavoring food or for medicine.

herd [hɚd] *n* a group of animals kept together. *Ex* There is a herd of cows on my uncle's farm.

here [hir] *adv* in, to, or at this place.

hero ['hirow] **1.** *n* a man or boy who does something brave. **2.** *n* the most important man in a book, play, or opera.

heroine ['hɛrowɪn] **1.** *n* a girl or woman who does something brave. **2.** *n* the most important woman in a book, play, or opera.

heroism ['hɛrowɪzm̩] *n* great bravery.

hers [hɚz] *pro* that which belongs to her. *Ex* That car is hers.

herself [hɚ'sɛlf] *pro* she and no one else.

he's [hiz] *cont* he is; he has.

hesitate ['hɛzəteyt] *v* to pause because you are not sure what to do or say next.

hexagon ['hɛksəgɑn] *n* a six-sided shape.

hibernate ['haybɚneyt] *v* to sleep all through the winter as some animals do.

hiccup ['hɪkəp] **1.** *n* a sharp noise in your throat made when you have eaten or drunk too quickly. *Ex* You do not make hiccups on purpose, and sometimes it is difficult to stop. **2.** *v* to make a sharp noise in the throat when you have eaten or drunk too quickly. Also spelled hiccough.

hid [hɪd] *v* the past tense of hide.

hidden ['hɪdn̩] *v* the past participle of hide.

hide [hɑyd] **1.** *v* to go where no one can see or find you; to put something where no one can see it or find it. *pt* hid. *pp* hidden. **2.** *n* the skin of an animal.

hide-and-seek [hɑydn̩'sik] *n* a game where one person hides and other people try to find him.

hideous ['hɪdiəs] *adj* very ugly; horrible.

hifi ['hɑyfɑy] *n* a good-quality record player. Short for the words high fidelity.

high [hɑy] *adj* a long way up; tall. *Ex* That is a very high mountain.

high chair ['hɑy tʃɛr] *n* a tall chair which makes it possible for an infant to eat at the table with adults.

high rise ['hɑy rɑyz] *n* a very tall apartment or office building.

high school ['hɑy skuwl] **1.** *n* the last three or four year period of school after grade school. **2.** *n* the building where high school is held.

highway ['hɑywey] *n* a public road where cars, buses, and trucks can move at high speed.

hike [hɑyk] **1.** *v* to go for a very long walk, usually in the country. **2.** *n* a very long walk in the country.

hill [hɪl] *n* a part of the ground which is higher than the rest but lower than a mountain.

him [hɪm] *pro* the objective form of he. *Ex* I did it for him.

himself [hɪm'sɛlf] *pro* he and no one else.

hinder ['hɪndɚ] *v* to delay or prevent someone from doing something.

hinge [hɪndʒ] *n* a folding joint, usually made of metal. *Ex* Doors are fitted with hinges so that they can be opened and shut.

hint [hɪnt] **1.** *v* to suggest something without actually saying it in so many words. **2.** *n* a suggestion.

hip [hɪp] *n* one of the sides of the body just below the waist.

hire [haɪr] *v* to employ someone.

his [hɪz] *pro* belonging to a male. *Ex* This is his car.

hiss [hɪs] **1.** *v* to make a noise that sounds like s-s-s-s-s. *Ex* Cats hiss when they are angry. **2.** *n* a noise that sounds like s-s-s-s-s.

historian [hɪs'torɪən] *n* a person who studies the past.

history ['hɪstɚi] *n* the study of what has happened in the past.

hit [hɪt] **1.** *v* to knock something. *pt* hit. *pp* hit. **2.** *n* a show or a song which is a big success.

hive [haɪv] *n* the place where bees live.

hoard [hord] *n* a store or stock of something hidden away. *Ex* Squirrels have a hoard of nuts hidden away for the winter.

hoarse [hors] *adj* having a rough-sounding voice, as when you have a sore throat. *Ex* I was hoarse for a week after my cold.

hobby ['habi] *n* something you like to do very much in your spare time, such as stamp collecting.

hockey ['haki] *n* a game where you try to hit a ball into the goal with a long stick curved at one end. *Ex* Hockey is usually played on the ice.

hoe [how] **1.** *n* a long-handled garden tool used for clearing weeds and loosening the soil. **2.** *v* to clear weeds and loosen the soil with a special tool.

hold [howld] **1.** *v* to have in your hands or your arms; to contain. **2.** *n* the part of a ship where cargo is kept. *pt* held. *pp* held.

hole [howl] *n* an opening in or through something. *Ex* Don't fall into that hole! There is a hole in my sock.

holiday ['hɑlədey] *n* a time when you do not have to work or to go to school.

hollow ['hɑlow] *adj* having a space or hole inside. *Ex* A basketball is hollow. The earth is not hollow.

holly ['hɑli] *n* an evergreen tree with prickly leaves and bright red berries. *Ex* Holly is often used for decoration at Christmas.

holster ['howlstɚ] *n* a leather case on a belt for holding a gun.

holy ['howli] *n* anything belonging to, or having to do with God or religion.

home [howm] *n* the place where you live.

home ec. [howm 'ɛk] *n* short for home economics; the study of managing a household.

homeowner ['howmownɚ] *n* a person who owns a house or apartment.

home plate ['howm 'pleyt] *n* a base in baseball where the batter stands and where a player must run to to win a point.

homework ['howmwɚk] *n* work done at home, usually schoolwork.

honest ['ɑnəst] *adj* truthful; not likely to steal from others.

honey ['hɐni] *n* a sweet food made by bees.

honeymoon ['hənimuwn] *n* a short vacation taken by the bride and groom just after they are married.

honk [hɔŋk] **1.** *n* the cry of a goose; the sound of the horn on a vehicle. **2.** *v* for a goose to make its cry; to sound the horn of a vehicle.

honor ['ɑnɚ] **1.** *v* to show respect for someone or something. **2.** *n* a privilege; respectability.

honors ['ɑnɚz] *n* special recognition given to a very good student.

hood [hʊd] *n* a loose cloth covering for the head. *Ex* Some coats and jackets have hoods.

hoof [hʊf] *n* the hard part of a horse's foot. The plural is hooves. *Ex* Cattle, deer, and some other animals also have hooves.

hook [hʊk] *n* a curved, pointed piece of metal for catching, holding, or pulling things.

hoop [huwp] *n* a large ring made of metal or wood.

hoot [huwt] **1.** *v* to shout scornfully at someone. **2.** *n* the cry of an owl in the night; the sound of a horn.

hop [hɑp] **1.** *v* to move in short jumps; to jump on one leg. **2.** *n* a short jump.

hope [howp] **1.** *v* to wish that something may happen although you know it may not. **2.** *n* a belief or trust that something good will happen.

hopeful ['howpfl̩] *adj* hoping; full of hope.

hopeless ['howpləs] *adj* without hope; impossible.

horde [hord] *n* a crowd or mass of people.

horizon [hə'rɑyzn̩] *n* the place where the sky and the earth appear to meet.

horizontal [horə'zɑntl̩] *adj* level with the ground; parallel to the horizon.

horn [horn] **1.** *n* one of the sharp, bony parts that grow out of the heads of cows, deer, and some other animals. **2.** *n* a musical instrument which is blown to make musical sounds.

horrible ['horəbl̩] *adj* ugly and awful; terrible.

horrid ['horəd] *adj* nasty; very unpleasant.

horror ['horɚ] *n* a very great fear or loathing.

horse [hors] *n* an animal used for riding and pulling things.

horseback ['horsbæk] *n* the back or top of a horse.

horseshoe ['horsʃuw] *n* a curved iron shoe which is nailed to the bottom of a horse's hoof.

hose [howz] **1.** *n* a long, thin tube used for carrying water from a tap. **2.** *n* socks or stockings.

hospital ['hɑspɪtl̩] *n* a place where people who are ill or hurt are looked after by doctors and nurses.

host [howst] **1.** *n* a boy or man who has other people as his guests. **2.** *n* a crowd or a large number.

hostess ['howstəs] *n* a girl or woman who has other people as her guests.

hot [hɑt] *adj* very warm.

hot chocolate [hɑt 'tʃɔklət] *n* a hot drink made from milk and cocoa.

hot dog ['hɑt dɔg] **1.** *n* a wiener; a special sausage made for sandwiches. **2.** *n* a sandwich made with a wiener, a long bun, and mustard or ketchup.

hotel [how'tɛl] *n* a building with many rooms and a place to eat. *Ex* People stay in hotels when they are traveling.

hound [hɑwnd] *n* a hunting dog.

hour ['ɑwɚ] *n* a period of time equal to 60 minutes.

house [hɑws] *n* a building to live in.

houseboat ['hɑwsbowt] *n* a large, flat-bottomed boat used as a floating house.

household ['hɑwshowld] *n* all of the people who live in the same house; the people and possessions in a house.

House of Representatives [hɑws əv rɛprə'zɛntətɪvz] *n* one of the two parts of the United States Congress.

houseplant ['hɑwsplænt] *n* any plant which grows well inside a house.

hover ['həvɚ] *v* to float or stay in one place in the air.

how [hɑw] *adv* in what way.

however [hɑw'ɛvɚ] *adv* in what way; to what degree; except that; but.

howl [hɑwl] **1.** *v* to make a long, crying sound. *Ex* Dogs and wolves howl. **2.** *n* a long, crying noise.

hub [həb] *n* the middle of a wheel.

huddle ['hədl̩] *v* to crowd closely together, perhaps to get warm.

hug [həg] **1.** *v* to hold someone or something close to you in your arms. **2.** *n* an act of hugging.

huge [hyuwɑ̃ʒ] *adj* enormous; very big.

hum [həm] *v* to make a musical sound in your nose as though you are saying m-m-m-m without opening your mouth.

human ['hyuwmən] **1.** *n* a man, woman, or child. **2.** *adj* having to do with people, not animals or plants.

human being [hyuwmən ˈbiɪŋ] *n* a person; a man, woman, or child.

humble [ˈhəmbl̩] *adj* meek; the opposite of proud.

humidity [hyuwˈmɪdəti] *n* the moisture in the air.

humor [ˈhyuwmɚ] *n* fun; jokes.

humorist [ˈhyuwmɚɪst] *n* someone who makes people laugh at jokes and sayings; a comedian.

humorous [ˈhyuwmɚəs] *adj* funny; amusing.

hump [həmp] *n* a lump or large bump; the mound of fat on a camel's back.

hundred [ˈhəndrəd] *n* the number 100 which is 10 X 10.

hung [həŋ] *v* a past tense and past participle of hang.

hunger [ˈhəŋgɚ] *n* the need for food.

hungry [ˈhəŋgri] *adj* feeling the desire or need for food.

hunt [hənt] **1.** *v* to chase after something in order to catch it or shoot it. **2.** *n* a chase after something such as wild game; a search.

hunter [ˈhəntɚ] *n* someone who hunts wild animals or birds for food or sport.

hurdle [ˈhɚdl̩] *n* a kind of fence which people or horses have to jump over in races; anything that stops a person's progress.

hurl [hɚl] *v* to throw something hard.

hurricane [ˈhɚəkeyn] *n* a very great windstorm.

hurry [ˈhɚi] *v* to move fast in order to get somewhere more quickly, or to finish doing something sooner.

hurt [hɚt] **1.** *v* to give pain. *pt* hurt. *pp* hurt. **2.** *n* pain; grief; an injury.

husband ['həzbn̩d] *n* a married man.

hush [həʃ] **1.** *v* to become quiet or silent. **2.** *n* a sudden period of silence.

hustle ['həsl̩] *v* to hurry; to make someone hurry along by pushing and shoving.

hut [hət] *n* a small, wooden house.

hyphen ['hɑyfn̩] *n* the sign (-) which connects some pairs of words.

hypothesis [hɑy'pɑθəsəs] *n* a theory; an idea which will be discussed and tested.

I [ɑy] *pro* the person who is talking; yourself. *Ex* I am talking to you. I am tired. I am reading a dictionary.

ice [ɑys] *n* water which has been frozen solid.

ice cream [ɑys 'krim] *n* a frozen food made with milk and sugar.

ice skates ['ɑys skeyts] *n* a pair of shoes with blades attached so that they can be used to glide on the ice.

icicle ['ɑysɪkl] *n* a long, thin spike of ice, usually hanging from something.

icing ['ɑysɪŋ] *n* a sugar coating on cakes and cookies.

I'd [ɑyd] *cont* I would; I had.

idea [ɑy'diə] *n* a plan which you think of; a picture in your mind.

ideal [ɑy'dil] *adj* perfect; exactly right.

identical [ɑy'dɛntəkl] *adj* exactly the same.

identification [ɪdɛntəfə'keyʃn̩] *n* cards or papers you carry with you to show who you are.

idiot ['ɪdiət] *n* a person whose mind does not work properly; a crazy person.

idle ['ɑydl̩] *adj* lazy; not working; doing nothing.

idol ['ɑydl̩] *n* an image or statue of a person or animal that is worshiped as a god.

if [ɪf] *conj* in case that; whether. *Ex* Please tell me if you can come. I will if I can. If it rains, I will not come.

igloo ['ɪgluw] *n* a hut made of blocks of hard snow. *Ex* Eskimos build igloos to live in.

ignorant ['ɪgnɚənt] *adj* without knowledge; not knowing.

ignore [ɪg'nor] *v* to take no notice; to pretend someone or something is not there.

ill [ɪl] *adj* sick; not healthy.

I'll [ɑyl] *cont* I will.

illegal [ɪ'ligl̩] *adj* against the law; unlawful.

illuminate [ɪ'luwmɘneyt] *v* to light; to throw light upon.

illustrate ['ɪlɘstreyt] *v* to give an example; to draw a helpful picture.

illustration [ɪlɘ'streyʃn̩] *n* a picture; a drawing; an example.

I'm [ɑym] *cont* I am.

image ['ɪmɪdʒ] *n* an exact likeness or copy of something; a statue.

imaginary [ɪ'mædʒɘnɛri] *adj* something you think of that is not real.

imagine [ɪ'mædʒn̩] *v* to picture in your mind what something or someone is like.

imitate ['ɪmɘteyt] *v* to copy; to do something the same as someone else.

immediately [ɪ'midɘtli] *adv* at once.

immense [ɪ'mɛn(t)s] *adj* enormous; very big.

immigrate ['ɪmɘgreyt] *v* to move into a country.

immigration [ɪmə'greyʃn̩] **1.** *n* moving into a country. **2.** *n* the government office in charge of people moving into or visiting a country.

imperative [ɪm'pɛrətɪv] *n* a kind of sentence which makes a demand. *Ex Close the door!* is an imperative.

importance [ɪm'pɔrtn̩(t)s] *n* value; significance.

important [ɪm'pɔrtn̩t] *adj* of great value; of great significance; well-known and respected.

impossible [ɪm'pɑsəbl̩] *adj* not able to be done.

impress [ɪm'prɛs] **1.** *v* to make something stay in someone's mind. **2.** *v* to press a dent or hollow into something.

impression [ɪm'prɛʃn̩] **1.** *n* an idea or thought that is fixed firmly in your mind. **2.** *n* marks that are made by pressing or printing.

impressive [ɪm'prɛsɪv] *adj* making a deep impression on the mind.

improve [ɪm'pruwv] *v* to make better; to become better.

improvement [ɪm'pruwvmənt] *n* a change for the better.

impudent ['ɪmpyədənt] *adj* not respectful; rude.

in [ɪn] **1.** *prep* at the inside of; within. *Ex* Please go in the house right now. **2.** *adv* to or at the inside. *Ex* Please go in now.

inch [ɪntʃ] **1.** *n* one twelfth of a foot. **2.** *v* to crawl along very slowly, an inch at a time.

incident ['ɪn(t)sədənt] *n* something that happens; an event.

include [ɪn'kluwd] *v* to count something in; to contain. *Ex* Please include me on your list.

income ['ɪnkəm] *n* the money that comes to you because you work; wages.

income tax ['ɪnkəm tæks] *n* a federal, city, or state tax on the money people earn.

increase [ɪn'kris] *v* to grow larger in size or number; to make larger in size or number.

indeed [ɪn'did] *adv* without question; as a matter of fact.

indent [ɪn'dɛnt] *v* to skip a few spaces before writing the first line of a new paragraph.

independent [ɪndə'pɛndənt] *adj* not ruled by another person or country.

index ['ɪndɛks] *n* a long list in alphabetical order, usually at the end of a book. *Ex* An index lists the numbers of the pages where things are mentioned in a book.

index finger ['ɪndɛks fɪŋgɚ] *n* the finger right next to the thumb; the finger that is often used for pointing.

Indian ['ɪndiən] **1.** *n* a person from India; an East Indian. **2.** *n* a person descended from the people who lived in the Americas before the Europeans came; an American Indian.

indignant [ɪn'dɪgnənt] *adj* annoyed or angry about something you think is wrong.

individual [ɪndə'vɪdʒəwəl] **1.** *adj* having to do with just one; separate. **2.** *n* a person; one person. *Ex* Do you think that an individual should own two cars?

indoor ['ɪndor] *adj* inside a building; the opposite of outdoor.

indoors [ɪn'dorz] *adv* to or at the inside of a building.

industry ['ɪndəstri] **1.** *n* hard work; constant work. **2.** *n* manufacturing; making things in factories.

infant ['ɪnfn̩t] *n* a baby; a young child.

infinity [ɪn'fɪnəti] **1.** *n* a number of indefinite size. **2.** *n* an unlimited number, length, or time period.

infirmary [ɪn'fɚ·mə·i] *n* a small hospital; a place in a school or factory where a person can receive medical treatment.

inflammable [ɪn'flæməbl̩] *adj* easily set on fire; burnable. *Ex* Paper is inflammable.

influenza [ɪnfluw'ɛnzə] *n* a disease like a cold, but usually worse. It is also called flu.

inform [ɪn'form] *v* to tell or give information.

information [ɪnfɚ·'meyʃn̩] *n* facts; knowledge; an explanation of something.

infuriate [ɪn'fyuwrieyt] *v* to make very angry.

inhabit [ɪn'hæbət] *v* to live in or occupy.

initial [ɪ'nɪʃl̩] **1.** *adj* first; beginning. **2.** *n* the first letter of a word or name. *Ex* Gene Jones' initials are G.J.

injection [ɪn'dʒɛkʃn̩] *n* a shot; the act of sticking a hollow needle into the body and pushing liquid medicine into the body. The medicine is to treat an illness or stop a person from getting one. *Ex* The doctor gave Martha an injection to keep her from getting the flu.

injure ['ɪndʒɚ·] *v* to harm or hurt.

injury ['ɪndʒɚ·i] *n* a hurt; a wound; an insult.

ink [ɪŋk] *n* a colored liquid used in writing with a pen.

inn [ɪn] *n* a small hotel.

innocent ['ɪnəsn̩t] *adj* without guilt.

input ['ɪnput] **1.** *n* information given to a person or a group; information given to a computer. **2.** *v* to give information to a computer.

inquire [ɪn'kwɑyr] *v* to ask; to ask about something.

inquisitive [ɪn'kwɪzətɪv] *adj* eager to find out about something; curious; nosey.

insect ['ɪnsɛkt] *n* a very small animal with six legs. *Ex* Ants, bees, and beetles are insects. Spiders have eight legs and are not really insects.

inside [ɪn'sɑyd] **1.** *prep* in; within. *Ex* The cow is inside the barn. **2.** *adv* to, at, or into the interior of something. *Ex* Please put this inside.

insist [ɪn'sɪst] *v* to demand; to say or ask over and over again.

inspect [ɪn'spɛkt] *v* to look carefully at something; to examine.

inspector [ɪn'spɛktɚ] **1.** *n* someone who examines things to make sure everything is all right. **2.** *n* a police officer who is in charge of other police officers.

installment [ɪn'stɔlmənt] **1.** *n* one part of the money owed for something which is to be paid for bit by bit. **2.** *n* one of the parts of a serial story or film; an episode.

instantly ['ɪnstəntli] *adv* at once; without delay.

instead [ɪn'stɛd] **1.** *prep* in place of. *Ex* She wanted red instead of green. **2.** *adv* as a different choice. *Ex* She wanted red instead.

instinct ['ɪnstɪŋkt] *n* the ability to do something without being taught. *Ex* Baby ducks are able to swim by instinct.

instruct [ɪn'strəkt] *v* to teach or inform someone.

instructor [ɪn'strəktɚ] *n* a teacher.

instrument ['ɪnstrəmənt] **1.** *n* a tool; a measuring device; a piece of apparatus. **2.** *n* something which makes musical sounds. *Ex* Mary plays the trumpet and other instruments too.

insulation [ɪnsə'leyʃn̩] **1.** *n* a covering or coating which helps hold in heat. *Ex* My new coat provides good insulation against the cold. Our apartment is cold because the building does not have good insulation. **2.** *n* a covering on an electrical wire or an electronic part to keep it from touching other wires, other parts, or people.

insult 1. *v* [ɪn'səlt] to say something rude or hurtful. **2.** *n* ['ɪnsəlt] something rude said about a person or thing.

insurance [ɪn'ʃɚən(t)s] *n* a contract with a company in which the company promises to pay money if you die or have some other loss.

integer ['ɪntədʒɚ] *n* any whole number including zero and numbers like -1 and -2.

intelligent [ɪn'tɛlədʒn̩t] *adj* smart; good at learning things.

intend [ɪn'tɛnd] *v* to mean to do something, as when you intend to pay someone back.

intense [ɪn'tɛn(t)s] *adj* very great. *Ex* I have an intense dislike for spinach.

interest ['ɪntrəst] **1.** *n* a wish to know more about something. **2.** *n* money paid as a fee for money borrowed. **3.** *v* to cause someone to be curious.

interested ['ɪntɚɛstəd, 'ɪntrəstəd] *adj* curious; paying attention; involved.

interesting ['ɪntɚɛstɪŋ, 'ɪntrəstɪŋ] *adj* holding a person's attention. *Ex* That is a very interesting story.

interfere [ɪntɚ'fir] *v* to meddle; to hinder; to try to stop something from going on.

interior [ɪn'tiriɚ] *n* the inside of something.

interjection [ɪntɚ'dʒɛkʃn̩] *n* a word or a phrase used as an exclamation. *Ex Good heavens!* is an interjection.

intermediate [ɪntɚ'midiət] *adj* at a middle point or level.

intermission [ɪntɚ'mɪʃn̩] *n* a break or rest period between the parts of a play, concert, opera.

Internal Revenue [ıntɚnl̩ 'rɛvənuw] *n* the name of the department which collects taxes for the federal government.

international [ıntɚ'næʃn̩l] *adj* having to do with two or more countries; having to do with foreign countries or people from foreign countries. *Ex* Maria is interested in international politics.

interrogative [ıntə'rɑgətıv] **1.** *adj* questioning; asking a question. **2.** *n* a sentence which asks a question; a question word. *Ex How, why,* and *what* are interrogatives.

interrupt [ıntə'rəpt] *v* to break in on something which is happening. *Ex* Please don't interrupt me when I am speaking.

intersect [ıntɚ'sɛkt] *v* to pass through; to cut across. *Ex* Please draw a line that intersects this line.

interstate ['ıntɚsteyt] **1.** *adj* having to do with something that affects two or more of the U.S. states. **2.** *n* a highway which goes between major cities in the U.S. states; an interstate highway.

interval ['ıntɚvl̩] *n* a period of time between two events.

interview ['ıntɚvyuw] **1.** *v* to talk with someone; to ask questions of someone. **2.** *n* a talk with someone, often broadcast or reported in a newspaper.

into ['ıntuw, ın'tuw] *prep* to the interior; toward the inside of.

introduce [ıntrə'duws] **1.** *v* to tell people each other's names when they meet for the first time. **2.** *v* to bring a new idea into whatever you are talking or writing about.

introduction [ıntrə'dəkʃn̩] **1.** *n* the act of introducing one person to another. **2.** *n* the act of bringing up a new topic.

invade [ın'veyd] *v* to attack; to go into a place or a country by force.

invalid 1. *n* ['ınvələd] a person who is ill. **2.** *adj* [ın'væləd] false; no longer usable.

invent [ɪn'vɛnt] *v* to think up or make something which is completely new and has never been thought of before.

investigate [ɪn'vɛstəgeyt] *v* to try to find out the cause of something; to examine a problem.

investment [ɪn'vɛstmənt] *n* the placing of money into a bank in order to get the money which the bank pays for the use of the money; money spent in the hope of increasing the amount in the future. *Ex* Money in the bank is a good investment. Buying a home is a good investment.

invisible [ɪn'vɪzəbl̩] *adj* not able to be seen.

invitation [ɪnvə'teyʃn̩] *n* asking someone to come to a party or some other event.

invite [ɪn'vɑyt] *v* to ask a person to be your guest.

iris ['ɑyrəs] **1.** *n* the round, colored part of the eye. **2.** *n* a garden plant with large flowers and long, pointed leaves.

iron ['ɑyɚn] **1.** *n* a strong, gray metal. **2.** *n* a heavy tool used to take the wrinkles out of clothing. **3.** *v* to use an iron to take the wrinkles out of clothes.

irony ['ɑyrəni] *n* a kind of mockery where the words used do not fit the situation.

irregular [ɪ'rɛgyələ˞] *adj* not regular; not following a regular pattern.

irritate ['ɪrəteyt] *v* to annoy or make angry.

is [ɪz] *v* a present tense form of the verb *be* used with the third person singular: *he, she,* and *it.*

island ['ɑylənd] *n* a piece of land with water all around it.

isle [ɑyl] *n* an island.

isn't ['ɪzn̩t] *cont* is not.

issue ['ɪʃuw] **1.** *n* a result; a problem. **2.** *v* to send; to give out something.

isthmus ['ɪsməs] *n* a narrow strip of land connecting two larger pieces of land.

it [ɪt, ət] **1.** *pro* a thing talked about before. *Ex* Give it to me. It is a very large one. **2.** *pro* a state; a condition; the weather. *Ex* It is raining. It is hard to believe. How is it going?

italics [ɪ'tælɪks] *n* a special kind of print which slants to the right. *Ex This sentence is in italics.*

itch [ɪtʃ] *n* a tickling feeling on the skin which makes you want to scratch.

it'd ['ɪtəd] *cont* it would; it had.

it'll ['ɪtl̩] *cont* it will.

its [ɪts, əts] *pro* belonging to it. *Ex* Where is its lid? Its knob needs polishing.

it's [ɪts] *cont* it is; it has.

itself [ɪt'sɛlf] *pro* it and it alone.

I've [ɑyv] *cont* I have.

ivy ['ɑyvi] *n* a climbing plant which grows on walls, fences, and posts.

J

jab [dʒæb] *v* to poke or stab at something suddenly.

jacket ['dʒækət] **1.** *n* a short coat. **2.** *n* a loose paper cover on a book.

jagged ['dʒægəd] *adj* having sharp or rough edges.

jail [dʒeyl] *n* a place where people are locked up as a punishment.

jam [dʒæm] *n* fruit cooked together with sugar until it is thick and soft. *Ex* Please give me some jam for my bread.

janitor ['dʒænətɚ] *n* the person who cleans a building and carries the keys to the doors; a custodian.

jar [dʒɑr] *n* a pottery or glass container with a wide opening.

jaw [dʒɔ] *n* the bones of the head in which the teeth grow.

jazz [dʒæz] *n* a kind of lively dance music.

jealous ['dʒɛləs] *adj* wishing you had something someone else has; full of envy.

jeans [dʒinz] *n* trousers made of strong cloth; blue jeans.

jeep [dʒip] *n* a small, open car used by the army.

jeer [dʒir] *v* to make fun of someone in an unkind way.

jelly ['dʒɛli] *n* fruit juice boiled with sugar until it is elastic and wobbly. *Ex* I like peanut butter and jelly sandwiches.

jerk [dʒɚk] *n* a short, sudden movement.

jersey [ˈdʒɚzi] *n* a knitted sweater, often worn while playing sports.

jet [dʒɛt] **1.** *n* a rush of liquid or gas through a small opening in a pipe or hose. **2.** *n* a kind of airplane without propellers.

jewel [ˈdʒuwəl] *n* a valuable stone, such as a diamond or emerald.

jeweler [ˈdʒuw(ə)lɚ] *n* a person whose job is making, repairing, and selling jewelry.

jewelry [ˈdʒuw(ə)lri] *n* necklaces, bracelets, rings, and other ornaments made of jewels and precious metals such as gold and silver.

jigsaw [ˈdʒɪgsɔ] *n* a fine saw that can make short curved and straight cuts.

jigsaw puzzle [ˈdʒɪgsɔ pəzl] *n* a puzzle made of odd-shaped pieces cut by a jigsaw. They are put together to make a picture.

jingle [ˈdʒɪŋgl̩] *n* a clinking sound made by coins or bells.

job [dʒɑb] *n* work done, usually for money.

jockey [ˈdʒɑki] *n* a person, usually a boy or man, who rides a horse in a race.

jog [dʒɔg] **1.** *v* to move along more quickly than walking, but not as fast as running. **2.** *n* a bend or turn in a path or roadway.

join [dʒoyn] **1.** *v* to put together or fasten. **2.** *v* to become a member of a group.

joint [dʒoynt] *n* the place where two parts of something come together. *Ex* Knees and elbows are joints.

joke [dʒowk] **1.** *n* something a person does or says to make other people laugh; a short, funny story. **2.** *v* to tell a short, funny story; to tell funny stories and say funny things with other people.

jolly ['dʒɑli] *adj* cheerful; full of fun.

jolt [dʒowlt] **1.** *v* to move forward in jerky movements. **2.** *n* a bump; a shaking-up; a shock.

jostle ['dʒɑsl̩] *v* to push or knock against someone, usually in a crowd.

journal ['dʒɚnl̩] *n* a magazine or a newspaper.

journalism ['dʒɚnl̩ɪzm̩] **1.** *n* the business of writing or publishing a magazine or a newspaper. **2.** *n* a school subject where people learn how to write for newspapers or magazines.

journey ['dʒɚni] *n* a trip; the act of traveling from one place to another.

jovial ['dʒowviəl] *adj* cheerful; jolly.

joy [dʒoy] *n* a feeling of great happiness.

judge [dʒədʒ] **1.** *n* the person in authority in a court of law who decides how to punish someone who has done something wrong. **2.** *v* to make a decision about someone or something.

judgment ['dʒədʒmənt] *n* an act of judging; an opinion; a decision.

jug [dʒəg] *n* a heavy container for liquids, sometimes with a handle used for pouring.

juggler ['dʒəglɚ] *n* a person who is skilled at balancing things and keeping them moving in the air.

juice [dʒuws] *n* the liquid in oranges, lemons, tomatoes, and other fruits and vegetables.

jukebox ['dʒuwkbɑks] *n* a machine which plays phonograph records when you put money into it.

jumble [ˈdʒəmbl̩] *n* a mixture of odd things.

jump [dʒəmp] **1.** *v* to leap off the ground; to leap over something. **2.** *n* a leap up; a leap over something.

junction [ˈdʒəŋkʃn̩] *n* a place where two or more things meet, such as roads or railroad tracks.

jungle [ˈdʒəŋgl̩] *n* a forest in hot countries where plants and trees grow so thickly that it is hard to find a way through.

junior [ˈdʒuwnyɚ] **1.** *adj* younger; of lower rank. *Ex* Clara is a junior executive. **2.** *n* a person who is younger or less important than others. **3.** *n* a boy or man with the same name as his father.

junk [dʒəŋk] **1.** *n* something that is of no use or value; rubbish. **2.** *n* a kind of Chinese sailing ship.

jury [ˈdʒɚi] *n* people chosen to make a decision about the facts in a law trial.

just [dʒəst] **1.** *adj* right; fair; reasonable. **2.** *adv* exactly; completely. **3.** *adv* almost; barely.

justice [ˈdʒəstəs] **1.** *n* fairness; rightness. **2.** *n* the legal system; a legal judgment. **3.** *n* a judge; a judge of the U.S. Supreme Court.

K

kaleidoscope [kə'laɪdəskowp] *n* a toy which is a tube which uses mirrors to reflect beautiful designs from bits of colored glass.

kangaroo [kæŋɡə'ruw] *n* an Australian animal which can jump a long way. *Ex* The mother kangaroo has a pocket for her baby.

keep [kip] **1.** *v* to hold on to something and not give it away. *Ex* Please keep this book for me. **2.** *v* to continue; to persist; to remain. *Ex* Please keep quiet! *pt* kept. *pp* kept.

keeper ['kipɚ] *n* someone who looks after or guards something, like a gamekeeper or a keeper at a zoo.

kennel ['kɛnl̩] *n* a small house or a shelter for a dog.

kept [kɛpt] *v* the past tense and past participle of keep.

kernel ['kɝnl̩] *n* the inside part of a nut which can be eaten; a grain of corn.

kerosene ['kɛrəsin] *n* a liquid fuel sometimes used for cooking or heating.

ketchup ['kɛtʃəp] *n* a sauce made of tomatoes and spices; the same as catsup.

kettle ['kɛtl̩] *n* a metal container used for boiling water, sometimes called a teakettle. *Ex* A kettle has a lid, a handle, and sometimes a spout.

key [ki] **1.** *n* a small piece of metal, shaped so that it will open a lock. **2.** *n* a lever on a piano or a typewriter.

keyboard ['kibord] *n* the keys of a piano, organ, or typewriter.

keyhole ['kihowl] *n* a hole specially shaped so that a key will fit in.

kick [kɪk] *v* to hit something or someone with the foot. *Ex* He kicked the ball very hard.

kid [kɪd] **1.** *n* a young goat. **2.** *n* a young child.

kidnap ['kɪdnæp] *v* to take someone away by force.

kill [kɪl] *v* to cause someone or something to die.

kilogram ['kɪləgræm] *n* a unit of weight equal to 1,000 grams and equal to 2.2046 pounds.

kilometer [kə'lamətɚ] *n* a unit of length equal to 1,000 meters and equal to 0.62 miles.

kind [kaynd] **1.** *n* type; sort; variety. **2.** *adj* friendly; good to other people.

kindergarten ['kɪndɚgartn̩] *n* a school or class for very young children.

king [kɪŋ] *n* a man who rules a country, usually because his family did so before him.

kingdom ['kɪŋdəm] *n* a country ruled by a king or queen.

kiss [kɪs] **1.** *v* to touch with your lips someone you like. **2.** *n* an act of kissing.

kitchen ['kɪtʃn̩] *n* a room where cooking is done.

kite [kayt] *n* a toy made of paper or cloth on light wood. It is flown on the end of a string when it is windy.

kitten ['kɪtn̩] *n* a young cat.

Kleenex ['klinɛks] *n* the trademarked brand name of a soft paper used for wiping the nose or the eyes.

knapsack ['næpsæk] *n* a bag for food and clothing that you carry on your back. *Ex* Some people carry books in a knapsack.

knee [ni] *n* the joint in the middle of the leg.

kneel [nil] *v* to get down on your knees. *pt* knelt. *pp* knelt.

knelt [nɛlt] *v* the past tense and past participle of kneel.

knew [nuw] *v* the past tense of know.

knife [nɑyf] *n* a thin, sharp piece of metal with a handle. It is used for cutting. The plural is knives.

knit [nɪt] *v* to weave yarn into clothing with long needles.

knob [nɑb] *n* a round handle, like a door handle.

knock [nɑk] **1.** *v* to hit something hard; to bump into something; to tap on a door with your knuckles. **2.** *n* an act of knocking; the sound of knocking.

knot [nɑt] *n* the place where two pieces of string or ribbon have been tied together.

know [now] *v* to understand and be sure about something you have read or seen. *pt* knew. *pp* known.

knowledge ['nɑlɪdʒ] *n* what you have learned and what you understand about things.

known [nown] *v* the past participle of know.

knuckle ['nəkl] *n* a finger joint.

L

lab [læb] *n* short for the word laboratory.

label ['leybl] **1.** *n* a small piece of paper or cardboard with writing or printing on it. *Ex* I couldn't tell what was in the can because I couldn't read the label. **2.** *v* to make a label; to put a label on something.

labor ['leybɚ] **1.** *n* hard work. **2.** *n* workers; people who work. **3.** *v* to work hard.

laboratory ['læbrətori] *n* a room or building where scientific tests are done. It is also called a lab.

lace [leys] **1.** *v* to fasten your shoestrings. **2.** *n* a special string used to fasten shoes. **3.** *n* material woven with a pretty pattern of holes.

lad [læd] *n* a boy.

ladder ['lædɚ] *n* a set of wooden or metal rungs between two long pieces of wood or metal. *Ex* Ladders are used for climbing up or down.

ladle ['leydl] *n* a spoon shaped like a small cup with a long, straight handle. *Ex* Ladles are used for serving soup or other liquids.

lady ['leydi] *n* another word for woman.

lag [læg] *v* to follow along slowly behind others.

laid [leyd] *v* the past tense and past participle of lay.

lain [leyn] *v* the past participle of lie.

lake [leyk] *n* a very large pool of water with land all around it.

lamb [læm] *n* a young sheep.

lame [leym] *adj* not able to walk easily because you have hurt your leg or your foot.

lamp [læmp] **1.** *n* a decorative device which holds a light, usually electric. **2.** *n* an electric light bulb.

lance [læn(t)s] **1.** *n* a long spear. **2.** *v* to cut open a boil so that the fluid can drain away.

land [lænd] **1.** *n* the parts of the earth that are not covered by water. **2.** *v* to come down from the air onto the land or water; for a ship to come to shore.

landing ['lændɪŋ] **1.** *n* coming back to land from the sea or the air. **2.** *n* the place where boats tie up at shore. **3.** *n* the floor at the top of the stairs.

landlady ['lændleydi] *n* a woman who owns a house or apartment where other people pay to live.

landlord ['lændlord] *n* a man who owns a house or apartment where other people pay to live.

lane [leyn] **1.** *n* a little road, usually in the country. **2.** *n* one of the pathways for vehicles on a very wide road. *Ex* Please keep in your own lane.

language ['læŋgwɪdʒ] **1.** *n* human speech or writing. **2.** *n* the kind of speech used in a particular country, such as German in Germany or French in France.

lantern ['læntɚn] *n* a metal and glass container for a lighted candle or other flame; a very large electric flashlight.

lap [læp] **1.** *n* the top part of your legs when you are sitting. **2.** *n* one time around a racetrack or a swimming pool.

lard [lɑrd] *n* fat from pigs, used in cooking.

large [lɑrdʒ] *adj* big; very big.

laser ['leyzɚ] *n* a very powerful kind of light beam. This word is an acronym for *light amplification by stimulated emission of radiation.*

lash [læʃ] **1.** *v* to hit someone with a whip; to tie up firmly. **2.** *n* a whip. **3.** *n* an eyelash.

lasso ['læsow] *n* a long rope with a big loop at one end. *Ex* A lasso is used to catch wild horses and cattle.

last [læst] **1.** *adj* coming at the end; after all others. **2.** *v* to hold out or endure; to continue to live.

late [leyt] *adj* behind time; not early.

lather ['læðɚ] *n* a foam made by using soap and water together.

latitude ['lætətuwd] *n* the distance north or south of the equator measured in degrees. The equator is at zero degrees latitude. *Ex* Washington, D.C. is at approximately 39 degrees north latitude.

laugh [læf] **1.** *v* to make a noise to show you feel happy or think something is funny. **2.** *n* a noise people make when something is funny.

launch [lɔntʃ] **1.** *v* to start something on its way, such as a ship or a rocket. **2.** *n* a large, open motorboat.

laundromat ['lɔndrəmæt] *n* a place where laundry is taken to be washed in coin-operated washers and dryers.

laundry ['lɔndri] **1.** *n* the place where dirty clothes are washed. **2.** *n* dirty clothes which are waiting to be washed; clothes which have just been washed.

lava ['lavə] *n* rock which has flowed out of a volcano in a liquid form.

lavatory ['lævətori] **1.** *n* a room containing a washbasin and a toilet; a bathroom. **2.** *n* a washbasin.

lavender ['lævəndɚ] *n* a light purple color.

law [lɔ] **1.** *n* a rule which tells people what they can or cannot do; all of the rules of government. In the U.S. there are federal, state, and local laws. **2.** *n* the study of the rules of government.

lawn [lɔn] *n* a smooth area of grass which is cut and looked after carefully.

lawn mower ['lɔn mowɚ] *n* a machine used to cut the grass on a lawn.

lawyer ['loyɚ] *n* a person who takes care of another person's legal matters.

lay [ley] **1.** *v* to put something down. *pt* laid. *pp* laid. **2.** *v* the past tense of lie.

layer ['leyɚ] *n* a flat covering or thickness. *Ex* Please bake me a layer cake.

lazy ['leyzi] *adj* not wanting to work; not wanting to make any effort.

lead 1. *v* [lid] to be first; to show other people the way. *pt* led. *pp* led. **2.** *n* [lɛd] a heavy, soft, gray metal.

leader ['lidɚ] *n* a person who is in front or at the head of a group of people.

leaf [lif] *n* the flat, green part of a plant or tree. The plural is leaves.

leak [lik] **1.** *v* for a liquid to escape from a hole or a crack. **2.** *n* the accidental escape of a fluid from a hole or crack in a pipe or container.

lean [lin] **1.** *adj* thin; without fat. **2.** *v* to rest against something; to tilt against something; to place something against something else at a slant.

leap [lip] *v* to jump up; to jump over.

leap year ['lip yir] *n* a year with 366 days, having 29 days in February. *Ex* Leap year comes every four years.

learn [lɚn] *v* to find out about things or how to do something.

lease [lis] *n* a written contract which states that you have the right to use certain property which is not yours.

least [list] **1.** *n* the smallest amount. *Ex* That was the least we could do. **2.** *adj* the smallest in size or importance.

leather ['lɛðɚ] *n* the skin of animals, used to make things like shoes and gloves.

leave [liv] **1.** *v* to go away from somewhere. **2.** *v* to let something stay where it is. *pt* left. *pp* left.

lecture ['lɛktʃɚ] *n* a talk given to an audience or a class at school.

lecturer ['lɛktʃɚɚ] *n* a person who gives a lecture; a person who teaches a class.

led [lɛd] *v* the past tense and past participle of lead.

ledge [lɛdʒ] *n* a narrow shelf.

left [lɛft] **1.** *adj* the opposite side of right. *Ex* When you face north, west is on your left side. **2.** *v* the past tense and past participle of leave.

leg [lɛg] **1.** *n* the part of the body which joins on to the foot. *Ex* Human beings have two legs. **2.** *n* one of the pieces of wood that hold up a chair or table.

legal ['ligl̩] **1.** *adj* in keeping with the law; lawful. **2.** *adj* having to do with laws.

legend ['lɛdʒn̩d] *n* a story from long ago which may or may not be true.

legion ['lidʒn̩] *n* a large group of soldiers; a large number.

lemon ['lɛmən] *n* a sour, yellow citrus fruit.

lemonade [lɛmən'ɑyd] *n* a drink made from lemon juice and sugar.

lend [lɛnd] *v* to let someone have something of yours which will be given back. *pt* lent. *pp* lent.

length [lɛŋ(k)θ] *n* how long something is.

lengthen ['lɛŋ(k)θņ] *v* to make longer; to grow longer.

lens [lɛnz] *n* a curved piece of glass used in eyeglasses or in instruments such as telescopes and cameras. The plural is lenses.

lent [lɛnt] *v* the past tense and past participle of lend.

less [lɛs] *adj* a smaller amount.

lesson ['lɛsņ] *n* something to be learned.

let [lɛt] *v* to agree that someone may do something; to give permission. *pt* let. *pp* let.

let's [lɛts] *cont* let us.

letter ['lɛtɚ] **1.** *n* one of the symbols used to write words. *Ex* Our alphabet has 26 letters. **2.** *n* a written message that is put in an envelope.

lettuce ['lɛtəs] *n* a garden plant with large green leaves which you can eat without cooking. *Ex* Lettuce is used in salads.

level ['lɛvļ] *adj* flat; with no bumps; parallel to the horizon.

lever ['lɛvɚ] *n* a bar pushed down at one end so that it lifts something on the other end.

liar ['lɑyɚ] *n* a person who tells lies.

liberty ['lɪbɚti] *n* freedom to do as you think is right.

librarian [lɑy'brɛriəṇ] *n* a person who is trained to work in a library.

library ['lɑybrɛri] *n* a room or a building full of books.

license ['lɑysṇ(t)s] *n* a special piece of printed paper that you must have before you can do certain things. *Ex* You need a license to go fishing, or to drive a car.

lick [lɪk] *v* to touch something with your tongue, like a lollipop or an ice cream cone.

licorice ['lɪkrɪʃ] *n* a black candy with a rubbery feeling.

lid [lɪd] *n* the top which can be taken off something, such as a box or a saucepan.

lie [lɑy] **1.** *v* to say something that you know is not true. *pt* lied. *pp* lied. **2.** *v* to rest flat; to recline. *pt* lay. *pp* lain.

life [lɑyf] *n* the time between birth and death. The plural is lives.

lifeboat ['lɑyfbowt] *n* a special boat kept ready to rescue people who have been shipwrecked.

lifeguard ['lɑyfgɑrd] *n* a person whose job is to watch over swimmers at the beach or at a pool.

lift [lɪft] *v* to move or raise something up.

light [lɑyt] **1.** *adj* not heavy. **2.** *n* something which shines brightly so that the darkness is gone. *Ex* Please turn the light out.

light bulb ['lɑyt bəlb] *n* a hollow glass ball which can be screwed into an electric lamp. *Ex* The wires inside the light bulb give off light when the lamp is turned on.

lighten ['lɑytṇ] **1.** *v* to cause to be less heavy. **2.** *v* to make less dark.

lighter ['laytɚ] **1.** *adj* not as heavy. **2.** *n* something used to make fire, such as a cigarette lighter.

lightly ['laytli] *adj* gently; not heavily.

lightning ['laytnɪŋ] *n* a sudden bright flash of light in the sky when there is a thunderstorm.

likable ['laykəbḷ] *adj* pleasant; easy to get along with. Also spelled likeable.

like [layk] **1.** *v* to be fond of; to be pleased with. **2.** *prep* the same as; almost the same as.

likely ['laykli] **1.** *adj* probable; expected to happen. **2.** *adv* probably.

lily ['lɪli] *n* a tall garden plant with large white or brightly colored flowers.

limb [lɪm] *n* an arm or a leg; a branch.

lime [laym] **1.** *n* a white powder made from limestone, used for making mortar. **2.** *n* a green citrus fruit.

limit ['lɪmət] *n* the place where something ends.

limp [lɪmp] **1.** *adj* without stiffness; wilted. **2.** *v* to walk in a lame way.

line [layn] *n* a thin mark; a wire such as a telephone line or an electric power line.

linen ['lɪnən] **1.** *n* cloth made from the flax plant. **2.** *n* sheets, pillowcases, towels, and other household items made of cloth.

linger ['lɪŋgɚ] *v* to hang about; to delay leaving.

link [lɪŋk] *n* one of the rings in a chain.

linoleum [lə'nowliəm] *n* a stiff, shiny floor covering. *Ex* Sometimes linoleum is used on drainboards.

lint [lɪnt] *n* bits of fluff which gather on clothing or carpets.

lion ['laɪən] *n* a strong and dangerous wild animal, like a very big cat.

lioness ['laɪənəs] *n* a female lion.

lip [lɪp] *n* one of the two soft edges of the mouth. *Ex* You have an upper lip and a lower lip.

lipstick ['lɪpstɪk] *n* a kind of crayon in a case, used by girls and women to color their lips red or pink.

liquid ['lɪkwɪd] *n* anything which is wet and flows like water.

list [lɪst] *n* words or bits of information placed under each other in a column. *Ex* There are twelve items on my shopping list.

listen ['lɪsn̩] *v* to try to hear something.

liter ['litɚ] *n* a unit of liquid measure equal to 1.057 quarts.

literature ['lɪtɚətʃɚ] **1.** *n* poems, stories, and books. **2.** *n* any writing or explanation. *Ex* Did your new lawn mower come with any literature on how to operate it?

litter ['lɪtɚ] **1.** *n* rubbish or wastepaper left lying about. **2.** *n* all the babies born to a mother animal at one time.

litterbug ['lɪtɚbəg] *n* a name for a person who is careless and leaves rubbish lying about.

little ['lɪtl̩] *adj* not big; small.

live 1. *v* [lɪv] to have life; to be alive. **2.** *adj* [laɪv] living; not dead; alive.

lively ['laɪvli] *adj* jolly; active; full of life.

liver ['lɪvɚ] *n* an inside part of the body; an organ of the body.

living room ['lɪvɪŋ ruwm] *n* a room with comfortable furniture where the family gathers together to talk, read, watch television, or entertain visitors.

lizard ['lɪzɚd] *n* a scaly reptile with four legs.

load [lowd] **1.** *n* all that can be carried at one time, like a load of bricks or a load of bananas. **2.** *v* to put bullets into a gun to make it ready for shooting.

loaf [lowf] *n* a shaped mass of baked bread.

loan [lown] **1.** *v* to lend. **2.** *n* something lent; something borrowed.

loathe [lowð] *v* to hate or despise greatly.

lobby ['lɑbi] *n* the entrance hall in a large building.

lobster ['lɑbstɚ] *n* a shellfish with two large, strong claws.

local ['lowkl̩] *adj* nearby; near or close by a certain place.

lock [lɑk] *n* a strong fastening for a door or gate that can only be opened with a key.

locker ['lɑkɚ] *n* a place where you can lock up your clothing or books. *Ex* I can't remember which gym locker is mine.

locomotive [lowkə'mowtɪv] *n* a train engine, especially an old one which runs on steam power.

locust ['lowkəst] *n* an insect something like a large grasshopper. *Ex* Locusts destroy crops.

lodge [lɑdʒ] *n* a small house in the country. *Ex* Hunters stay overnight in a lodge.

loft [lɔft] *n* a large space under the roof which can be used for storage or large projects. *Ex* Chin Wu takes ballet lessons in a loft on Clark Street.

log [lɔg] **1.** *n* a thick, round piece of wood. **2.** *n* a record book for all of the things which happen aboard ship.

loiter ['loytɚ] *v* to linger; to dawdle; to hang around.

lollipop ['lɑlipɑp] *n* a large piece of candy on the end of a stick.

lone [lown] *adj* single; the only one.

lonely ['lownli] *adj* feeling sad because you are alone.

long [lɔŋ] *adj* of a large distance.

long division [lɔŋ dɪ'vɪʒn̩] *n* divison in mathematics where all of the steps are performed and are shown on your paper.

longhand ['lɔŋhænd] **1.** *n* the kind of writing where the letters flow together; cursive writing. **2.** *adj* having to do with writing that flows together; not printed letter by letter.

longitude ['lɔndʒətuwd] *n* east and west distance measured in degrees. *Ex* Greenwich, England is at zero degrees longitude.

look [lʊk] *v* to watch; to try to see.

loom [luwm] *n* a machine for weaving thread into cloth.

loop [luwp] *n* a ring of wire, string, or ribbon.

loose [luws] *adj* the opposite of tight; not properly fastened.

loosen ['luwsn̩] *v* to make something less tight; to grow less tight.

lose [luwz] *v* to be responsible for something's disappearance; not to be able to find something. *pt* lost. *pp* lost.

loss [lɔs] *n* the lack of something that you once had; a disappearance; the death of someone you love.

lost [lɔst] *v* the past tense and past participle of lose.

lost and found ['lɔst ən 'fɑwnd] *n* a place where things people find are put. *Ex* If you lose a glove, you should check the lost and found.

lot [lɑt] **1.** *n* a large number; a great many. **2.** *n* a piece of land; a section of land where a house can be built.

lotion ['lowʃn̩] *n* a soothing liquid medicine that you can put on sore places on your skin.

lotus ['lowtəs] *n* a water lily that grows in some hot countries.

loud [lɑwd] *adj* noisy; easily heard.

loudspeaker ['lɑwdspikɚ] *n* the part of a radio, record player, or P.A. system that makes the sound.

lounge [lɑwndʒ] **1.** *n* a room with comfortable chairs in a club, hotel, or other building. **2.** *v* to lie about in a lazy way.

lovable ['ləvəbl̩] *adj* worth loving; cute and cuddly.

love [ləv] **1.** *v* to be very fond of; to like someone or something very much. **2.** *n* a strong feeling of fondness that you have for someone.

lovely ['ləvli] *adj* beautiful; pretty; nice.

low [low] *adj* not high; not tall.

lower ['lowɚ] **1.** *adj* not as high. **2.** *v* to let down; to bring down. *Ex* You should lower the flag at night.

loyal ['loyəl] *adj* faithful; true to someone.

luck [lək] *n* something that happens by chance. *Ex* I had bad luck fishing, and I caught nothing.

lucky ['ləki] *adj* having good luck.

luggage ['ləgɪdʒ] *n* baggage; suitcases and trunks. *Ex* His luggage is new.

lukewarm ['luwk'worm] *adj* between cool and warm.

lumber ['ləmbɚ] *n* timber; timber which has been cut into boards.

lump [ləmp] *n* a piece of something, usually without any special shape, like a lump of clay or dough.

lunar ['luwnɚ] *adj* having to do with the moon.

lunch [ləntʃ] *n* the meal eaten at midday.

lunch box ['ləntʃ bɑks] *n* a box used for carrying a lunch to school or work.

lunchroom ['ləntʃruwm] *n* the room in a school or other place where lunch is eaten; a cafeteria.

lunge [ləndʒ] **1.** *v* to make a sudden thrust or rush at something. **2.** *n* a jump or a rush at something or someone.

lurch [lɚtʃ] *v* to jerk forward or to one side.

lurk [lɚk] *v* to hide yourself while you are waiting for someone or something; to prowl about.

luscious ['ləʃəs] *adj* delicious; lovely.

luxury ['ləkʃɚi] *n* something expensive and pleasant that you would like to have but don't really need; great comfort.

M

macaroni [mækə'rowni] *n* long, stiff tubes of dried wheat paste that become soft when cooked in boiling water; a kind of pasta.

machine [mə'ʃin] *n* an instrument, usually made of metal, which does some special job, like a sewing machine or a washing machine.

machinery [mə'ʃinəɾi] *n* the working parts of a machine; machines in general.

mad [mæd] **1.** *adj* angry. **2.** *adj* crazy.

made [meyd] *v* the past tense and past participle of make.

magazine ['mægəzin] *n* a thin book that comes out every week, every month, or every few months. *Ex* There is a magazine for almost every subject.

maggot ['mægət] *n* a tiny worm or grub that is found in bad meat, cheese, or fruit.

magic ['mædʒɪk] *n* an imaginary power that makes wonderful things happen; tricks that appear to make impossible things happen.

magician [mə'dʒɪʃn̩] *n* a person who can do magic.

magnet ['mægnət] *n* a piece of iron or steel that has the power to pull other pieces of metal to it.

magnetic [mæg'nɛtɪk] **1.** *adj* the ability to attract metal objects. **2.** *adj* the ability to attract people. *Ex* Susan has a magnetic personality.

magnificent [mæg'nɪfəsṇt] *adj* splendid; very grand.

maid [meyd] *n* a woman servant.

mail [meyl] **1.** *n* anything sent through the post office, such as letters or packages. **2.** *v* to send letters or packages through the post office.

mailbox ['meylbaks] *n* a container where you put mail for the post office to pick up and send; a box where you receive mail.

mail carrier ['meyl kɛriɚ] *n* a person who delivers mail to homes and offices.

main [meyn] **1.** *adj* most important. **2.** *n* a very large water pipe, usually called a water main.

majesty ['mædʒəsti] **1.** *n* a title given to kings or queens. **2.** *n* power and dignity. *Ex* The judge spoke with great majesty.

major ['meydʒɚ] **1.** *adj* of great importance. **2.** *n* an officer in the army.

majority [mə'dʒɔrɪty] **1.** *n* a number greater than half; usually used in the counting of votes. *Ex* Twelve people voted, and Martha got 7 votes, which is a majority. **2.** *n* the greatest number of people.

make [meyk] *v* to produce; to build; to create; to cause. *pt* made. *pp* made.

makeup ['meykəp] *n* face powder, lipstick, and coloring used around the eyes.

make up ['meyk 'əp] *v* to repeat work done badly; to take a test after the rest of the class. *Ex* John will not be allowed to make up the examination.

male [meyl] **1.** *n* a person or an animal that can become a father. **2.** *adj* having to do with the biological sex which relates to men and boys.

mammal ['mæməl] *n* the kind of animal whose females have milk to feed their babies.

man [mæn] **1.** *n* a grown-up male human being. The plural is men. **2.** *n* mankind; all human beings.

manage ['mænɪdʒ] *v* to look after or be responsible for something, such as a business or a household.

manager ['mænɪdʒɚ] *n* a person in charge of something such as a business, a baseball team, or a factory.

mane [meyn] *n* the long hair that some animals have on their necks. *Ex* Horses and male lions have manes.

mangle ['mæŋgl̩] *v* to tear or cut something up; to destroy something.

manicure ['mænəkyɚ] **1.** *v* to trim and polish the fingernails. **2.** *n* a trimming and polishing of the fingernails.

manicurist ['mænəkyɚɪst] *n* a person whose job is to manicure other people's hands.

mankind [mæn'kaynd] *n* all human beings; humans of both sexes.

manners ['mænɚz] *n* how you behave towards other people; the way in which you do things. *Ex* It is good manners to say "please" and "thank you."

mansion ['mæntʃn̩] *n* a very large house.

manure [mə'nuwr] *n* anything put into the ground to make plants and crops grow better; dung.

many ['mɛni] *adj* a lot.

map [mæp] *n* a special kind of drawing to show how to find your way about a place, a country, or the different parts of the world.

marble ['mɑrbl̩] **1.** *n* a hard kind of stone that is used in important buildings. *Ex* Marble is also carved into statues and beautiful ornaments. **2.** *n* one of the round, glass balls used in a game called marbles.

march [mɑrtʃ] *v* to walk in step. *Ex* Soldiers march in time to music in a parade.

mare [mɛr] *n* a female horse.

margarine ['mɑrdʒɚən] *n* a soft, yellow food which is like butter.

margin ['mɑrdʒn] *n* the blank edge on the side of a page where nothing is printed or written.

marine [mə'rin] **1.** *adj* having to do with the sea. **2.** *n* a soldier who serves on a ship.

marionette [mɛriə'nɛt] *n* a puppet made to move by pulling strings.

mark [mɑrk] *n* a spot or line on something.

market ['mɑrkət] *n* a shop; a store; a place where farmers and fishermen come to sell their goods.

maroon [mə'ruwn] **1.** *n* a dark reddish color. **2.** *v* to leave someone stranded. *Ex* The family was marooned on an island for two weeks.

marriage ['mɛrɪdʒ] *n* the ceremony by which a man and woman become husband and wife.

marry ['mɛri] *v* to become husband and wife; to unite a man and a woman as husband and wife.

marsh [mɑrʃ] *n* a piece of wet, swampy land which is unsafe to walk on because your feet sink down into it.

marshal ['mɑrʃl] *n* an official of the police; someone who guards prisoners; a sheriff.

marshmallow ['mɑrʃmɛlow] *n* a soft, puffy, white candy. *Ex* Marshmallows are very good when roasted over an open fire.

marshy ['mɑrʃi] *adj* wet; swampy.

marvel ['marvl] **1.** *v* to wonder; to be amazed; **2.** *n* a wonderful thing; a miracle.

marvelous ['marvələs] *adj* wonderful; thrilling.

mascot ['mæskat] *n* a person, animal, or charm that is supposed to bring good luck. *Ex* Our team's mascot is a lion.

masculine ['mæskyələn] *adj* like, or having to do with, men and boys.

mash [mæʃ] *v* to crush something so that it becomes soft and smooth. *Ex* Please mash the potatoes for dinner.

mask [mæsk] *n* a cover to hide the face. *Ex* Masks can be funny, pretty, or frightening.

mass [mæs] *n* a lump of something; a large quantity or number.

massive ['mæsɪv] *adj* huge; large and heavy.

mass media [mæs 'midiə] *n* newspapers, radio stations, television stations, and magazines which carry information to millions of people. This word is plural. *Ex* The mass media bring us news every day.

mast [mæst] *n* a very long pole, such as a flagpole.

master ['mæstɚ] *n* someone who is in control or in command of other people or of pets.

mat [mæt] *n* a piece of thick material on a floor or other surface. *Ex* Small mats are used on tables under hot plates.

match [mætʃ] **1.** *n* a thin piece of wood or cardboard with a tip that makes fire. **2.** *v* to find something that goes with something that you already have; to go with; to be the same as. *Ex* Chin Wu bought a blue skirt to match her blue sweater.

mate [meyt] **1.** *n* a spouse; a wife's husband; a husband's wife. **2.** *v* to join together to produce and raise offspring. Usually said of animals.

material [mə'tiriəl] *n* the matter that something is made of; cloth.

math [mæθ] *n* short for the word mathematics.

mathematics [mæθə'mætɪks] *n* the study of numbers, measurements, and quantities.

matinee [mætə'ney] *n* an afternoon performance of a show.

mattress ['mætrəs] *n* the thick, soft part of the bed that you lie on.

may [mey] *v* a word which expresses permission, probability, or possibility. *Ex* I may go to the baseball game tomorrow. May I have another piece of pie? *pt* might.

maybe ['meybi] *adv* perhaps; possibly.

mayor ['meyɚ] *n* someone chosen to be the leader of a city or town.

maze [meyz] *n* a place with many paths that cross and turn so that it is hard to find the way. *Ex* Mazes are used in a laboratory where rats or mice try to learn how to get through.

me [mi] *pro* the objective form of I. *Ex* Give it to me.

meadow ['mɛdow] *n* a field of grass where cows can graze.

meal [mil] *n* food eaten at certain times of the day. *Ex* Breakfast, lunch, dinner, and supper are the names of meals.

meal ticket ['mil tɪkət] *n* a card which allows you to eat in the cafeteria without paying cash each time.

mean [min] **1.** *adj* unkind; cruel; selfish. **2.** *v* to signify; to stand for. *Ex* Red means stop. Elderly means old. *pt* meant. *pp* meant.

meaning ['minɪŋ] *n* the sense or explanation of something said or written.

meant [mɛnt] *v* the past tense and past participle of mean.

meanwhile ['minhwɑyl] *n* the time between two events or happenings.

measles ['mizl̩z] *n* an illness. *Ex* When you have measles you have a high fever and small, itchy, red spots.

measure ['mɛʒɚ] **1.** *v* to find out the size of something. **2.** *n* an amount; a measured amount.

measurement ['mɛʒɚmənt] *n* the size or amount of something.

meat [mit] *n* the parts of an animal that are cooked and eaten.

mechanic [mə'kænɪk] *n* a person who cares for machines, especially cars and trucks.

mechanical [mə'kænɪkl̩] *adj* machine-like; operated by a machine.

medal ['mɛdl̩] *n* an award in the form of a special metal coin given for great skill or courage.

meddle ['mɛdl̩] *v* to interfere with what someone else is trying to do.

media ['midiə] *n* newspapers, magazines, radio, and television; the mass media. The singular is medium.

medicine ['mɛdəsn̩] *n* something you eat or drink or rub on yourself to feel better when you are ill.

medium ['midiəm] **1.** *adj* middle-sized; in between. **2.** *n* a channel or a means of carrying information. *Ex* Radio is an important medium. The plural is media.

meek [mik] *adj* gentle and patient; too gentle and patient for your own good.

meet [mit] **1.** *v* to come together with someone or something.

pt met. *pp* met. **2.** *n* a game, match, or tournament. *Ex* Are you going to the track meet?

meeting ['mitɪŋ] *n* coming together for a purpose.

melt [mɛlt] *v* to turn to liquid when heated. *Ex* Butter melts when it is heated.

member ['mɛmbɚ] *n* someone who belongs to a team, club, or some other group of people.

memo ['mɛmow] *n* a note to help you remember something; a note from someone at your office or business.

memorial [mə'moriəl] *n* something, such as a ceremony or object, which helps keeps memories alive.

memory ['mɛmɚi] *n* the part of the mind that remembers things.

men [mɛn] *n* the plural of man.

mend [mɛnd] *v* to fix; to repair; to put something right.

mental ['mɛntl̩] *adj* having to do with the mind; worked out in your head and not written out.

mention ['mɛntʃn̩] *v* to speak briefly about something.

menu ['mɛnyuw] *n* a card or a piece of paper that lists what there is to eat at a restaurant or a cafe.

mercy ['mɚsi] *n* pity; forgiveness.

mere [mir] *adj* lowly; nothing more than. *Ex* That creature is not a pet; it is a mere pest!

merit ['mɛrət] **1.** *v* to deserve something such as a reward or punishment. **2.** *n* goodness; virtue; worth.

mermaid ['mɚmeyd] *n* an imaginary sea creature, supposed to be half woman and half fish, with a fish tail instead of legs.

merry ['mɛri] *adj* happy; enjoying yourself.

merry-go-round ['mɛrigowrɑwnd] *n* a ride at a carnival or fair which carries you around while you sit on a wooden pony or some other animal.

mess [mɛs] *n* confusion; a muddle; a mixed-up situation.

message ['mɛsɪdʒ] *n* information for a person who is not present. It can be a written message or a spoken one. *Ex* Please give this message to Billy.

messenger ['mɛsn̩dʒɚ] *n* a person who carries a message to someone.

met [mɛt] *v* the past tense and past participle of meet.

metal ['mɛtl̩] *n* a hard material, such as iron, steel, or lead.

meteor ['mitiɚ] *n* a piece of rock traveling in space, often called a shooting star. *Ex* Sometimes a meteor strikes the earth.

meter ['mitɚ] **1.** *n* an instrument for measuring a quantity of something, such as gas, water, or electricity. **2.** *n* a unit of measurement equal to 39.37 inches.

method ['mɛθəd] *n* a way of doing something.

metropolitan [mɛtrə'pɑlətn̩] *n* having to do with a large city.

mice [mɑys] *n* the plural of mouse.

microphone ['mɑykrəfown] *n* an instrument that picks up sounds for radio, television, or tape recorders.

microscope ['mɑykrəskowp] *n* an instrument with a tube that you look through, which makes very tiny things look much larger.

microwave ['mɑykroweyv] **1.** *adj* having to do with a kind of powerful radio signal which is used in home cooking. *Ex* We have a new microwave oven. **2.** *n* short for microwave oven. **3.** *v* to cook something in a microwave oven. *Ex* Clara's mother microwaved a chicken for dinner.

midday ['mɪd'dey] *n* the middle of the day; the period of time around the noon hour.

middle ['mɪdl̩] **1.** *adj* halfway; in the center. **2.** *n* the center; the halfway point.

middle name [mɪdl̩ 'neym] *n* a name between the first name and the last name. *Ex* Roger is John Roger Jones' middle name.

midnight ['mɪdnɑyt] *n* 12 o'clock at night; the middle of the night.

midst [mɪdst] *n* the middle; a place near the center; a part surrounded by the rest. *Ex* I got lost in the midst of the crowd.

might [mɑyt] **1.** *n* strength; power. **2.** *v* a word which expresses possibility or probability. **3.** *v* the past tense of may.

mighty ['mɑyti] *adj* powerful; strong.

migration [mɑy'greyʃn̩] *n* the movement from one place to another; usually said of groups of people or animals. *Ex* Ducks have an annual migration.

mild [mɑyld] *adj* not strong or severe; not too cold or too hot.

mile [mɑyl] *n* a measure of distance equal to 1,760 yards or 1.609 kilometers.

military ['mɪlətɛri] **1.** *adj* having to do with the army, navy, air force, or marines. **2.** *n* the government departments having to do with war and defense.

milk [mɪlk] **1.** *n* the white liquid that is used to feed babies. *Ex* Cow's milk is drunk in the U.S. **2.** *v* to take milk from a cow or other mammal.

milkman ['mɪlkmæn] *n* a person whose job is to bring milk to your house.

mill [mɪl] **1.** *n* a machine for grinding things like grain, coffee beans, and pepper into very small pieces. **2.** *n* a building or factory where cloth or steel is made.

millimeter ['mɪləmitɚ] *n* a measurement equal to a thousandth part of a meter, or 0.04 inches.

million ['mɪlyən] *n* one thousand times one thousand; 1,000,000.

millionaire [mɪlyə'nɛr] *n* a person who has money or property equal to at least $1,000,000.00.

mimeograph machine ['mɪmiəgræf məʃin] *n* a machine that produces copies of something which you have typed on special paper. The machine has a part that rotates and prints each copy with ink.

mimic ['mɪmɪk] **1.** *v* to copy or imitate someone else, usually in a mocking way. **2.** *n* a person who copies other people very well.

mind [maynd] **1.** *n* what you think with; your memory and the thinking power of the brain. **2.** *v* to obey. **3.** *v* to be careful and think about what you are doing.

mine [mayn] **1.** *n* a large, deep hole in the ground where miners dig for coal or gold. **2.** *pro* that which belongs to me. *Ex* That book is mine.

miner ['maynɚ] *n* someone who works in a mine.

mineral ['mɪnɚəl] *n* any substance in the earth which can be dug out and used, such as coal or metal.

mingle ['mɪŋgl̩] *v* to mix with or go about with, as when you mingle with a crowd at a football game.

miniature ['mɪn(i)ətʃɚ] **1.** *n* a small copy of something. **2.** *adj* small; smaller than normal.

minister ['mɪnəstɚ] *n* a clergyman, especially a Protestant clergyman; a preacher.

minor ['maynɚ] **1.** *adj* not important. **2.** *n* a person who is not yet an adult.

minority [mə'norəti] *n* a small number of people; a race or nationality of people who are few in number.

mint [mɪnt] **1.** *n* a place where coins are made. **2.** *n* a garden plant used for flavoring.

minus sign ['maynəs sɑyn] *n* the sign (-) which means to subtract. *Ex* 3 - 2 = 1.

minute ['mɪnət] *n* one minute is 60 seconds. *Ex* There are 60 minutes in an hour.

miracle ['mɪrəkl̩] *n* something wonderful or fortunate that you would not expect to happen.

mirage [mə'rɑʒ] *n* something you imagine you can see that is not really there, as when hot and thirsty travelers in the desert think they see water ahead.

mirror ['mɪrɚ] *n* a piece of glass with something behind it so that you can see yourself instead of seeing through the glass.

misbehave [mɪsbə'heyv] *v* to behave badly; to behave in a rude way.

mischief ['mɪstʃəf] *n* harm or damage; naughtiness.

miser ['mayzɚ] *n* someone who hoards all his money.

miserable ['mɪzɚəbl̩] *adj* feeling very sad and unhappy.

misery ['mɪzɚi] *n* unhappiness; sorrow.

misfortune [mɪs'fortʃn̩] *n* bad luck; a calamity.

miss [mɪs] **1.** *v* to fail to hit, catch, or find something. **2.** *n* a failure to hit, catch, or find something. **3.** *n* a girl or an unmarried young lady. **4.** *n* (*capitalized*) a title for a girl or unmarried woman.

mist [mɪst] *n* a very low cloud.

mistake [mɪ'steyk] **1.** *v* to confuse something with something else; to blunder; to misunderstand. *pt* mistook. *pp* mistaken. **2.** *n* an error; something wrong.

mistaken [mɪ'steykn̩] *v* the past participle of mistake.

mistletoe ['mɪsl̩tow] *n* an evergreen plant with pearl-like berries, which grows on the branches of trees. *Ex* Mistletoe is used for decoration at Christmas.

mistook [mɪ'stʊk] *v* the past tense of mistake.

mistrust [mɪs'trəst] **1.** *v* not to trust someone; not to believe someone. **2.** *n* disbelief; lack of trust.

misunderstanding [mɪsəndɚ'stændɪŋ] *n* a case where different people's meanings or intentions are not correctly understood.

mitten ['mɪtn̩] *n* one of a pair of coverings for the hands. *Ex* Mittens are like gloves but without places for the fingers.

mix [mɪks] *v* to put different things together.

mixture ['mɪkstʃɚ] *n* two or more things put together.

moan [mown] **1.** *n* a long, low sound made by a person in pain or sorrow. **2.** *v* to make a long, low sound when in pain or sorrow.

mock [mɑk] *v* to make fun of someone.

mockery ['mɑkɚi] *n* the act of making fun of something or someone.

model ['mɑdl̩] **1.** *n* a copy of something like a boat or airplane, usually smaller than the real thing. **2.** *n* someone who wears clothing to show it off to people who might want to buy it. **3.** *n* a person who stays quite still while being painted or drawn by an artist.

moderate ['mɑdɚət] *adj* fair; not extreme.

modern ['mɑdɚn] *adj* at this time; not old-fashioned; up-to-date.

moist [moyst] *adj* damp; slightly wet.

moisture ['moystʃɚ] *n* dampness; slight wetness.

mold [mowld] **1.** *n* a fungus or other growth which can be found in damp places. **2.** *n* a specially shaped cavity or hollow which gives its shape to clay, plaster, or plastic which is poured in. **3.** *v* to make an object through the use of a mold.

mole [mowl] **1.** *n* a small animal with sharp claws, tiny eyes, and thick fur. *Ex* Moles dig long tunnels in the ground. **2.** *n* a dark spot on the skin.

moment ['mowmənt] *n* a very short time.

monarch ['mɑnɑrk] *n* a king, queen, emperor, or empress.

monastery ['mɑnəstɛri] *n* a building where monks live.

money ['məni] *n* coins and paper bills.

money order ['məni ordɚ] *n* a check issued by a bank or post office. *Ex* When you buy a money order, you must pay a small fee.

mongrel ['mɑngrl̩] *n* a dog which is a mixture of different types.

monk [məŋk] *n* a member of a religious group living in a monastery.

monkey ['məŋki] *n* a small, lively animal with a long tail. *Ex* Monkeys are very good at climbing trees and swinging from branch to branch.

monster ['mɑn(t)stɚ] *n* an enormous, horrible creature; a plant or animal of unusual or frightening appearance.

month [məntθ] *n* a time period of about four weeks. *Ex* There are twelve months in a year.

monument ['mɑnyəmənt] *n* a statue or a building that is put up to make people remember someone or some event.

mood [muwd] *n* how you feel; the state of your mind. *Ex* You can be in a good mood when you are happy, or in a bad mood when something has made you cross or unhappy.

moon [muwn] *n* the largest and brightest light seen in the sky at night.

mop [mɑp] **1.** *n* pieces of sponge or thick cotton yarn fastened to a long stick. *Ex* Mops are used to clean floors. **2.** *v* to clean a floor with a mop.

moral ['morəl] **1.** *adj* good; virtuous. **2.** *n* a lesson learned from a story.

more [mor] *adj* of a greater number; of a larger amount. *Ex* Please give me more potatoes.

morning ['mornɪŋ] *n* the time between dawn and midday.

mortar ['mortɚ] *n* a mixture of cement, sand, and water used in building to make bricks or stones stick together.

mosaic [mow'zeyɪk] *n* a pattern or picture made by arranging lots of small pieces of colored glass or stones.

mosquito [mə'skitow] *n* a small, flying insect which bites.

moss [mɔs] *n* a very small, green plant that looks like velvet. *Ex* Moss grows close to the ground in damp places, especially in the woods.

most [mowst] **1.** *adj* of the greatest number; of the largest amount. **2.** *pro* the greatest number; the largest amount.

moth [mɔθ] *n* an insect rather like a butterfly, except that it only flies at night. *Ex* Moths are attracted to light.

mother ['məðɚ] *n* a woman who has children.

motion ['mowʃn̩] *n* movement.

motion picture [mowʃn̩ 'pɪktʃɚ] *n* a movie; a moving picture; what you see in a movie theater.

motion picture theater [mowʃn̩ pɪktʃɚ 'θiətɚ] *n* the building where movies are shown; a cinema.

motor ['mowtɚ] *n* a machine which makes something work or move.

motorbike ['mowtɚbayk] *n* a kind of heavy bicycle with a motor.

motorcycle ['mowtɚsaykl̩] *n* a heavy and powerful kind of bicycle with a motor; a large motorbike.

motto ['matow] *n* a short saying which gives a rule for behavior, such as *Be prepared.*

mound [mawnd] *n* a heap of stones or earth; a small, rounded hill.

mount [mawnt] **1.** *n* a mountain. **2.** *v* to get up onto something, like a horse or a bicycle.

mountain ['mawntn̩] *n* a very high hill.

mouse [maws] *n* a little animal with a long tail and sharp teeth.

mouth [mawθ] **1.** *n* the opening in the face used for speaking and eating. **2.** *n* the end of a river which flows into a lake or the ocean; the place where you enter a river from the ocean or a lake.

move [muwv] **1.** *v* to go from one place to another; to make something go from one place to another. **2.** *n* a step in the playing of a game such as chess.

movement ['muwvmənt] *n* the act of moving.

movie ['muwvi] *n* a motion picture; what you see at a cinema.

mow [mow] *v* to cut grass or hay.

Mr. ['mɪstɚ] *n* an abbreviation of mister, a title for men.

Mrs. ['mɪsəz] *n* an abbreviation of mistress, a title for married women.

Ms. [mɪz] *n* a title for married or unmarried women.

much [mətʃ] **1.** *adj* a great amount of. *Ex* Is there much snow in February? **2.** *n* a lot; a large amount. *Ex* Don't give me much!

mud [məd] *n* soft, wet earth.

muffin ['məfn̩] *n* a soft bread, usually served warm. *Ex* Some muffins are made with raisins or other fruit.

muffler ['məflɚ] **1.** *n* a wooly scarf. **2.** *n* a part of the car which makes the engine noises quieter.

mug [məg] *n* a large, heavy cup with straight sides.

mule [myuwl] *n* an animal whose parents are a donkey and a horse.

multiplication [məltəplə'keyʃn̩] *n* the part of arithmetic where one number is multiplied by another. *Ex* 2 × 2 = 4.

multiplication sign [məltəplə'keyʃn̩ sɑyn] *n* the sign (×) which indicates that you should multiply one number by another; the times sign. *Ex* 2 × 2 = 4.

multiplication table [məltəplə'keyʃn̩ teybl̩] *n* a chart which shows multiplication problems and their answers.

multiplier ['məltəplɑyɚ] *n* a number by which another number is multiplied.

multiply ['məltəplay] *v* to increase; to make something a number of times greater.

mumble ['məmbḷ] *v* to speak with your mouth nearly closed so that your words are not heard clearly.

mumps [məmps] *n* an illness which makes your neck swell up and makes it hurt to swallow.

munch [mənt∫] *v* to chew with a crunching sound.

municipal [myuw'nɪsəpḷ] *adj* having to do with a city.

murder ['mɚdɚ] *v* to kill someone on purpose and against the law.

murderer ['mɚdɚɚ] *n* a person who kills someone on purpose and against the law.

murmur ['mɚmɚ] **1.** *n* a gentle, soft sound that goes on and on. **2.** *v* to make a gentle, soft sound; to talk very softly.

muscle ['məsḷ] *n* the parts of the body that tighten and loosen to make it move.

museum [myuw'ziəm] *n* a place where interesting collections of things are set out for people to look at.

mushroom ['mə∫ruwm] *n* a small fungus plant shaped like an umbrella. *Ex* Some mushrooms can be eaten; some of them are poisonous.

music ['myuwzɪk] *n* pleasing sounds that you sing or play on a musical instrument.

musician [myuw'zɪ∫n̩] *n* a person whose job or hobby is to make music of some kind.

must [məst] *v* to have to do something, such as going to school every day. *Ex* I must wash the dishes today.

mustache ['məstæ∫] *n* the hair growing on a man's upper lip, especially if it is allowed to grow long.

mustard ['məstəd] *n* a spicy, bright yellow sauce which is eaten on hamburgers and hot dogs.

mutiny ['myuwtṇi] *n* a refusal by soldiers, sailors, or airmen to obey their officers.

mutter ['mətə˞] *v* to speak so softly that it is hard to understand the words.

muzzle ['məzḷ] **1.** *n* the jaws and nose of an animal. **2.** *n* a set of straps built to fasten on an animal's nose and mouth to keep it from biting.

my [mɑy] *pro* belonging to me. *Ex* That is my car.

myself [mɑy'sɛlf] *pro* me and no one else.

mystery ['mɪstə˞i] *n* something strange that has happened, but that cannot be explained or easily understood.

myth [mɪθ] *n* a very old story which explains how something began or happened; an imaginary person or event.

N

***

nag [næg] *v* to keep scolding or finding fault. *Ex* Please don't nag me about my homework.

nail [neyl] **1.** *n* the hard part at the end of a finger or toe. **2.** *n* a thin, sharp piece of metal used to join pieces of wood. *Ex* Please hammer the nail into this wood.

naked ['neykəd] *adj* not wearing any clothes or covering.

name [neym] **1.** *n* what a person or thing is called. **2.** *v* to give a name to someone or something; to list things; to say the names of things. *Ex* Please name the U.S. Presidents.

nap [næp] *n* a short sleep.

napkin ['næpkɪn] *n* a square piece of cloth or paper used to wipe your mouth and fingers when you eat.

narrow ['nɛrow] *adj* slim; thin; not wide.

nasty ['næsti] *adj* not nice; not pleasant.

nation ['neyʃn̩] *n* a country; all of the people who live in one country under one government.

national ['næʃənl̩] *adj* belonging to one nation or country.

nationality [næʃə'næləti] *n* the country of a person's citizenship; the country to which a person belongs.

native ['neytɪv] **1.** *n* a person belonging to a particular place or country. *Ex* I am a native of southern Indiana. **2.** *adj* having to do with a particular place. *Ex* That flower is not native to this country.

natural ['nætʃɚəl] *adj* part of nature; not man-made.

nature ['neytʃɚ] *n* everything in the world that is not man-made.

naughty ['nɔti] *adj* having to do with bad behavior; wicked.

nausea ['nɔziə] *n* a sick feeling in your stomach; the feeling that you are going to vomit.

navigate ['nævəgeyt] *v* to steer or guide a ship or airplane.

navy ['neyvi] *n* a nation's warships and the sailors who run them.

near [nir] **1.** *adv* close. *Ex* Please come near. **2.** *adj* close. *Ex* Wow, that was a near miss! **3.** *prep* close to. *Ex* Please don't get near me.

nearly ['nirli] *adv* very close; almost; not far from. *Ex* I nearly fell down.

nearsighted ['nirsɑytəd] *adj* able to see close better than far.

neat [nit] *adj* tidy; in good order.

necessary ['nɛsəsɛri] *adj* having to be done; needed.

neck [nɛk] *n* the part of your body between your head and your shoulders.

necklace ['nɛkləs] *n* a string of beads or a thin chain worn around the neck.

nectar ['nɛktɚ] *n* a sweet juice found in some flowers.

need [nid] *v* to have to have something. *Ex* You need clothes to keep you warm.

needle ['nidl] *n* a long, thin pointed piece of metal used for sewing. There are also special needles for knitting.

negative ['nɛgətɪv] *adj* meaning or saying no; not positive.

neglect [nə'glɛkt] *v* to be careless about looking after some‐
thing. *Ex* Please don't neglect your homework.

neighbor ['neybɚ] *n* a person who lives near you.

neighborhood ['neybɚhʊd] *n* the area in which you live. *Ex*
There are many restaurants in our neighborhood.

neither ['niðɚ] **1.** *adj* not one or the other. *Ex* Neither student
could answer the question. **2.** *pro* not one or the other. *Ex*
Neither could answer the question.

nephew ['nɛfyuw] *n* the son of a brother or sister.

nerve [nɚv] **1.** *n* one of the small, thread-like parts of your
body that carry messages to and from the brain so you can
move and feel. **2.** *n* courage and daring.

nervous ['nɚvəs] *adj* jumpy; easily frightened. *Ex* Examina‐
tions make me nervous.

nest [nɛst] *n* a bird's home, where the eggs are laid and
hatched; the home of some kinds of insects such as wasps.

net [nɛt] *n* something like a cloth woven with enormous spaces
between the threads.

network ['nɛtwɚk] **1.** *n* an arrangement of ropes, wires, or
lines running in many different directions and crossing one
another. **2.** *n* a radio or television broadcasting company
connected to the many stations which send out its programs.

neutral ['nuwtrəl] **1.** *adj* in between; not on one side or the
other. **2.** *n* a gear on a vehicle which lets the engine run
without the vehicle going anywhere.

neutron ['nuwtrɑn] *n* a part of the atom which has no electrical
charge.

never ['nɛvɚ] *adj* not ever; not at any time. *Ex* We never have
enough time to do our work.

new [nuw] *adj* only just made; not old; not seen before.

adj just born.

...s that have just happened; stories and
...hat have just happened. This word is
...ngular, and there is no plural form. *Ex* Have you heard the good news? The news is good.

newspaper ['nuwzpeypɚ] *n* the paper which has the news of the day printed in it.

newsstand ['nuwzstænd] *n* the place where newspapers and magazines are sold. *Ex* Please buy me a newspaper at the newsstand.

next [nɛkst] *adj* the nearest; the one after.

nibble ['nɪbl̩] **1.** *v* to take very small bites. **2.** *n* a very small bite of food.

nice [nɑys] *adj* kind; friendly; pretty; pleasant.

nick [nɪk] *n* a little cut in something; a chipped place in something. *Ex* There is a nick in my cup, but it's not broken.

nickel ['nɪkl̩] **1.** *n* a silvery-gray metal. **2.** *n* a coin worth five cents.

nickname ['nɪkneym] *n* a name you give to someone for fun. *Ex* John's nickname is Shorty because he is not very tall.

niece [nis] *n* the daughter of a brother or sister.

night [nɑyt] *n* the time between sunset and sunrise, when the sky is dark.

nightgown ['nɑytgɑwn] *n* a garment worn in bed by girls and women.

nip [nɪp] **1.** *v* to pinch or bite off a little bit of something. **2.** *n* a little bit or pinch of something.

no [now] **1.** *adv* the opposite of yes. **2.** *adj* not yes.

noble ['nowbļ] *adj* great; grand.

nobody ['nowbɑdi] **1.** *pro* no person; not anyone. **2.** *n* a person of no importance. *Ex* He's just a nobody.

nod [nɑd] **1.** *v* to bend the head forward and back to show agreement. **2.** *v* to let the head fall forward when sleepy.

noise [noyz] *n* a sound; a very loud or unpleasant sound; an unmusical sound.

nomad ['nowmæd] *n* one of a group of people who have no permanent home, but who roam about looking for food for themselves and their animals.

nominal ['nɑmənļ] *n* a noun; a word or group of words used as a noun.

none [nən] *pro* not one; not any.

nonfiction [nɑn'fɪkʃṇ] *n* literature which is not fiction; literature written about true events and people.

nonsense ['nɑnsɛn(t)s] *n* talk which means nothing.

noon [nuwn] *n* midday; 12 o'clock in the day.

noose [nuws] *n* a loop in a rope that can be tightened by pulling it.

nor [nor] *conj* and not; and not this one. *Ex* They found comfort neither here nor there.

normal ['norməl] *adj* ordinary; usual.

north [norθ] *n* the direction which is the opposite of south. *Ex* North is on your left as you face the rising sun.

North Pole ['norθ 'powl] *n* the farthest northern point in the world; 90 degrees north latitude.

nose [nowz] *n* the part of the face through which air is brought into the body.

nosey ['nowzi] *adj* wanting to know all about other people's belongings and activities.

nostril ['nɑstrəl] *n* one of the two openings in the nose.

not [nɑt] *adv* indicates the negative of verbs. *Ex* She does not run fast.

note [nowt] **1.** *n* a written message; a short letter. **2.** *n* a sound in music. **3.** *n* a piece of paper money.

notebook ['nowtbʊk] *n* a little book in which you write things down that you don't want to forget.

nothing ['nəθɪŋ] *pro* not anything.

notice ['nowtəs] **1.** *v* to see something. **2.** *n* a piece of paper announcing something; a printed announcement of something.

noun [nɑwn] *n* a word which is the name of something.

nourish ['nɚɪʃ] *v* to feed.

novel ['nɑvḷ] **1.** *adj* new and different. **2.** *n* a long story about imaginary people.

novelty ['nɑvḷti] *n* something new and different.

now [nɑw] *adv* at this time.

nowhere ['nowhwɛr] *adv* not anywhere or any place.

nozzle ['nɑzḷ] *n* a spout at the end of a pipe or hose.

nuclear ['nuwkliɚ] *adj* having to do with atomic weapons; having to do with atomic energy.

nucleus ['nuwkliəs] *n* the central part of a cell or an atom.

nude [nuwd] *adj* naked; not wearing clothing.

nudge [nədʒ] *v* to poke or push something or someone gently with your elbow.

nuisance ['nuwsṇ(t)s] *n* something or someone who gets in the way of what others want to do.

null set ['nəl 'sɛt] *n* zero.

numb [nəm] *adj* not able to feel, as when your fingers are numb with cold.

number ['nəmbɚ] *n* a written or spoken symbol telling how many. *Ex* Both four and 4 are numbers.

numeral ['nuwmɚl] *n* a figure indicating how many. *Ex* The figure 4 is a numeral.

numerator ['nuwmɚeytɚ] *n* the part of the fraction which is above or to the left of the line. *Ex* In the fraction 3/4, the 3 is the numerator, and the 4 is the denominator.

numerous ['nuwmɚəs] *adj* very many.

nun [nən] *n* a female member of a religious group who sometimes lives in a convent.

nurse [nɚs] *n* someone who helps the doctor take care of people who are ill.

nursery ['nɚs(ə)ri] *n* a room or a building where very young children sleep or play.

nut [nət] **1.** *n* a fruit or seed with a very hard shell. **2.** *n* a piece of metal with a hole through it that you screw on to a bolt.

nylon ['naylɑn] *n* a man-made material used for making clothing, brushes, and other useful things.

O

oak [owk] *n* a kind of tree which can grow very big and lives to a very old age. *Ex* An oak has acorns as its fruit.

oar [or] *n* a long piece of wood with one flat end that is used to row a boat.

oasis [ow'eysəs] *n* a place in the desert where plants and trees grow because there is water.

oath [owθ] *n* a solemn promise that you will speak the truth or keep your word.

oatmeal ['owtmil] *n* a hot, thick breakfast cereal made from ground-up oats.

oats [owts] *n* a kind of grain used mostly for feeding animals, especially horses.

obedience [ow'bidiən(t)s] *n* doing as you are told.

obey [ow'bey] *v* to do as someone tells you to do. *Ex* You must obey your teacher.

obituary [ow'bɪtʃəwɛri] *n* a notice of someone's death, usually in the newspaper.

object 1. *n* ['abdʒɛkt] a thing; something you can see or handle. **2.** *v* [əb'dʒɛkt] to disagree with someone else's idea.

objection [əb'dʒɛkʃn̩] *n* a disagreement; a complaint against something.

oblige [ə'blaydʒ] **1.** *v* to do someone a favor. **2.** *v* to force someone to do something.

oblong ['ablɔŋ] **1.** *n* a rectangle. **2.** *adj* rectangular.

observe [əb'zɚv] **1.** *v* to watch carefully; to notice *Ex* Observe her careful movements. **2.** *v* to celebrate; to remember a special day. *Ex* They do not observe all holidays.

obstacle ['ɑbstəkl] *n* anything that stands in the way so that you cannot go forward.

obstinate ['ɑbstənət] *adj* wanting your own way; stubborn.

obtain [əb'teyn] *v* get; go and get; seek and get.

occasion [ə'keyʒn̩] *n* a particular event or happening.

occupation [ɑkyə'peyʃn̩] *n* the kind of work that a person does; a job.

occupy ['ɑkyəpɑy] **1.** *v* to live in; to dwell in. **2.** *v* to go into enemy land in wartime and take over towns and cities.

occur [ə'kɚ] *v* to happen.

ocean ['owʃn̩] *n* a very big sea with salty water.

o'clock [ə'klɑk] *n* the time by the clock. *Ex* It is three o'clock.

octopus ['ɑktəpʊs] *n* a sea creature with eight arms. *Ex* The octopus has suckers on its arms.

odd [ɑd] **1.** *adj* strange; queer. **2.** *adj* not even in number. *Ex* The numbers 1, 3, 5, 7, and 9 are odd numbers.

odor ['owdɚ] *n* a smell.

of [əv] *prep* from; made from; separate from.

off [ɔf] **1.** *prep* from; from the top; the opposite of on. **2.** *adv* away from; the opposite of on. *Ex* Please turn the light off.

offend [ə'fɛnd] *v* to displease; to do something wrong; to make someone angry.

offense [ə'fɛn(t)s] **1.** *n* a crime. **2.** *n* an action that causes hurt feelings or anger in another person.

offensive [ə'fɛn(t)sɪv] *adj* causing hurt; unpleasant.

offer ['ɔfɚ] *v* to say you will do or give something.

office ['ɔfɪs] *n* a building or room where people work with business papers.

officer ['ɔfəsɚ] **1.** *n* someone who commands others, as in the army, navy, or air force. **2.** *n* a police officer.

official [ə'fɪʃl] **1.** *n* an officer. **2.** *adj* authorized; genuine.

offspring ['ɔfsprɪŋ] *n* a child; children. This form is used in both the singular and the plural. *Ex* I am an offspring of my parents. Chicks are the offspring of chickens.

often ['ɔfn̩] *adv* many times; happening over and over.

oil [oyl] **1.** *n* a thick, greasy liquid which can come from animals or plants, or from under the ground. **2.** *v* to put oil on metal parts so they can move better.

ointment ['oyntmənt] *n* a soothing paste you put on sores or cuts.

okay ['ow'key] **1.** *adj* correct; all right. **2.** *v* to approve something. **3.** *n* approval; an act of approval. Also spelled O.K.

old [owld] *adj* having been alive or existing for a long time.

old-fashioned [owld'fæʃn̩d] *adj* not modern; from long ago.

omelette ['ɑmlət] *n* eggs beaten up and cooked for a while and then folded over.

omit [ow'mɪt] *v* to leave out; not to do something.

on [ɔn] **1.** *prep* upon; resting upon the surface of; the opposite of off. **2.** *adv* to a place resting on the surface of; the opposite of off. *Ex* Please turn the light on.

once [wən(t)s] **1.** *adv* for one time only. **2.** *adv* at a long time ago.

one [wən] **1.** *n* the number 1. **2.** *pro* any person; someone.

one-way ['wən'wey] *adj* having to do with a street where the traffic moves only in one direction.

onion ['ənyən] *n* a bulb-like vegetable with a strong smell and flavor.

online ['ɔnlɑyn] *adj* having to do with the direct control of a computer.

only ['ownli] **1.** *adj* single; one and no more. **2.** *adv* just; merely; just once.

open ['owpən] **1.** *adj* not shut; able to let things through. **2.** *v* to make open; to make a door open; to unfasten, unfold, unseal, or uncover. The opposite of shut and close.

opening ['owpənɪŋ] *n* an open place; a passageway; a hole or space.

opera ['ɑprə] *n* a musical performance including singing, orchestral music, and sometimes dance.

operate ['ɑpɚeyt] **1.** *v* to run; to function; to work. *Ex* This toy does not operate correctly. Do you know how to operate a tape recorder? **2.** *v* to perform surgery.

operation [ɑpə'reyʃn̩] **1.** *n* something that is done; a project. **2.** *n* surgery done in a hospital by a doctor.

opinion [ə'pɪnyən] *n* what you think about something.

opportunity [ɑpɚ'tuwnəti] *n* a chance to do something.

opposite ['ɑpəzɪt] *adj* as different as possible from something else; across from.

optical ['ɑptəkl̩] *n* having to do with eyes or seeing.

optician [ɑpˈtɪʃn̩] *n* a person who makes and sells eyeglasses and other things with lenses.

or [or] *conj* a word indicating a choice; if not one, then the other. *Ex* Please give me a red one or a blue one.

orange [ˈɔrəndʒ] **1.** *n* a sweet citrus fruit grown mostly in Florida and California. **2.** *n* a color between yellow and red.

orangutan [əˈræŋətæŋ] *n* a large, reddish-brown ape that lives in jungles.

orbit [ˈorbɪt] *n* the path in which something moves around another thing in space. *Ex* The moon's orbit is fairly close to the earth.

orchard [ˈortʃɚd] *n* a field or an area where fruit trees grow.

orchestra [ˈorkəstrə] *n* a group of musicians who play a variety of instruments.

order [ˈordɚ] **1.** *n* a command; a request for goods; a request for your choice of food at a restaurant. **2.** *v* to ask that something be done; to command that something be done. **3.** *n* neatness; tidiness.

ordinary [ˈordn̩ɛri] *adj* usual; not special or different.

ore [or] *n* rock or mineral from which metal is made.

organ [ˈorgən] **1.** *n* a large musical instrument with a keyboard and pipes that the sounds come from. **2.** *n* a body part, such as the heart, which performs a specific function.

organization [orgənəˈzeyʃn̩] *n* a group of people or of nations who get together to work for a particular purpose.

organize [ˈorgənayz] *v* to get a group of people together for a particular purpose; to plan and arrange something.

origin [ˈorədʒn̩] *n* the source; the cause of something.

ornament ['ornəmənt] *n* anything used to make something look prettier, such as jewelry or a vase.

orphan ['orfn̩] *n* a child whose mother and father are both dead.

other ['əðɚ] **1.** *n* the second of the two; the alternative. **2.** *adj* alternate; one that is not this one.

others ['əðɚz] *pro* other people. *Ex* We like this one, but others don't.

otherwise ['əðɚwɑyz] *adv* if not; if things are different.

ought [ɔt] *v* should.

ounce [ɑwn(t)s] *n* a measurement of weight. *Ex* There are 16 ounces to a pound.

our ['ɑwɚ] *pro* belonging to us. *Ex* That is our car.

ours ['ɑwɚz] *pro* that which belongs to us. *Ex* That car is ours.

out [ɑwt] **1.** *prep* toward the outside; the opposite of in. *Ex* The bird flew out the window. **2.** *adv* toward the outside; away from the inside; the opposite of in. *Ex* The bird flew out.

outburst ['ɑwtbɚst] *n* a sudden noise, such as cheering when a goal is scored at a football game.

outdoor ['ɑwtdor] *adj* outside a building; the opposite of indoor.

outdoors ['ɑwtdorz] *adv* to or at the outside of a building.

outfit ['ɑwtfɪt] *n* a set of clothing or equipment.

outing ['ɑwtɪŋ] *n* a pleasure trip or walk.

outlaw ['ɑwtlɔ] *n* a person who fights against the law; a person who is a criminal. *Ex* Robin Hood and his men were outlaws.

outlet ['ɑwtlɛt] **1.** *n* a place where something can flow out or go out. **2.** *n* the place where you put a plug in to get electricity.

outline ['ɑwtlɑyn] **1.** *v* to draw a line to show the shape of something. **2.** *n* a line drawn to show the shape of something around the outside edge. **3.** *n* a list of the main ideas of a story or a plan.

output ['ɑwtpʊt] **1.** *n* the amount of production of a factory. *Ex* This factory has a large output. **2.** *n* what a computer puts out; an answer from a computer; the result of a computer program.

outside ['ɑwt'sɑyd] **1.** *adj* out-of-doors; the opposite of in-doors. *Ex* They have an outside entrance to their garage. **2.** *adv* out; away from the inside. *Ex* It is raining, and I can't go outside.

oval ['owvḷ] **1.** *n* a shape like an egg; a shape like a long circle. *Ex* The letter O is an oval. **2.** *adj* egg-shaped.

oven ['əvṇ] *n* the inside part of a stove where things are baked.

over ['owvɚ] **1.** *prep* above. *Ex* The roof is over our heads. **2.** *adv* again. *Ex* You don't understand it. Please read it over.

overall ['owvɚɔl] *adj* complete; total.

overcame [owvɚ'keym] *v* the past tense of overcome.

overcoat ['owvɚkowt] *n* an outdoor coat to be worn over other clothing.

overcome [owvɚ'kəm] *v* to defeat; to get the better of someone or something. *pt* overcame. *pp* overcome.

overflow [owvɚ'flow] *v* to spill over the top of a container because it is too full.

overtake [owvɚ'teyk] *v* to catch up with and go in front of someone or something. *pt* overtook. *pp* overtaken.

overtaken [owvɚˈteykn̩] *v* the past participle of overtake.

overthrew [owvɚˈθruw] *v* the past tense of overthrow.

overthrow [owvɚˈθrow] *v* to destroy; to defeat completely. *pt* overthrew. *pp* overthrown.

overthrown [owvɚˈθrown] *v* the past participle of overthrow.

overtime [ˈowvɚtɑym] **1.** *n* time spent doing something after a time limit has been reached. *Ex* When a basketball score is tied at the end of the game, the game goes into overtime. When you work more hours than usual, it is called overtime. **2.** *n* payment for working more than normal hours.

overtook [owvɚˈtʊk] *v* the past tense of overtake.

owe [ow] *v* to need to pay for something you have bought.

owl [ɑwl] *n* a bird with big eyes and a sharp, curved beak. *Ex* Owls fly at night and sleep through the day.

own [own] *v* to have something that belongs to you; to have something as yours and yours alone.

ox [ɑks] *n* a cow; a bull.

oxen [ˈɑksn̩] *n* bulls and cows. The singular is ox.

oyster [ˈoystɚ] *n* a shellfish with a very hard, flat shell in two parts.

P

pace [peys] **1.** *n* a step or the length of a step. *Ex* The door is six paces in front of you. **2.** *v* to walk back and forth in a nervous or bored manner.

pack [pæk] **1.** *v* to put things into a container. *Ex* I must go and pack my suitcase. **2.** *n* a bundle of things carried on your back.

package ['pækɪdʒ] *n* a parcel; a bundle; a container. *Ex* Joel mailed two packages at the post office.

packet ['pækət] *n* a small parcel; a small package.

pad [pæd] **1.** *n* a lot of sheets of paper glued or sewn together at the top. **2.** *n* a piece of thick, soft material; a cushion. **3.** *v* to line with pads; to cushion with soft material. *Ex* I like to sit on a comfortably padded chair.

paddle ['pædl̩] **1.** *v* to swim with small strokes of the hands and feet or paws. *Ex* The dog paddled out to the boat. **2.** *v* to spank gently. *Ex* The mother paddled the child for breaking the chair. **3.** *n* a pole with a flat part at one end, like an oar, used to move a canoe through the water.

page [peydʒ] **1.** *n* one side of a sheet of paper in a book, magazine, or newspaper. **2.** *n* someone who calls people or runs errands. *Ex* The librarian sent a page to get the book. **3.** *v* to call a person for whom there is a message; to call a person over a P.A. system. *Ex* Please page Mr. Kim and tell him that there is a telephone call for him.

pageant ['pædʒṇt] *n* a show in costume, usually about things that happened long ago.

paid [peyd] *v* the past tense and past participle of pay.

pail [peyl] *n* a bucket; a container for water, milk, or some other liquid.

pain [peyn] **1.** *n* the feeling of hurt. **2.** *v* to cause hurt.

paint [peynt] **1.** *v* to color something with a brush and a special colored liquid; to make a picture using a brush and colored liquids. **2.** *n* a special colored liquid which gives color and protection to objects on which it is spread.

painting ['peyntɪŋ] *n* a colored picture painted on paper or canvas. *Ex* Paintings are found in museums and galleries.

pajamas [pə'dʒæməz] *n* the shirt and pants or similar clothing worn in bed.

palace ['pæləs] *n* the house where a king or queen lives.

pale [peyl] *adj* not having much color or brightness; looking washed out.

palm [pɑm] **1.** *n* the inside of your hand between your fingers and your wrist. **2.** *n* a tall tree with fan-shaped leaves at the top. *Ex* Palm trees grow in hot countries.

pan [pæn] *n* a metal container with a handle, used for cooking.

pancake ['pænkeyk] *n* a thin, round cake eaten hot. *Ex* Pancakes are cooked in a frying pan.

panic ['pænɪk] *n* sudden fear or terror that keeps people from thinking reasonably.

pansy ['pænzi] *n* a small garden plant with velvety, brightly colored flowers.

pant [pænt] *v* to gasp for breath.

pantomime ['pæntəmɑym] *n* a play in which the actors do not speak.

pantry ['pæntri] *n* a small room or cupboard where food is kept.

pants [pænts] *n* trousers.

paper ['peypɚ] *n* the material used to write on or wrap parcels in.

paper clip ['peypɚ klɪp] *n* a length of wire bent in a special way so that it will hold a few sheets of paper together.

paper cutter ['peypɚ kətɚ] *n* a device with a large blade used for cutting small stacks of paper neatly.

paper punch ['peypɚ pəntʃ] *n* a device used to punch holes in sheets of paper. It is also called a hole punch.

parachute ['pɛrəʃuwt] *n* a large piece of strong cloth which is fastened to a person who is going to jump from an airplane. *Ex* The parachute opens like an umbrella and lowers the person slowly to the ground.

parade [pə'reyd] *n* a lot of people walking or marching together, sometimes in costume.

paragraph ['pɛrəgræf] *n* a part of a piece of writing which is one or more sentences long. *Ex* Each new paragraph is indented at the beginning.

parallel ['pɛrəlɛl] **1.** *adj* going in the same direction the same distance apart and never meeting. *Ex* Railroad tracks are parallel. **2.** *n* a line of latitude. *Ex* Thirty-eight degrees latitude is the same as the thirty-eighth parallel.

paraphrase ['pɛrəfreyz] **1.** *v* to say or write something in a simpler way; to say or write something in your own words. **2.** *n* writing or other words which have been restated.

parcel ['pɑrsl̩] *n* a package; a wrapped-up package.

pardon ['pɑrdn̩] **1.** *v* to forgive. **2.** *n* forgiveness.

parent ['pɛrənt] *n* a mother or a father.

parentheses [pə'rɛnθəsiz] *n* () are parentheses. The singular is parenthesis. *Ex* (This sentence is in parentheses.)

parish ['pɛrɪʃ] **1.** *n* an area or neighborhood which has its own church. **2.** *n* one of the counties of the state of Louisiana.

park [pɑrk] **1.** *n* an open place with grass, trees, and a place for children to play. **2.** *v* to stop a vehicle and leave it in a parking space.

parliament ['pɑrləmənt] *n* the group of people elected to make the laws of a country; the name of the legislature in England and in many other countries.

parlor ['pɑrlɚ] *n* a living room.

parrot ['pɛrət] **1.** *n* a brightly colored bird often kept as a pet in a cage. *Ex* Some parrots can imitate talking. **2.** *v* to copy someone's words; to repeat someone's words.

part [pɑrt] **1.** *n* a piece of something. **2.** *v* to separate; to separate from; to divide. *Ex* He parts his hair on the left. They parted as friends.

participle ['pɑrtəsɪpl] *n* a special form of a verb. Present participles always end in *ing*. Regular past participles end in *ed*.

particle ['pɑrtɪkl] *n* a tiny bit or piece of something.

particular [pɚ'tɪkyəlɚ] **1.** *adj* single; special. **2.** *adj* fussy; very careful; choosy.

partner ['pɑrtnɚ] *n* a person who shares equally; a person who works well with some other person; a person who owns a business with you.

party ['pɑrti] *n* a celebration; a group of people having a good time in one place.

pass [pæs] **1.** *v* to move ahead of something or someone in front of you. **2.** *v* to hand something to someone.

passage ['pæsɪdʒ] *n* a way through something; a hallway.

passenger ['pæsṇdʒɚ] *n* someone who rides in a vehicle but is not the driver.

pass out ['pæs 'awt] **1.** *v* to faint; to become unconscious. **2.** *v* to hand out something to someone.

passport ['pæsport] *n* special papers from the government which help you travel in other countries.

past [pæst] **1.** *adj* ended; finished; just finished. **2.** *prep* up to and beyond. *Ex* He drove his car past me and didn't stop. **3.** *n* earlier times; history. *Ex* I love to hear stories of the past. **4.** *adj* having to do with something that happened before.

pasta ['pɑstə] *n* foods made from flour paste, such as macaroni, spaghetti, lasagne, and ravioli.

paste [peyst] *n* a thick, white liquid used to stick paper and other things together.

pastime ['pæstɑym] *n* a game or hobby that you like to do to pass the time.

pastry ['peystri] *n* a special kind of bread or cake made with flour, water, and butter. *Ex* Sometimes pastries are very fancy.

pasture ['pæstʃɚ] *n* a field where cattle and horses eat the grass.

P.A. system ['pi 'ey sɪstəm] *n* a public address system; an electronic device which makes the voice louder and broadcasts it to many people.

pat [pæt] **1.** *v* to hit something very lightly. **2.** *n* a very light tap. *Ex* He gave the dog a pat on the head.

patch [pætʃ] **1.** *n* a small piece of ground. *Ex* We grow pumpkins in the pumpkin patch. **2.** *n* a small piece of cloth used to cover a hole in clothing. **3.** *v* to sew a small piece of cloth over a hole in clothing. *Ex* I have a patch on the knee of my trousers.

patent ['pætn̩t] *n* a government paper that keeps other people from using an invention without permission.

path [pæθ] *n* a narrow way along which people may travel, usually on foot.

patience ['peyʃṇ(t)s] *n* the ability to wait for something without making a fuss or getting uncomfortable.

patient ['peyʃnt] **1.** *n* a sick person who is looked after by a doctor. **2.** *adj* able to wait for something without making a fuss or getting uncomfortable.

patio ['pætiow] *n* a paved outdoor living area next to a house. *Ex* We had a picnic on our patio last night.

patrol [pə'trowl] **1.** *v* to walk or drive around looking for people making trouble. *Ex* The police don't patrol this area enough. **2.** *n* one or more persons out on patrol; someone who helps move people through the halls or across the street.

patter ['pætɚ] **1.** *v* to tap lightly and quickly. **2.** *n* the sound of light tapping. *Ex* I hear the patter of rain on the roof.

pattern ['pætɚn] **1.** *n* a model or plan to help you make something. *Ex* I made this dress from a pattern. **2.** *n* curved or straight lines repeated many times, as on wallpaper.

pause [pɔz] **1.** *v* to stop doing something for a moment. **2.** *n* a stopping of something for a moment.

pavement ['peyvmənt] *n* the hard part of a road, sidewalk, or playground.

pavilion [pə'vɪlyən] *n* a large tent or canopy.

paw [pɔ] *n* the foot of a four-legged animal which has claws.

pay [pey] *v* to give money for something which you have bought or for work which has been done. *pt* paid. *pp* paid.

payment ['peymənt] *n* money given for goods or for work. *Ex* I have not received payment of my wages for two weeks.

P.E. ['pi 'i] *n* physical education; gym class.

pea [pi] *n* one of the round, green seeds which are used as food. *Ex* Peas grow in pods on a climbing plant.

peace [pis] *n* a time when no one is fighting; a time when there is no war.

peach [pitʃ] *n* a juicy, round fruit with a velvety skin and a stone-like seed.

peak [pik] *n* the topmost point; the top of a high mountain.

peal [pil] *n* a loud sound, such as loud bells ringing.

peanut ['pinət] *n* a kind of nut which grows underground in a pod.

peanut butter ['pinət bətɚ] *n* a paste made of ground-up peanuts. *Ex* Peanut butter is spread on bread, sometimes with jelly, to make a sandwich.

pear [pɛr] *n* a juicy fruit something like an apple, only softer and sort of cone-shaped.

pearl [pɝl] *n* a small, creamy-white jewel, used for necklaces and other jewelry. *Ex* Pearls grow inside some oyster shells.

peasant ['pɛznt] *n* a person who works the land or works as a laborer on someone's land. *Ex* Peasants are usually poor.

pebble ['pɛbl] *n* a small, smooth, roundish piece of stone.

peck [pɛk] *v* for a bird to jab with its beak. *Ex* Hens peck at their food.

peculiar [pəˈkyuwlyɚ] *adj* odd; strange; unusual.

pedal ['pɛdl] *n* a foot lever to make something work. *Ex* Bicycles, cars, and pianos all have pedals which do different things.

pedestrian [pəˈdɛstriən] *n* someone who is walking; a person on foot, not on a horse or in a car.

peel [pil] **1.** *n* the skin of fruits and vegetables. **2.** *v* to take the skin off of something, such as a piece of fruit.

peep [pip] **1.** *v* to take a quick look. **2.** *n* the sound made by a baby chick.

peer [pɪr] *v* to look very closely. *Ex* She peered at me for a very long time.

peg [pɛg] *n* a round rod of wood which you can use to hang things on or fasten things down. *Ex* Please hang your coat on the peg in the wall. Please help me hammer in this tent peg.

pellet ['pɛlət] *n* a tiny ball of something such as paper, clay, or metal.

pelt [pɛlt] **1.** *n* the hide or skin of an animal. **2.** *v* to throw; to throw down. *Ex* We pelted the kid with snowballs. The rain pelted us until we got home.

pen [pɛn] *n* a tool used for writing with ink.

penalty ['pɛnḷti] *n* a punishment for breaking a rule.

pencil ['pɛn(t)sḷ] *n* a thin tool for writing or drawing. *Ex* A pencil is made of wood with a stick of black or colored material in the center.

pencil sharpener ['pɛn(t)sḷ ʃɑrpənɚ] *n* a device which puts a new point on a pencil. *Ex* Some pencil sharpeners are electric.

pendulum ['pɛndʒələm] *n* a weight on the end of a rod that swings from side to side as in a clock.

peninsula [pə'nɪn(t)sələ] *n* an area of land which sticks far out into the sea. *Ex* The southern part of Florida is a peninsula.

penny ['pɛni] *n* a coin made of copper. It is worth one cent. *Ex* One hundred pennies equal one dollar.

people ['pipḷ] *n* men, women, boys, and girls.

pepper ['pɛpɚ] **1.** *n* a spicy powder used to flavor food. *Ex* Pepper tastes hot and can make you sneeze if you breathe it in. **2.** *v* to sprinkle pepper on food. *Ex* Mike always peppers his food whether it needs it or not. **3.** *n* a red or green vegetable, sometimes called a bell pepper.

peppermint ['pɛpɚmɪnt] *n* a green plant used for flavoring sauces, drinks, and candy.

percent [pɚ'sɛnt] *n* a fraction of one hundred. The percent sign is %. *Ex* The fraction 1/4 is 25%.

perch [pɚtʃ] **1.** *n* something a bird sits on or stands on, like a branch or a twig. **2.** *n* a kind of fish which is good to eat.

percolator ['pɚkəleytɚ] *n* a kind of coffeepot. *Ex* A percolator makes coffee by sending boiling water up and letting it run down through the ground-up coffee.

percussion [pɚ'kəʃn] **1.** *n* something striking something else. **2.** *n* musical instruments, such as drums and cymbals, that are struck.

perfect 1. *adj* ['pɚfɪkt] without any errors; without fault. **2.** *v* [pɚ'fɛkt] to make exactly right.

perform [pɚ'fɔrm] *v* to do or act; to play a part on the stage; to play a musical instrument.

performance [pɚ'fɔrmən(t)s] *n* an act; a play or other entertainment.

perfume [pɚ'fyuwm] *n* a sweet smell; a liquid having a sweet smell.

perhaps [pɚ'hæps] *adv* maybe; possibly.

peril ['pɛrəl] *n* great danger.

perimeter [pə'rɪmətɚ] *n* the outside measurement of a figure or area.

period ['pɪriəd] **1.** *n* a length of time. **2.** *n* a punctuation mark (.) which is found at the end of some kinds of sentences.

periodical [pɪri'adəkl̩] **1.** *adj* appearing at fixed intervals; published at fixed intervals. *Ex* A monthly magazine is a periodical publication. **2.** *n* a magazine or other publication which appears at fixed intervals. *Ex* The library has a large collection of periodicals.

periscope ['pɛrəskowp] *n* a tube containing mirrors used in submarines or underground so that people can see what is happening above them.

perish ['pɛrɪʃ] *v* to die; to be destroyed.

permanent ['pɚmənənt] **1.** *adj* long lasting; not ever changing. **2.** *n* a permanent wave in the hair, put into the hair to keep it curly or wavy for a long time.

permission [pɚ'mɪʃn̩] *n* freedom to do something. *Ex* The principal gave Frank permission to leave early.

permit 1. *v* [pɚ'mɪt] to allow; to give permission. **2.** *n* ['pɚmɪt] a license; a piece of paper which allows you to do something.

persist [pɚ'sɪst] *v* to keep trying to do something or asking for something.

person ['pɚsn̩] *n* a man, woman, or child.

personal ['pɚsənl̩] *adj* belonging to one person; private.

personnel [pɚsə'nɛl] **1.** *n* employees; people who work in a place. **2.** *n* an office in a company which takes care of hiring people and managing their benefits.

perspire [pɚ'spayr] *v* to give off sweat from your skin when you are very hot.

persuade [pɚ'sweyd] *v* to talk someone into doing something; to convince someone to do something.

pest [pɛst] *n* someone or something that makes difficulties for others; a nuisance; a bothersome creature such as a mouse, a cockroach, or a silverfish.

pet [pɛt] **1.** *n* an animal that is kept at home. *Ex* Dogs and cats are pets. **2.** *v* to pat and caress a person or a pet.

petal ['pɛtl̩] *n* the part of a flower that grows out from the middle; the colored part of a flower.

petticoat ['pɛtikowt] *n* a skirt worn under dresses by girls and women. Also called a slip.

petty ['pɛti] *adj* small; unimportant.

pew [pyuw] *n* a long, wooden bench with a back for people to sit on in a church.

pharmacist ['farməsɪst] *n* the person who runs a drugstore and fills prescriptions.

pharmacy ['farməsi] *n* a drugstore; a store or a department where prescriptions are filled.

phone [fown] **1.** *n* a telephone. **2.** *v* to make a telephone call.

phonograph ['fownəgræf] *n* a machine which plays phonograph records; a hifi; a stereo.

photograph ['fowtəgræf] *n* a picture taken with a camera.

photography [fə'tagrəfi] *n* using a camera to take pictures; the hobby or business of taking pictures with a camera.

phrase [freyz] *n* a group of words, usually part of a sentence.

phys. ed. ['fɪz 'ɛd] *n* physical education; P.E.

physical ['fɪzək l̩] *adj* having to do with nature or the body.

physical education [fɪzək l̩ ɛdʒə'keyʃn̩] *n* instruction in exercise and the use of the body; gym class; P.E.

physics ['fɪzɪks] *n* the science that studies force and motion.

piano [pɪ'yænow] *n* a large musical instrument with a keyboard. When you press a piano key, a hammer strikes a tightly stretched string and makes a sound.

pick [pɪk] **1.** *v* to choose; to gather. **2.** *n* a sharp tool used to break rock or hard ground.

pickle ['pɪkl̩] **1.** *v* to cook a vegetable in vinegar and spices and store it. *Ex* Last year we pickled beets. **2.** *n* a vegetable or a slice of a vegetable, usually a cucumber, which has been cooked and preserved in vinegar.

picnic ['pɪknɪk] *n* an outing where food is taken along to be eaten outside.

picture ['pɪktʃɚ] *n* a drawing, painting, or photograph.

pie [pɑy] *n* a food made of pastry on the outside and fruit or meat on the inside. *Ex* Pie usually means a piece of fruit pie eaten for dessert.

piece [pis] **1.** *n* a part or bit of something, but not all of it. **2.** *n* one of something, such as a piece of paper.

pier [pir] *n* a platform of stone, wood, or metal that reaches out over the water so that ships and boats can stop at the end of it.

pierce [pirs] *v* to make a hole with something sharp. *Ex* Chin Wu had her ears pierced yesterday.

pig [pɪg] *n* a fat farm animal with a curly tail. *Ex* We get ham and bacon from pigs.

pigeon ['pɪdʒn̩] *n* a plump bird with short legs, that makes a cooing sound. *Ex* Pigeons are often found around the buildings in a city.

pigtail ['pɪgteyl] *n* a braid of hair hanging from the back of the head.

pile [pɑyl] *n* a lot of things on top of each other, like a pile of books or a pile of junk.

pilgrim ['pɪlgrəm] **1.** *n* someone who travels a long way to visit a holy place. **2.** *n* one of the early settlers at Plymouth (New England) in 1620.

pill [pɪl] *n* a bit of medicine shaped like a tiny ball or a pellet which must be swallowed.

pillar ['pɪlɚ] *n* a large post of stone or wood, used to hold up part of a building.

pillow ['pɪlow] *n* a bag filled with feathers or some soft material, where you lay your head in bed.

pillowcase ['pɪlowkeys] *n* a covering for a pillow. It is also called a pillowslip.

pilot ['pɑylət] *n* a person who steers a ship into a harbor; a person who controls an airplane.

pimple ['pɪmpl̩] *n* a small, pointed swelling on the skin, usually on the face.

pin [pɪn] *n* a thin, pointed piece of metal wire used for fastening or holding things together.

pinch [pɪntʃ] **1.** *v* to squeeze something tightly; to clamp onto something; to press something hard between your thumb and index finger. **2.** *n* a squeezing; an act of pinching with the thumb and index finger.

pine [pɑyn] *n* an evergreen tree with cones and leaves like needles.

pineapple ['pɑynæpl̩] *n* a sweet tropical fruit with a very rough skin. *Ex* Pineapples grow in hot countries.

pink [pɪŋk] **1.** *n* a pale red color. **2.** *adj* pale red.

pint [pɑynt] *n* a measure for liquid equal to 16 ounces. *Ex* There are two pints in a quart.

pipe [pɑyp] **1.** *n* a tube, usually of metal, through which a liquid or gas flows. **2.** *n* a small bowl on the end of a tube, used for smoking tobacco.

pirate ['payrət] *n* someone who robs ships at sea.

pistol ['pɪstəl] *n* a small handgun that can be carried in the pocket.

pit [pɪt] *n* a hole in the ground.

pitch [pɪtʃ] **1.** *v* to throw something forward; to throw a baseball toward the batter. **2.** *v* to set up a tent. **3.** *n* tar; a black sticky substance. **4.** *n* the highness or lowness of a note.

pitcher ['pɪtʃɚ] **1.** *n* a large jug for holding or pouring liquids. **2.** *n* a person who throws a baseball toward the batter.

pitch pipe ['pɪtʃ payp] *n* a small musical instrument used only for giving the pitch to a chorus or for tuning other instruments.

pity ['pɪti] *n* a feeling of sadness you have because someone else is ill or unhappy.

pivot ['pɪvət] *n* the pin or center on which something turns.

pizza ['pitsə] *n* a food made of cheese, tomatoes, and other things on a disk of pastry.

place [pleys] **1.** *n* somewhere where something is. **2.** *v* to put something somewhere.

plague [pleyg] *n* a terrible illness that spreads from person to person very quickly.

plaid [plæd] *n* a piece of cloth with a checked pattern.

plain [pleyn] **1.** *adj* ordinary; not fancy or decorated. **2.** *n* a large, flat part of a country.

plan [plæn] **1.** *v* to think out how a thing can be done before you do it. **2.** *n* a model or drawing showing the shape and design of something, like a building or a town.

plane [pleyn] **1.** *n* an airplane. **2.** *n* a carpenter's tool used to make wood smooth.

planet ['plænət] *n* a body in the sky which, like the earth, goes around the sun.

plank [plæŋk] *n* a long, flat, heavy piece of wood, thicker than a board.

plant [plænt] **1.** *n* anything that grows up out of the earth, such as grass or flowers. **2.** *v* to put something into the ground so that it will grow.

plaster ['plæstɚ] **1.** *n* a mixture of sand, water, and lime which hardens when it is put on walls and ceilings. **2.** *v* to spread plaster onto walls and ceilings.

plastic ['plæstɪk] **1.** *adj* flexible; moldable. **2.** *n* material that can be molded into different shapes when it is soft. Later it becomes hard. *Ex* Combs, cups, and buckets are made of plastic.

plate [pleyt] *n* a round, flat dish for food.

platform ['plætform] **1.** *n* the raised part of a hall or theater for the speakers or actors. **2.** *n* the part of a railway station beside the tracks, where you get on a train.

play [pley] **1.** *v* to have fun; to take part in a game; to perform on a musical instrument. **2.** *n* a show acted on a stage, usually without music.

playground ['pleygrɑwnd] *n* a special place at school or in a park where children can play.

playmate ['pleymeyt] *n* someone you play with.

playtime ['pleytɑym] *n* a period of time for playing, not working or studying.

please [pliz] **1.** *v* to make someone feel happy. **2.** *adv* a word used to make a request seem more polite. *Ex* Please feed the cat.

pleasure ['plɛʒɚ] *n* a feeling of being glad and happy when you are enjoying yourself.

pleat [plit] *n* a fold in cloth, pressed or stitched down to keep it in place.

pledge [plɛdʒ] **1.** *v* to promise; to make a vow; to give your word. **2.** *n* a promise; a vow; giving your word of honor.

plenty ['plɛnti] *n* more than enough; all that is needed. *Ex* I have plenty of air in my tires. That boy is plenty of trouble.

pliers ['playɚz] *n* a tool which can pinch very hard. *Ex* Pliers are used to twist or bend wire and to tighten things.

plot [plɑt] **1.** *n* a small piece of land. *Ex* We will plant a few tomatoes on that plot. **2.** *n* the main happenings in a play or story; a wicked or evil plan. **3.** *v* to make a plan; to make an evil plan against something.

plow [plaw] **1.** *n* a farm tool which cuts into the ground and turns it over. *Ex* A plow is usually pulled by a tractor, but can be pulled by a horse or a mule. **2.** *v* to turn over the soil with a plow.

pluck [plək] *v* to pull at the strings of a musical instrument, such as a guitar.

plug [pləg] **1.** *n* a piece of metal or rubber made to fit into a hole so that liquid cannot get out. **2.** *n* the device at the end of an electric cord which is put into an outlet to get electrical power. **3.** *v* to put a plug into something. *Ex* Please plug in the lamp.

plum [pləm] *n* a juicy fruit with a stone in the middle.

plumber ['pləmɚ] *n* a person whose job is to connect up or repair water, gas, or sewer pipes.

plumbing ['pləmɪŋ] **1.** *n* the water, gas, and sewer pipes in buildings and leading to buildings. **2.** *n* bathroom facilities.

plump [pləmp] *adj* well-rounded; almost fat.

plunge [plənʤ] *v* to throw yourself into water; to rush into something.

plural ['plʊrəl] *n* the form of a word which indicates more than one. *Ex* The plural of cat is cats. The plural of child is children.

plus [pləs] **1.** *n* the sign (+) which shows that numbers are to be added together. *Ex* Put a plus before the number 4. **2.** *prep* increased by. *Ex* 2 + 2 = 4.

plus sign ['pləs sɑyn] *n* the sign (+) which indicates that numbers are to be added together; a plus.

plywood ['plɑywʊd] *n* a piece of wood made of very thin layers of wood glued together.

pneumonia [nə'mownyə] *n* a painful illness of the lungs.

poach [powtʃ] **1.** *v* to cook foods, such as fish or eggs without their shells, in very hot water. **2.** *v* to catch animals or fish on someone else's land without permission.

P.O. Box ['pi ow 'bɑks] *n* a post office box; a numbered and locked box in a post office where you can receive your mail; the number of a post office box. *Ex* Please send your payment to P.O. Box 4365.

pocket ['pɑkət] *n* a little bag sewn into clothes to put things in.

pocketknife ['pɑkətnɑyf] *n* a small folding knife which can be carried in the pocket.

pod [pɑd] *n* the outside covering of seeds.

poem ['powəm] *n* a piece of writing, like a song without music, that shows your thoughts and feelings.

poet ['powət] *n* someone who writes poems.

poetry ['powətri] **1.** *n* the art of writing poetry; the writing of poems. **2.** *n* poetry or poems. *Ex* Maria just bought a book of poetry.

point [poynt] **1.** *n* the sharp end of something, like a pin or a pencil. *Ex* That needle has a very sharp point. **2.** *v* to indicate something; to aim the index finger at something. *Ex* Don't point at people!

pointed ['poyntəd] *adj* sharp; with a point; like the end of a pin.

poison ['poyzṇ] **1.** *n* something swallowed or injected that can cause illness or death. **2.** *v* to give poison to a living creature; to put poison into something that a living creature will eat or drink.

poke [powk] *v* to jab or push something or someone suddenly.

poker ['powkɚ] **1.** *n* a metal rod used for stirring a fire. **2.** *n* a kind of a card game.

polar ['powlɚ] *adj* having to do with the North Pole or the South Pole. *Ex* Polar bears live near the North Pole.

pole [powl] **1.** *n* a long, rounded piece of wood or metal, used to hold something up, such as a flag. **2.** *n* the north or south ends of the earth's axis; the north or south ends of a magnet.

police [pə'lis] **1.** *n* people whose job is to see that the laws are obeyed; people whose job is to enforce the law. **2.** *v* to act as a police officer; to patrol.

policeman [pə'lismən] *n* a male member of a police force.

policy ['paləsi] **1.** *n* a plan for dealing with something; a course of action. **2.** *n* a contract for insurance.

polish ['palɪʃ] **1.** *v* to make something shiny by rubbing it hard, usually with a special powder, paste, or liquid. **2.** *n* a special powder, paste, or liquid for use in polishing.

polite [pə'layt] *adj* having good manners.

political [pə'lɪtəkḷ] *adj* having to do with politics.

politics ['palətɪks] *n* the activity of running government; the activity of controling government; the activity of working with and controling any group of people.

pollen ['pɑlən] *n* a yellow powder in the middle of flowers. *Ex* Pollen gives me hay fever.

poncho ['pɑntʃow] *n* an outer garment like a blanket with a hole for the head to go through.

pond [pɑnd] *n* a small lake.

pony ['powni] *n* a little horse; a young horse.

poodle ['puwdḷ] *n* a kind of dog with very curly hair, often called a French poodle.

pool [puwl] *n* a small area of water, sometimes no bigger than a puddle; a swimming pool.

poor [puwr] **1.** *adj* having little money or few belongings. **2.** *adj* not good; of low quality. *Ex* The soil is poor there, and nothing will grow.

pop [pɑp] **1.** *n* a sharp, exploding sound. **2.** *adj* popular. *Ex* I really like to listen to pop music.

popcorn ['pɑpkorn] *n* a special kind of corn that makes a popping sound and bursts open when it is heated.

popular ['pɑpyəlɚ] *adj* liked by most people. *Ex* Andy is very popular.

population [pɑpyə'leyʃṇ] **1.** *n* the people living in any country, city, town, or village. *Ex* The population of Springfield is quite small. **2.** *n* the number of people living in a country, city, town, or village. *Ex* The population of Springfield is 2,365.

porch [portʃ] *n* a covered entrance to a building.

porcupine ['porkyəpɑyn] *n* a wild animal with a coat of sharp needles or spines mixed with hairs.

pork [pork] *n* the meat of pigs and hogs.

port [port] *n* a harbor; a town with a harbor.

portable ['portəbl̩] *adj* able to be carried . *Ex* Elaine has a new portable television set.

porter ['portɚ] *n* a person whose job is to carry luggage at airports and train stations.

portion ['porʃn̩] *n* a part; a helping or serving of food.

portrait ['portrət] *n* a painting or drawing of a person.

position [pə'zɪʃn̩] **1.** *n* place; location. *Ex* Please move that chair into a new position. **2.** *n* a job. *Ex* Joel has a new position at his office.

positive ['pɑzətɪv] *adj* meaning yes; absolutely sure; not negative.

possess [pə'zɛs] *v* to own; to have.

possessive [pə'zɛsɪv] **1.** *adj* owning; having; selfish. **2.** *adj* having to do with words which show ownership. *Ex* The word *his* is a possessive pronoun.

possible ['pɑsəbl̩] *adj* able to be done.

possibly ['pɑsəbli] *adv* perhaps; maybe.

post [powst] *n* a long piece of wood or metal fastened in the ground so that it stands up; a pole.

postage ['powstɪdʒ] *n* the charge for sending something through the mails; stamps.

postcard ['pows(t)kard] *n* a thin piece of cardboard on which you can write to your friends. *Ex* Many postcards have pictures on the back.

poster ['powstɚ] *n* a large notice or picture that tells you about something that is going to happen.

postman ['pows(t)mən] *n* a man whose job is to collect and deliver the mail.

post office ['post ɔfəs] *n* the place where you buy stamps and send off letters and parcels.

postpone [pows(t)'pown] *v* to put off until another time.

pot [pɑt] *n* a deep pan for cooking; a teapot; a flowerpot.

potato [pə'teytow] *n* a vegetable grown under the ground. *Ex* Potatoes can be baked, fried, or boiled.

potter ['pɑtɚ] *n* a person who makes pots and other things out of clay.

pottery ['pɑtɚi] *n* crockery; ornaments and other things made of baked clay.

pouch [pɑwtʃ] *n* a small bag.

poultry ['powltri] *n* chickens, ducks, and geese.

pounce [pɑwn(t)s] *v* to spring or jump down on something suddenly.

pound [pɑwnd] **1.** *n* a measurement of weight equal to 16 ounces or 0.453 kilograms. **2.** *v* to beat or hammer on something. *Ex* He pounded in the nail with a hammer.

pour [por] *v* to make liquid run out of a container by tipping it forward.

pout [pɑwt] *v* to close your lips and push them out to show that you are not pleased.

powder ['pɑwdɚ] *n* very tiny dust-like bits of something. *Ex* Flour and cocoa are powders.

powder room ['pɑwdɚ ruwm] *n* a bathroom with only a toilet and a sink; a very polite name for a bathroom.

power ['pɑwɚ] *n* ability to do something.

practical ['præktɪkl̩] *adj* useful; sensible.

practice ['præktəs] **1.** *v* to do something over and over until you are good at it. **2.** *n* the doing of something over and over until you are good at it.

prairie ['prɛri] *n* a large area of flat, grassy land with very few trees.

praise [preyz] **1.** *v* to say very nice things about someone or something. **2.** *n* very nice things said about someone or something.

pray [prey] *v* to request humbly; to ask God for help.

prayer ['prɛɚ] *n* the act of praying.

preach [pritʃ] *v* to speak to others about being good, usually in church.

preacher ['pritʃɚ] *n* a minister of a church; a clergyman who preaches sermons.

precinct ['prisɪŋkt] *n* a subdivision of a county or city. *Ex* You must vote in your own precinct.

precious ['prɛʃəs] *adj* very valuable, worth lots of money.

prefer [prəˈfɚ] *v* to like one better than the other.

prefix ['prifɪks] *n* a syllable at the beginning of a word which changes its meaning. If you put *un* before the word *pleasant* it changes the meaning to *not pleasant*.

pregnant ['prɛgnənt] *adj* carrying a baby or babies not yet born.

preliminary [prəˈlɪmənɛri] *adj* first; early; before the final.

prepare [prəˈpɛr] *v* to make or get something ready. *Ex* I hardly have time to prepare dinner.

preposition [prɛpəˈzɪʃn̩] *n* a kind of word that goes before a noun or pronoun to show how it is related to other words. *Ex In, out, up, down,* and *around* are prepositions.

prescription [prə'skrɪpʃn̩] *n* a piece of paper from a doctor which states what kind of medicine you should get from a drugstore. *Ex* The pharmacist filled my prescription.

present 1. *adj* ['prɛznt] now; at this time. **2.** *adj* ['prɛznt] in attendance; not absent. **3.** *n* ['prɛznt] a gift; something nice given to someone. **4.** *v* [prɪ'zɛnt] to give something like a gift; to perform something like a play.

president ['prɛzədənt] *n* the elected head of a government or other organization.

press [prɛs] **1.** *v* to push against; to push down. **2.** *n* all of the newpapers and magazines, the companies which publish them, and the people who write what is printed in them.

pressure ['prɛʃɚ] *n* force or weight pushing against something.

pretend [prɪ'tɛnd] *v* to make believe; to do play acting.

pretty ['prɪti] *n* nice-looking; lovely; almost beautiful.

prevent [prɪ'vɛnt] *v* to stop something from happening.

previous ['priviəs] *adj* happening or occurring before some other event.

prey [prey] *n* a bird or animal that is hunted for food by another bird or animal.

price [prɑys] *n* the amount of money you must pay for something.

prick [prɪk] *v* to make a tiny hole with something sharp.

pride [prɑyd] *n* a good opinion of how clever you are and how nice you look; a feeling of pleasure about something you have done well.

priest [prist] *n* a man who is in charge of a church and who leads the prayers there.

primary ['praymɛri] **1.** *adj* first of all; initial. **2.** *n* a first election to see who will run for office in the final election.

prince [prɪn(t)s] *n* the son of a king or queen.

princess ['prɪn(t)səs] *n* the daughter of a king or queen.

principal ['prɪn(t)səpl] **1.** *n* the person in charge of a school. **2.** *adj* main; major; most important. *Ex* Your principal problem is your lack of speed.

principle ['prɪn(t)səpl] *n* a rule or standard of behavior.

print [prɪnt] **1.** *v* to press words and pictures on paper with a heavy machine. **2.** *v* to draw letters one at a time rather than writing longhand. **3.** *n* the letters that appear on a page; neatly formed letters rather than writing.

prison ['prɪzn̩] *n* a very large jail run by a state or the federal government.

prisoner ['prɪz(ə)nɚ] *n* someone who has been locked up in a jail as a punishment.

private ['prayvət] **1.** *adj* belonging to one person or a group of people; not public; personal. **2.** *n* a low-ranking soldier in the army.

prize [prayz] **1.** *n* a reward for doing something well. **2.** *v* to value something highly. *Ex* I prize that vase very highly.

probable ['prabəbl] *adj* likely to happen.

probably ['prabəbli] *adv* maybe; perhaps; likely.

problem ['prabləm] *n* a question that is difficult to answer or decide; a happening that causes trouble; something that must be solved.

proceed [prə'sid] *v* to go ahead; to go on.

procession [prə'sɛʃn̩] *n* a large number of people or vehicles moving along in a straight line.

prod [prɑd] *v* to poke; to jab.

produce 1. *v* [prə'duws] to make; to cause; to bring into being. **2.** *n* ['prowduws] fruits and vegetables.

producer [prə'duwsɚ] *n* someone who produces a film or a play; a company that produces something.

product ['prɑdəkt] *n* something which has been produced or manufactured.

profession [prə'fɛʃn̩] *n* a kind of work that needs special study and training, such as the nursing profession or the teaching profession.

professor [prə'fɛsɚ] *n* a teacher in a college or university.

profit ['prɑfət] **1.** *n* gain; the money left after all expenses have been paid. **2.** *v* to gain from; to make money from.

program ['prowgræm] **1.** *n* a printed piece of paper giving information about a performance. **2.** *n* the order of events; a course of action. **3.** *n* the coded instructions given to a computer; a computer program. **4.** *v* to give coded instructions to a computer.

progress ['prɑgrɛs] *n* movement forward or onward; improvement.

prohibit [prə'hɪbət] *v* to forbid; to prevent.

projector [prə'dʒɛktɚ] *n* a machine which shows a strong light through a film so that the picture on the film can be seen on a screen or the wall.

promise ['prɑmɪs] **1.** *v* to say that you will or will not do something without fail. **2.** *n* a pledge that you will or will not do something.

prompt [prɑmpt] *adj* quickly; at once; without delay.

prong [prɔŋ] *n* one of the sharp spikes on a fork.

pronoun ['prownɑwn] *n* a word which stands for another word. *Ex He, she,* and *it* are pronouns.

pronounce [prə'nɑwn(t)s] *v* to speak or sound out words.

pronunciation [prənən(t)si'eyʃn̩] *n* the saying of speech sounds; the way of saying speech sounds.

proof [pruwf] *n* a way of showing that what is said is true.

prop [prɑp] *n* a long piece of wood or metal that is put under something to keep it from falling down.

propel [prə'pɛl] *v* to drive forward.

propeller [prə'pɛlɚ] *n* the spinning part of a ship and of some airplanes which drives them forward.

proper ['prɑpɚ] *adj* right; as it should be.

property ['prɑpɚti] *n* something that belongs to someone.

prophecy ['prɑfəsi] *n* what someone says will happen in the future.

prophesy ['prɑfəsɑy] *v* to say what will happen in the future.

propose [prə'powz] *v* to suggest something, such as a plan of action or way of going about things.

prosecute ['prɑsəkyuwt] *v* to present the negative side of a case against a person in a court of law.

protect [prə'tɛkt] *v* to guard or defend.

protest 1. *v* [prə'tɛst] to object to something; to disagree. **2.** *n* ['prowtɛst] a complaint; a group of people all complaining about the same thing.

proton ['prowtɑn] *n* a very tiny part of an atom.

protractor ['prowtræktɚ] *n* an instrument used in measuring and drawing angles.

proud [prɑwd] *adj* having a feeling of pride; pleased that you are good at something.

prove [pruwv] *v* to show that what is said is true.

proverb ['provɚb] *n* a well-known short saying which is often used to show you how you should act, like *He who laughs last laughs longest.*

provide [prə'vɑyd] *v* to supply; to give what is needed.

provision [prə'vɪʒn̩] **1.** *n* the act of providing something for someone. **2.** *n* a rule; a part of a rule or a law. *Ex* There is a provision in your lease that says you can't keep pets.

prowl [prɑwl] *v* to move about silently and secretly.

pry [prɑy] *v* to peer into or try to find out about things that do not concern you.

psychiatrist [sə'kɑyətrəst] *n* a person whose profession is treating mental illness, sometimes with medicine. *Ex* A psychiatrist is a special kind of doctor.

psychologist [sɑy'kɑlədʒəst] *n* a person who studies behavior. *Ex* Some psychologists treat mental illness.

public ['pəblɪk] *adj* open to or belonging to everyone; the opposite of private.

publication [pəblə'keyʃn̩] **1.** *n* a book, magazine, or newspaper; anything which is printed and offered to the public. **2.** *n* the act of publishing.

publish ['pəblɪʃ] *v* to print many copies of and offer them to the public, usually for a price.

pudding ['pudɪŋ] *n* a soft, sweet food eaten at the end of a meal.

puddle ['pədl̩] *n* a small pool of water left on the ground after a rain.

puff [pəf] **1.** *v* to blow air or smoke out of the mouth. **2.** *n* a small, sudden gust of wind; a bit of air or smoke blown out of the mouth.

pull [pʊl] *v* to get hold of something and bring it towards you.

pulley ['pʊli] *n* a wheel with a hollow rim. *Ex* You put a rope around the pulley and pull on it to lift heavy things.

pullover ['pʊlowvɚ] *n* a knitted garment with sleeves; a kind of sweater.

pump [pəmp] **1.** *n* a machine used to raise water to a higher level, such as pumping it out of a well; a machine used to force air into a tire. **2.** *v* to use a pump to force liquid or air into something or to a higher level.

pumpkin ['pəmpkn̩] *n* a large yellow- or orange-colored fruit that grows on a vine on the ground.

punch [pəntʃ] *v* to hit hard, usually with your fists.

punch card ['pəntʃ kɑrd] *n* a card into which little holes are punched in a pattern that a computer can understand.

punctual ['pəŋktʃəwəl] *adj* on time; not late.

punctuate ['pəŋktʃəweyt] *v* to divide writing into phrases or sentences by using special marks, such as a period (.), a question mark (?), or a comma (,).

puncture ['pəŋktʃɚ] **1.** *v* to make a hole in something. *Ex* A nail punctured my bicycle tire. **2.** *n* a hole made by puncturing. *Ex* There is a puncture in my bicycle tire.

punish ['pənɪʃ] *v* to make someone suffer or pay for doing something wrong.

punishment ['pənɪʃmənt] *n* something that makes a person suffer or pay for doing something wrong.

pupil ['pyuwpl̩] **1.** *n* a person taught by a teacher; a student. **2.** *n* the round, dark circle in the middle of your eye through which you see.

puppet ['pəpət] *n* a doll which can be moved by pulling strings or putting your hand inside it.

puppy ['pəpi] *n* a young dog; a baby dog.

purchase ['pɚtʃəs] **1.** *v* to buy something. **2.** *n* something that you have bought; something which you are going to buy.

pure [pyuwr] *adj* clean; without fault.

purple ['pɚpl̩] **1.** *n* a color made by mixing red and blue. **2.** *adj* of a color between red and blue.

purpose ['pɚpəs] *n* something you plan to do.

purr [pɚ] **1.** *n* the sound a cat makes when it is happy. **2.** *v* to make the sound of a happy cat.

purse [pɚs] *n* a small bag to keep money in.

pursue [pɚ'suw] *v* to go after; to follow.

push [puʃ] *v* to move something away from you without lifting it.

put [put] *v* to place something somewhere. *pt* put. *pp* put.

puzzle ['pəzl̩] *n* a kind of game or question. *Ex* You have to do lots of clever thinking to get the answer to a puzzle.

puzzled ['pəzl̩d] *adj* confused.

pyramid ['pɪrəmɪd] *n* a solid shape with four flat, triangular sides, usually on a square base.

python ['paɪθɑn] *n* a large, dangerous snake that can kill living creatures by squeezing them in its coils.

Q

quack [kwæk] **1.** *n* the noise a duck makes. **2.** *v* to make the noise a duck makes.

quadrangle [ˈkwɑdræŋgl̩] *n* any four-sided shape.

quaint [kweynt] *adj* old-fashioned; slightly odd.

quake [kweyk] **1.** *v* to tremble; to shake. **2.** *n* short for earthquake.

quality [ˈkwɑləti] *n* how good or bad something is. *Ex* Clothes of good quality usually cost more but will last longer than clothes of poor quality.

quantity [ˈkwɑntəti] *n* the size, number, or amount of things.

quarrel [ˈkwɑrəl] *v* to argue or disagree with someone in an angry way.

quarry [ˈkwori] **1.** *n* a place where stone for building is dug out. **2.** *n* an animal which is being hunted.

quart [kwort] *n* a measure of liquid equal to two pints or 0.946 liters. *Ex* There are four quarts in a gallon.

quarter [ˈkwortɚ] **1.** *n* one fourth of anything; a fourth part. **2.** *n* a coin equal to one quarter of a dollar, or twenty-five cents.

queen [kwin] *n* a woman who is the royal ruler of a country; the wife of a king.

queer [kwir] *adj* odd; strange; not ordinary.

question [ˈkwɛstʃn̩] **1.** *n* something someone wants to know; something that someone asks. *Ex* I want to ask you a question. **2.** *v* to ask someone something. *Ex* The police questioned her about the accident.

question mark ['kwɛstʃn̩ mɑrk] *n* the sign (?) used in writing to indicate that a question is being asked. *Ex* Please put a question mark at the end of each question.

quick [kwɪk] *adj* fast; in a very short time.

quiet ['kwɑyət] *adj* not making a noise; silent; at rest.

quilt [kwɪlt] *n* a thick, padded bed cover.

quit [kwɪt] *v* to stop doing something; to leave off doing something; to leave. *Ex* Please quit bothering me. *pt* quit. *pp* quit.

quite [kwɑyt] *adv* completely; positively.

quiz [kwɪz] *n* a lot of questions to find out how much someone knows; a small examination.

quotation [kwow'teyʃn] *n* someone's exact words used again. *Ex* He read us a quotation from Shakespeare.

quotation marks [kwow'teyʃn̩ mɑrks] *n* the signs (") and (") which are put around someone's exact words and other special words.

quote [kwowt] *v* to read, write, or say someone's exact words.

quotient ['kwowʃn̩t] *n* the answer to a division problem in mathematics.

R

rabbit ['ræbət] *n* a small, furry animal with long ears. *Ex* We saw a rabbit hopping through the woods.

race [reys] **1.** *v* to move very quickly to get to a place before someone else does. **2.** *n* a contest to see who can get to a goal first. **3.** *n* a large group of people having a similar appearance, especially the same skin color. *Ex* Europeans, Africans, and Chinese belong to different races.

racetrack ['reystræk] *n* the path or course where a race is run.

rack [ræk] *n* a framework to keep things on, such as a hat rack.

racket ['rækət] **1.** *n* an oval frame with a network of strings and a handle. *Ex* A racket is used to strike a ball in tennis and other games. **2.** *n* a loud noise; a lot of loud noises.

radar ['reydɑr] *n* a special kind of radio which helps find objects in the dark and in fog. The word is an acronym for *radio detecting and ranging. Ex* Radar is used by ships and airplanes.

radiant ['reydiənt] **1.** *adj* bright; shining. **2.** *adj* joyful; bright and very cheerful.

radiate ['reydieyt] **1.** *v* to send out rays of heat or light. **2.** *v* to spread out in many directions from a center.

radiator ['reydieytɚ] **1.** *n* a large, iron object used to put heat into a room. **2.** *n* the part of a car engine which gives off the heat from the engine.

radio ['reydiow] *n* an instrument that brings broadcast music and voices through the air from far away.

radius ['reydiəs] *n* a straight line from the center of a circle to its outer edge.

raft [ræft] *n* floating logs or boards fastened together.

rag [ræg] *n* a piece of cloth that is old and often full of holes.

rage [reydʒ] *n* great anger; fury.

raid [reyd] *n* a quick surprise attack.

rail [reyl] **1.** *n* a wooden or metal bar used as part of a fence or railing; a bar which you hold on to when going up or down stairs. **2.** *n* one of the two (or three) metal bars used to make railroad tracks.

railing ['reylɪŋ] *n* a fence of posts and rails; a low wall made of bars to keep people from falling off of something.

railroad ['reylrowd] *n* a very long track of metal bars which trains run on. It is also called a railway.

rain [reyn] **1.** *n* drops of water that fall from the clouds. **2.** *v* for drops of water to fall from the sky.

rainbow ['reynbow] *n* a beautifully colored arch seen in the sky when the sun shines after a rain.

raincoat ['reynkowt] *n* a coat made of rubber or some other material that doesn't let the rain through.

rainfall ['reynfɔl] *n* the amount of rain that falls in a certain period of time.

raise [reyz] **1.** *v* to lift up. *Ex* Maria raised her hand to ask a question. **2.** *v* to collect. *Ex* We raised fifty dollars for charity. **3.** *v* to increase. *Ex* The landlord raised the rent.

raisin ['reyzn̩] *n* a dried grape used in baking, or eaten by itself.

rake [reyk] **1.** *n* a garden tool with a long handle and metal teeth. **2.** *v* to use a rake to pull out loose grass from the lawn or to gather leaves that have fallen from the trees.

ram [ræm] **1.** *n* a male sheep. **2.** *v* to push hard; to crash into something.

ramble ['ræmbl̩] **1.** *v* to walk about for pleasure. **2.** *v* to talk for a long time without making much sense.

ramp [ræmp] **1.** *n* a long, slanted walkway that lets people move between floors of different levels without using stairs. **2.** *n* the special road which leads cars onto a highway or expressway.

ran [ræn] *v* the past tense of run.

ranch [ræntʃ] *n* a very big farm where large numbers of cattle, horses, or sheep are raised.

rang [ræŋ] *v* the past tense of ring.

ranger ['reyndʒɚ] *n* a person whose job is to look after a forest or a large area of land.

rank [ræŋk] **1.** *n* the position of a soldier or sailor in the armed forces. *Ex* His rank is major. **2.** *n* a row or line of things or people.

ransack ['rænsæk] *v* to search through something in a rather rough and untidy way.

ransom ['ræn(t)səm] *n* money paid for the safe return of someone who has been captured or kidnapped.

rap [ræp] *v* to hit sharply.

rapid ['ræpəd] *adj* quick; speedy.

rapids ['ræpədz] *n* a rocky part of a river where the water flows very fast.

rare [rɛr] *adj* unusual; valuable.

rascal ['ræskl̩] *n* a dishonest person; a person who makes trouble and cannot be trusted.

rash [ræʃ] **1.** *n* a lot of red spots on the skin, usually as part of a disease or an allergy. **2.** *adj* without careful thought. *Ex* That was a rash decision.

raspberry ['ræzbɛri] *n* a small, soft, red fruit with lots of seeds.

rat [ræt] *n* an animal like a large mouse, with long, sharp teeth.

rate [reyt] **1.** *n* how fast something happens. **2.** *n* the cost of a unit of something. *Ex* The rate for renting a car is $45.00 a day.

rather ['ræðɚ] *adv* to some extent; somewhat; a little bit.

ratio ['reyʃow] *n* the relationship in size or number of two or more things; a proportion.

ration ['ræʃn̩] *n* a share or a portion; a limited portion.

rattle ['rætl̩] **1.** *v* to shake something so that it makes a lot of clicking noises. **2.** *n* a lot of little clicking noises heard when you shake something. **3.** *n* a baby's toy that makes lots of clicking noises when it is shaken.

rattlesnake ['rætl̩sneyk] *n* a poisonous snake with rattling, bony rings on its tail.

raw [rɔ] *adj* not cooked.

ray [rey] *n* a thin line of light like a sunbeam.

rayon ['reyɑn] *n* a man-made, silky material. *Ex* Dresses, blouses, ties, and other clothes are made of rayon.

razor ['reyzɚ] *n* a very sharp instrument, used to shave hair off.

reach [ritʃ] **1.** *v* to stretch out far enough to touch or get hold of something. **2.** *v* to get to a place; to arrive.

react [ri'ækt] *v* to make a response to something. *Ex* I don't know how to react to this problem.

reaction [ri'ækʃn̩] *n* a response to something.

read 1. *v* [rid] to follow and understand printed or written words. *pt* read. *pp* read. **2.** *v* [rɛd] the past tense and past participle of read.

reading ['ridɪŋ] **1.** *n* for someone to read. **2.** *n* the study of how to read; a school course in how to read.

ready ['rɛdi] *adj* prepared; able to do something at once.

real [ril] *adj* true; not made up or imaginary.

real estate ['ril əsteyt] **1.** *n* land; a piece of land and the house on it. **2.** *n* the business of selling land, or land and houses.

realize ['ri(ə)laɪz] *v* to understand clearly.

really ['rili] *adv* without question; in fact.

reap [rip] *v* to cut and gather in crops of grain.

rear [rir] **1.** *n* the back part. **2.** *v* to raise offspring.

reason ['rizn̩] *n* why something is done or said; an explanation.

reasonable ['rizənəbl̩] *adj* sensible; fair; good enough.

rebel [rɪ'bɛl] *v* to go against someone in authority.

receipt [ri'sit] *n* a written or printed note that proves you have paid for something.

receive [rɪ'siv] *v* to take something that is given to you or sent to you.

receiver [rɪ'sivɚ] **1.** *n* a person who receives something. **2.** *n* the part of a telephone which you hold to your ear and mouth.

recent ['risn̩t] *adj* happening a short time ago.

receptionist [rɪ'sɛpʃənɪst] *n* a person whose job is to greet people and find out what they want when they come into an office.

recess 1. *v* [rɪ'sɛs] to take a break in a meeting or some other activity. *Ex* Congress recessed for the holidays. **2.** *n* ['risɛs] a place set back in a wall. *Ex* The drinking fountain is in a recess in the west wall. **3.** *n* ['risɛs] a rest from work or lessons; a time when schoolchildren can go out to play between classes.

recipe ['rɛsəpi] *n* information that tells how to cook something and what to put into it.

recite [rɪ'sɑyt] *v* to say something aloud that you have learned by memory. *Ex* Jorge recited the poem.

reckless ['rɛkləs] *adj* careless; not thinking or caring about what could happen.

recognize ['rɛkəgnɑyz] *v* to know something because you have seen it before.

recommend [rɛkə'mɛnd] *v* to state that something or someone is worthy.

record 1. *v* [rɪ'kord] to write down something; to copy sounds or images onto tape or film. **2.** *n* ['rɛkɚd] a phonograph disk; a phonograph recording. **3.** *n* ['rɛkɚd] the best that someone has ever done in a contest. *Ex* Margie broke the record for the 50 meter race.

recorder [rɪ'kordɚ] **1.** *n* an instrument which records sounds or images on tape. **2.** *n* a musical instrument you blow into to make musical sounds.

record player ['rɛkɚd pleyɚ] *n* an instrument for playing phonograph records; a hifi; a stereo.

recover [rɪ'kəvɚ] **1.** *v* to find or get something back that has been lost. **2.** *v* to get better after being ill.

recreation [rɛkri'eyʃn̩] *n* something people like to do in their free time, such as sports or gardening.

rectangle ['rɛktæŋgl̩] *n* a shape that has four sides and four right angles but is not a square. Two of the sides are longer than the other two. *Ex* A dollar bill is shaped like a rectangle.

rectangular [rɛk'tæŋgyəlɚ] *adj* shaped like a rectangle.

recur [rɪ'kɚ] *v* to happen again.

red [rɛd] **1.** *n* the color of fire engines and seven of the stripes of the U.S. flag. **2.** *adj* of a red color.

redhead ['rɛdhɛd] *n* a person with reddish or copper-colored hair.

reduce [rɪ'duws] **1.** *v* to make something smaller. **2.** *v* to grow smaller; to lose weight.

reed [rid] *n* a tall, stiff grass that grows in or near water. *Ex* Reeds are usually hollow.

reef [rif] *n* a line of rocks lying just under the water, so that the waves break over it.

reek [rik] *v* to smell very strong and bad. *Ex* That cheese really reeks.

reel [ril] *n* a plastic or metal holder for recording tape or movie film.

refer [rɪ'fɚ] **1.** *v* to mention or speak of. *Ex* Please don't refer to that problem again. **2.** *v* to suggest that someone look in a particular place for something; to suggest that someone ask a particular person. *Ex* He referred me to the dictionary for the answer to my question.

referee [rɛfə'ri] *n* someone who has to see that rules are obeyed in games and sports.

reference ['rɛf(ə)rən(t)s] **1.** *n* the mention of something. *Ex* Joel made reference to my new bicycle. **2.** *adj* having to do with the kind of book in which you look up information, such as a dictionary or encyclopedia. *Ex* Please look it up in a reference work.

reflect [rɪˈflɛkt] *v* to throw back light or heat from a shiny surface.

refreshment [rɪˈfrɛʃmənt] *n* a light snack or a drink that makes you feel better when you are tired.

refrigerator [rɪˈfrɪdʒəˌeytɚ] *n* a machine which keeps the food inside cold and fresh. *Ex* The refrigerator in our kitchen is broken.

refuge [ˈrɛfyuwdʒ] *n* a shelter; a safe place for people or animals.

refuse [rɪˈfyuwz] *v* to say that you will not do something you are asked to do.

regard [rɪˈgɑrd] **1.** *v* to look at. **2.** *v* to think well or affectionately of someone. **3.** *n* a good or affectionate thought about someone. *Ex* John sent his regards to our family.

region [ˈridʒn̩] *n* an area; an area of a country.

register [ˈrɛdʒəstɚ] **1.** *v* to sign up for something; to enroll in a school or a class. **2.** *n* a written list of names or things for a special purpose.

regret [rɪˈgrɛt] *v* to feel sorry about something.

regular [ˈrɛgyəlɚ] *adj* usual; always happening at the same time.

regulate [ˈrɛgyəleyt] *v* to control; to provide rules and enforce them.

regulation [rɛgyəˈleyʃn̩] **1.** *n* an act of regulating. **2.** *n* a rule or part of a law.

regulator [ˈrɛgyəleytɚ] *n* a thing or person which regulates or controls.

rehearse [rɪˈhɚs] *v* to practice for a performance.

reign [reyn] *n* the period of time that a king or queen rules a country.

reindeer ['reyndir] *n* a kind of large deer that lives in very cold places. *Ex* They say that Santa Claus's sleigh is pulled by reindeer.

reins [reynz] *n* the leather straps used to guide a horse.

rejoice [rɪ'dʒoys] *v* to feel full of joy; to celebrate and express your happiness.

relative ['rɛlətɪv] *n* a person who is part of your family. *Ex* Your mother, father, brothers, sisters, grandparents, aunts, uncles, etc., are all your relatives.

relax [rɪ'læks] *v* to rest and take it easy.

release [rɪ'lis] *v* to let go; to set free.

relent [rɪ'lɛnt] *v* to become less angry at someone; to forgive; to give in.

reliable [rɪ'layəbl̩] *adj* able to be trusted.

relief [rɪ'lif] *n* freedom from pain or trouble; the state of having trouble or pain just taken away.

relieve [rɪ'liv] **1.** *v* to give help; to reduce pain or worry. **2.** *v* to take over work from someone else.

religion [rɪ'lɪdʒn̩] *n* a system of beliefs in God or gods.

religious [rɪ'lɪdʒəs] *adj* believing in and worshipping God or gods.

rely [rɪ'lay] *v* to trust or depend on.

remain [rɪ'meyn] *v* to stay behind; to be left behind.

remainder [rɪ'meyndɚ] **1.** *n* the number left after subtracting another number; anything which remains or is left over. **2.** *n* the number left in a division problem. *Ex* A remainder is left because it is smaller than the divisor and cannot be divided.

remark [rɪ'mɑrk] *n* something that is said.

remember [rɪ'mɛmbɚ] *v* to keep something in your memory; to bring something into your thinking from your memory; the opposite of forget.

remind [rɪ'mɑynd] *v* to make someone remember something; to help someone remember something.

remote control [rɪmowt kn̩'trowl] **1.** *n* controling something from a distance. **2.** *n* a device that will control something from a distance. *Ex* The remote control for our television is broken.

remove [rɪ'muwv] *v* to take away; to take out; to take off.

renew [rɪ'nuw] **1.** *v* to make new; to make something seem like new. **2.** *v* to get permission from a librarian to borrow a book for a time longer than you had asked for at first. *Ex* John had to renew his library book because he had not finished it.

rent [rɛnt] **1.** *v* to pay someone money for the use of something. *Ex* We rent our apartment from a landlord. **2.** *v* to charge someone money for the use of your property. *Ex* Our landlord rents an apartment to us. **3.** *n* money paid or collected for renting. *Ex* I paid the rent yesterday.

repair [rɪ'pɛr] *v* to mend; to fix; to make things right.

repeat [rɪ'pit] *v* to say or do over again.

repent [rɪ'pɛnt] **1.** *v* to stop doing wrong and promise to do right. **2.** *v* to be sorry; to regret.

replace [rɪ'pleys] *v* to put back; to substitute one for the other.

reply [rɪ'plɑy] **1.** *v* to answer. **2.** *n* an answer.

report [rɪ'port] **1.** *v* to write or tell about something that has happened. **2.** *n* a piece of writing or a speech telling about something that has happened. **3.** *n* the noise made by a cannon or a gun.

report card [rɪ'pɔrt kɑrd] *n* a card or piece of paper which tells how well you are doing in school.

reporter [rɪ'pɔrtɚ] *n* a person whose job is to gather news for radio, television, or a newspaper.

represent [rɛprə'zɛnt] *v* to speak or act for someone or something else.

representative [rɛprə'zɛntətɪv] **1.** *n* a person who speaks or acts for someone else. **2.** *n* a person elected to a legislature; a person elected to the U.S. House of Representatives.

reproach [rɪ'prowtʃ] *v* to scold or blame a person for doing something wrong.

reproduction [riprə'dəkʃn̩] *n* the process of producing babies.

reptile ['rɛptɑyl] *n* a cold-blooded, scaly animal, such as a snake or a crocodile.

republic [ri'pəblɪk] *n* a type of government or a type of country where the voters elect people to make the laws and people to run the government.

Republican [rɪ'pəblɪkn̩] *n* one of the two major political parties in the U.S.

request [rɪ'kwɛst] *v* to ask someone to do something; to ask for something.

require [rɪ'kwɑyr] *v* to need.

requirements [rɪ'kwɑyrmənts] *n* a set of things you must do to achieve something. *Ex* What are the requirements for joining your club?

rescue ['rɛskyuw] **1.** *v* to save; to take someone away from danger. **2.** *n* saving someone or something from danger.

resemble [rɪ'zɛmbl] *v* to look like someone or something else. *Ex* You resemble your older brother.

reservoir ['rɛzɚvwɑr] *n* a man-made lake for storing water.

resist [rɪ'zɪst] *v* to struggle or fight against someone who is trying to make you do something you do not want to do.

resolve [rɪ'zɑlv] **1.** *v* to decide to do something; to make up your mind. **2.** *v* to settle an argument; to find a solution to some difficulty.

respect [rɪ'spɛkt] **1.** *v* to admire or have a very good opinion of someone. **2.** *n* a good opinion about someone.

responsibility [rɪspɑnsə'bɪləti] **1.** *n* a duty or task. **2.** *n* the state of being responsible for something.

responsible [rɪ'spɑnsəbl] *adj* looking after the safe keeping of someone or something. *Ex* Your parents are responsible for you.

rest [rɛst] **1.** *v* to stop working or playing and be quiet for a time. *Ex* I have worked very hard, and now it is time to rest. **2.** *n* a period when someone or something stops working; a time when someone sits or lies down. *Ex* I have worked very hard, and I need a rest. **3.** *n* the remainder; the part that is left. *Ex* I will eat the rest of the bread.

restaurant ['rɛst(ə)rənt] *n* a place where a person can buy and eat food. *Ex* You don't usually eat snacks at a restaurant, only full meals.

restrain [rɪ'streyn] *v* to hold back.

restroom ['rɛstruwm] *n* a bathroom in a public building. There is not usually a bathtub in a restroom, only toilets and sinks.

result [rɪ'zəlt] *n* whatever happens at the end of some action. *Ex* If you go out without your coat, you may catch cold as a result.

retire [rɪ'tɑyr] **1.** v to go away; to go to bed. **2.** v to end a job or career, usually when you have grown old.

retreat [rɪ'trit] v to go back or run away from danger.

return [rɪ'tɚn] v to come back; to give something back.

reveal [rɪ'vil] v to show something that is hidden or secret.

revenge [rɪ'vɛndʒ] **1.** v to get even with someone who has hurt or injured you; to punish someone who has hurt or injured you. **2.** n an act of getting even with someone.

reverse [rɪ'vɚs] **1.** adj in the opposite way; in the other way. Ex Please put these numbers into reverse order. **2.** v to make something turn around or go the other way. Ex You must reverse the letter which you have printed backwards. **3.** n the gear in a car which makes the car go backwards. Ex Please put the car into reverse and back up.

review [rɪ'vyuw] **1.** v to go over something; to look at something like a book or a film and then tell about it. **2.** n the act of studying or going over something; a piece of writing which tells about a book or a film.

revolt [rɪ'vowlt] **1.** v to rebel against authority; to turn against the government; to make war against the government. **2.** n a revolution; a turning against authority.

revolution [rɛvə'luwʃn̩] n the overthrowing of a government by rebels who want another kind of government.

revolve [rɪ'vɑlv] v to turn around in a circle; to make something turn around in a circle.

revolver [rɪ'vɑlvɚ] n a kind of pistol.

revolving door [rɪvɑlvɪŋ 'dor] n a special kind of doorway which is shaped like an X when you look at it from above. The X turns, and you get in or out by walking between the arms of the X while it is turning.

reward [rɪ'word] **1.** n something you get in return for something you have done, such as a prize for winning a race. **2.** *v* to give someone a prize for winning or doing something well.

rhyme [raym] **1.** *n* words that have the same sounds at the end. *Ex* Blue, shoe, and zoo make a rhyme. **2.** *v* for words to have the same sounds at the end. *Ex* Blue, shoe, and zoo rhyme.

rhythm ['rɪðəm] *n* a regular pattern or beat of music that you can keep time to.

rhythm band ['rɪðəm bænd] *n* a school band where the students strike different instruments in time with music.

rib [rɪb] *n* one of the curved bones running from the backbone to the front of the body.

ribbon ['rɪbən] *n* a narrow piece of silky or velvety cloth. *Ex* She put a yellow ribbon in her hair. Mary wrapped the gift and tied the package with a ribbon.

rice [rays] *n* the seeds of a food plant which is grown where it is very wet, sometimes in a flooded field. *Ex* A grain of rice is hard, but it becomes soft when it is cooked.

rich [rɪtʃ] **1.** *adj* having lots of money. **2.** *adj* very fatty, creamy, or sweet. *Ex* This ice cream is very rich.

rid [rɪd] *v* to remove entirely; to become free of something; to make something free of something. *Ex* You must rid this house of pests. *pt* rid. *pp* rid.

ridden ['rɪdn̩] *v* the past participle of ride.

riddle ['rɪdl] *n* a special kind of question. *Ex* You have to be clever to guess the answer to a riddle.

ride [rayd] *v* to be carried in a vehicle or on an animal. *pt* rode. *pp* ridden.

rider ['raydɚ] *n* someone who rides.

ridge [rɪdʒ] *n* a long, narrow top of a hill between valleys; a narrow, raised strip of something.

ridicule ['rɪdəkyuwl] *v* to make fun of or laugh at someone.

ridiculous [rɪ'dɪkyələs] *adj* silly; foolish; laughable.

rifle ['rɑyfl̩] *n* a long gun.

right [rɑyt] **1.** *n* the right-hand side; the opposite of left. **2.** *adj* correct; proper; the opposite of wrong.

right angle ['rɑyt 'æŋgl̩] *n* an angle of 90 degrees. *Ex* The letter L has one right angle. The corners of a square or a rectangle are right angles.

rim [rɪm] *n* the outside edge of something round, like the rim of a wheel.

ring [rɪŋ] **1.** *n* a piece of circular jewelry that is worn on a finger. *Ex* My mother takes off her rings when she washes the dishes. **2.** *n* a circle. *Ex* Please draw a ring around the correct answer. **3.** *n* a bell-like sound. **4.** *v* to make a bell ring. *pt* rang. *pp* rung.

ringmaster ['rɪŋmæstɚ] *n* a man who announces the acts in a circus.

rink [rɪŋk] *n* a large circle of ice that people can ice-skate on; a large, smooth floor that people can roller-skate on.

rinse [rɪn(t)s] *v* to take soap away by washing in clear water.

riot ['rɑyət] *n* a noisy disturbance by a lot of people, often dangerous and violent.

rip [rɪp] **1.** *v* to tear something. **2.** *n* a torn place in something.

ripe [rɑyp] *adj* ready to eat, usually said of fruit or vegetables.

ripple ['rɪpl̩] *n* a small wave or movement on the surface of water.

rise [rɑyz] *v* to move upwards; to go higher. *pt* rose. *pp* risen.

risen ['rɪzn̩] *v* the past participle of rise.

risk [rɪsk] **1.** *n* a chance that you may lose something or be harmed in some way. **2.** *v* to take a chance; to take a chance of losing or getting injured.

river ['rɪvɚ] *n* a large amount of water that flows across the land into a lake or sea.

roach [rowtʃ] *n* short for the word cockroach, an insect pest.

road [rowd] *n* a hard, level surface used for vehicles to travel on.

roam [rowm] *v* to wander about.

roar [ror] **1.** *n* a loud, deep noise. *Ex* The tiger's roar is frightening. The roar of the sea woke me up. **2.** *v* to make a loud, deep noise.

roast [rowst] **1.** *v* to cook meat in an oven. **2.** *n* a large piece of meat like beef or pork that is cooked in an oven.

rob [rɑb] *v* to take something that is not yours; to steal by force.

robber ['rɑbɚ] *n* someone who steals by force.

robbery ['rɑbɚi] *n* a theft; stealing.

robe [rowb] *n* a loose garment that covers a person down to the ankles.

robin ['rɑbən] *n* a wild bird with an orange breast and brown and gray feathers.

robot ['rowbɑt] *n* a machine built to look like a human; a machine built to do the work of a human.

rock [rɑk] **1.** *n* a large piece of stone. **2.** *v* to move back and forth or from side to side. *Ex* Babies like to be rocked.

rocket ['rɑkət] **1.** *n* a machine that is shot up into space, sometimes carrying astronauts. **2.** *n* a type of fireworks that is shot up into the air.

rod [rɑd] *n* a long, thin stick or bar, usually of wood or metal.

rode [rowd] *v* the past tense of ride.

roll [rowl] **1.** *v* to move along by turning over and over; to move something by turning it over and over. **2.** *n* a kind of bread or pastry.

roller ['rowlɚ] **1.** *n* something that rolls things flat and smooth. **2.** *n* a hair curler.

roller skates ['rowlɚ skeyts] *n* skates with wheels.

rolling pin ['rowlɪŋ pɪn] *n* a tube-shaped piece of wood or metal used to flatten dough or pastry before it is cooked.

roof [rʊf, ruwf] *n* the covering on top of a building or a car.

room [ruwm] *n* a part of the inside of a house, such as a bedroom or kitchen.

rooster ['ruwstɚ] *n* an adult male chicken; a cock.

root [rʊt, ruwt] *n* the part of a plant or tree that grows underground.

rope [rowp] *n* a very thick string or cord.

rose [rowz] **1.** *n* a beautiful, sweet-smelling flower with a prickly stem. **2.** *v* the past tense of rise.

rot [rɑt] *v* to decay; to go bad. *Ex* The apples fell off the tree and rotted on the ground.

rotate ['rowteyt] *v* to turn around; to turn something around.

rotten ['rɑtn̩] *adj* rotted; decayed; spoiled. *Ex* The apples on the ground are rotten.

rough [rəf] *adj* not smooth; bumpy.

round [rɑwnd] *adj* curved like a circle; in the shape of a ball.

route [rɑwt, ruwt] *n* the exact way to get from one place to another.

row 1. *n* [row] a line of things or people. **2.** *v* [row] to move a boat through the water, using oars. **3.** *n* [rɑw] a noisy fight or quarrel.

royal ['roy(ə)l] *adj* having to do with a king or a queen.

rub [rəb] *v* to move something against something else, such as putting polish on furniture with a cloth. *Ex* He rubbed the brass until it shined brightly.

rubber ['rəbɚ] *n* a material that stretches.

rubber band [rəbɚ 'bænd] *n* a ring made of rubber, used for holding papers or other things together.

rubber stamp [rəbɚ 'stæmp] *n* a small block of wood with a layer of rubber on it. The rubber is molded with letters spelling out a message. A rubber stamp is used with a stamp pad.

rubbish ['rəbɪʃ] *n* something which is worthless; trash; garbage.

ruby ['ruwbi] *n* a jewel, deep red in color.

rudder ['rədɚ] *n* a piece of wood or metal at the back of a boat or an airplane, used for steering.

rude [ruwd] *adj* bad-mannered; the opposite of polite.

rug [rəg] *n* a small floor mat or carpet; a carpet.

rugged ['rəgəd] *adj* rough and strong.

ruin ['ruwən] **1.** *v* to spoil or destroy; to make something useless. **2.** *n* an old building that is falling down.

rule [ruwl] **1.** *n* a ruler used for measuring. **2.** *n* a law or a regulation; what a person must or must not do. **3.** *v* to run a country or a government, as a king or a queen.

ruler ['ruwlɚ] **1.** *n* a straight piece of wood used for measuring things. **2.** *n* a person who is the head of a country.

rum [rəm] *n* a liquor made of sugarcane.

rumble ['rəmbl̩] *n* a low-pitched, deep, rolling sound, like faraway thunder.

rumor ['ruwmɚ] *n* something said about a person or events that may or may not be true.

run [rən] **1.** *v* to move quickly on your feet. *pt* ran. *pp* run. **2.** *n* the act of moving quickly on your feet from one place to another.

rung [rəŋ] **1.** *n* a piece of wood or metal used as a step in a ladder. **2.** *v* the past participle of ring.

rural ['rʊrəl] *adj* having to do with the country; the opposite of urban.

rush [rəʃ] **1.** *v* to hurry; to move quickly to get somewhere on time. **2.** *n* a great hurry. **3.** *n* a tall kind of grass growing near water.

rust [rəst] **1.** *n* a brownish-red coating that appears on iron or steel after it has been wet for some time. **2.** *v* for iron or steel to get a brownish-red coating after being wet for some time.

rustle ['rəsl̩] *n* a soft, whispering sound, such as is made by dry leaves rubbing together.

rut [rət] *n* a deep track made by a wheel in soft ground; a deep track or groove.

rye [rɑy] **1.** *n* a kind of grain which is used in a special kind of bread. **2.** *n* rye bread; rye bread used for a sandwich. *Ex* Please give me a ham on rye sandwich.

S

sack [sæk] *n* a large bag made of cloth, paper, or plastic.

sacred ['seykrəd] *adj* holy.

sad [sæd] *adj* not happy; feeling sorry.

saddle ['sædl̩] *n* a leather seat for a rider on a horse or a bicycle.

safari [sə'fɑri] *n* an expedition in Africa in search of wild animals.

safe [seyf] **1.** *adj* out of danger; not able to be hurt. **2.** *adj* having arrived safely at a base or at home plate in baseball. **3.** *n* a very strong metal box used to lock money and valuable things away safely.

safety ['seyfti] *n* freedom from harm or danger.

safety pin ['seyfti pɪn] *n* a wire pin, folded so that the sharp point is hidden in a metal cover.

sag [sæg] *v* to sink down or bend in the middle; to hang limply or droop.

said [sɛd] *v* the past tense and past participle of say.

sail [seyl] **1.** *n* a piece of cloth fastened to a ship's mast. *Ex* Sails catch the wind so that the ship is moved along. **2.** *v* for a ship to move along using sails to catch the wind.

sailor ['seylɚ] *n* someone who works on a ship; a person who sails a boat for fun.

saint [seynt] *n* a very good and holy person.

salad ['sæləd] *n* a mixture of cold vegetables, such as lettuce, tomatoes, and celery. *Ex* Some salads have meat, fish, or eggs added to them. Other salads are made only of fruit.

salary ['sæl(ə)ri] *n* money paid regularly for work done.

sale [seyl] **1.** *n* the exchange of something for money; an act of selling. **2.** *n* a period when stores sell their goods more cheaply.

salesclerk ['seylzklək] *n* a person who sells things in a store.

saliva [sə'lɑyvə] *n* the liquid that keeps the inside of your mouth moist.

salmon ['sæmən] *n* a large fish with silvery scales and pink flesh.

salt [sɔlt] **1.** *n* a white powder that we get from the earth and from seawater. *Ex* It is used in cooking and at meals to make food taste better. **2.** *v* to put salt on food.

salute [sə'luwt] **1.** *v* to greet someone by raising your right hand to your forehead. **2.** *n* a greeting where the right hand is raised to the forehead.

same [seym] *adj* not different; like something else.

sample ['sæmpl] *n* one of, or a small part of, something that shows what the rest is like. *Ex* Please give me a sample of that candy.

sand [sænd] *n* small grains of rock which we find in large quantities at the beach or in the desert.

sandals ['sændlz] *n* light shoes held on the feet with straps.

sandwich ['sændwɪtʃ] *n* two pieces of bread with meat or some other food between them.

sang [sæŋ] *v* the past tense of sing.

sanitary ['sænətɛri] *adj* free from germs; very clean.

sanitation [sænə'teyʃn̩] **1.** *n* cleanliness. **2.** *n* the name of a department in a city which cares for the sewers and collects the garbage.

sank [sæŋk] *v* the past tense of sink.

sap [sæp] *n* the juice of plants and trees.

sardine [sɑr'din] *n* a small fish, usually sold in flat cans.

sash [sæʃ] **1.** *n* a thin strip of ribbon worn around the waist or over the shoulder. **2.** *n* the part of a window that slides up and down.

sat [sæt] *v* the past tense and past participle of sit.

satellite ['sætl̩ayt] *n* a small planet or other object that revolves around another planet. *Ex* The moon is the earth's satellite.

satin ['sætn̩] *n* a soft, shiny cloth.

satisfactory [sætəs'fæktɚi] *adj* good enough; pleasing.

satisfy ['sætəsfɑy] *v* to do all you can to please someone, or to fill a need.

sauce [sɔs] *n* a liquid that is poured over food to give it more flavor.

saucepan ['sɔspæn] *n* a cooking pot with a lid and a handle.

saucer ['sɔsɚ] *n* a small, curved plate put under a cup.

sausage ['sɔsɪdʒ] *n* a meat mixture chopped up very small and put into a thin tube made of animal skin.

savage ['sævɪdʒ] *adj* fierce and cruel; wild.

save [seyv] **1.** *v* to keep something for use later on. **2.** *v* to help someone who is in danger; to rescue someone or something.

savings ['seyvɪŋz] *n* money that you have saved; money that you keep in a bank to earn interest.

saw [sɔ] **1.** *n* a metal tool with pointed teeth on one edge, used for cutting wood. **2.** *v* the past tense of see.

sawdust ['sɔdəst] *n* powder from wood that has been sawed.

say [sey] *v* to speak; to tell something. *pt* said. *pp* said.

saying ['seyɪŋ] *n* something which is said over and over. *Ex* I am tired of hearing old sayings from you.

scab [skæb] *n* the dry crust on a sore place or wound when it begins to heal.

scald [skɔld] *v* to burn someone or something with a very hot liquid or steam.

scale [skeyl] **1.** *n* one of the many small, hard flakes that cover the skin of snakes and fish. **2.** *n* a set of notes in music. **3.** *n* a machine used for weighing things.

scar [skɑr] *n* the mark left on your skin after a sore or wound has healed.

scarce [skɛrs] *adj* not enough; difficult to find; rare.

scarcely ['skɛrsli] *adv* hardly; not enough.

scarcity ['skɛrsɪti] *n* a shortage or absence of something.

scarecrow ['skɛrkrow] *n* something, usually like the dummy figure of a man, which is put in a field to frighten the birds away from the crops.

scared [skɛrd] *adj* afraid; frightened.

scarf [skɑrf] *n* a long, thick piece of material you wear to keep your neck or head warm.

scarlet ['skɑrlət] **1.** *n* a bright red color. **2.** *adj* of a bright red color.

scatter ['skætɚ] *v* to throw things around in all directions, like scattering bread crumbs on the ground for birds to eat.

scene [sin] *n* a view; the place where something happens; part of a play.

scenery ['sin(ə)ri] **1.** *n* what you see when you look around you, such as hills, fields, and trees. **2.** *n* the things used on a stage to make it look like a real place.

scent [sɛnt] *n* a smell; the smell which an animal leaves behind.

schedule ['skɛdʒuwl]] **1.** *n* a list of things and the times they are supposed to happen. **2.** *v* to put something or someone's name on a schedule.

scholar ['skɑlɚ] *n* a person who studies; a pupil or a student.

scholarship ['skɑlɚʃɪp] **1.** *n* knowledge or learning. **2.** *n* a sum of money given to a student because of high grades. *Ex* Maria got a scholarship to help her go to college.

school [skuwl] *n* a place where people go to learn.

science ['sɑyən(t)s] *n* knowledge gotten by careful study and testing of things, often having to do with nature. *Ex* Chemistry is a natural science.

scientist ['sɑyəntəst] *n* someone who finds out why things happen on earth and in space.

scissors ['sɪzɚz] *n* a cutting tool like two knives fastened together in the middle. *Ex* A pair of scissors is used to cut paper or cloth.

scold [skowld] *v* to speak crossly to a person who has done something wrong.

scoop [skuwp] **1.** *n* a tool shaped like a deep shovel. *Ex* A scoop is used to dig up earth or sand. Small scoops are used to measure dry foods such as sugar or flour. **2.** *v* to dig or measure with a scoop.

scooter ['skuwtɚ] *n* a small, two-wheeled vehicle, moved by pushing with one foot or by an engine.

scorch [skortʃ] *v* to burn slightly; to dry up with heat. *Ex* Mother scorched my new blouse with the iron.

score [skor] **1.** *n* the number of points or goals made in a game. **2.** *v* to make points or goals in a game.

scoreboard ['skorbord] *n* a large panel or board used to show the score of a game.

scorn [skorn] **1.** *v* to think that something or someone is not worth bothering about, or no good. **2.** *n* distaste; sneering. *Ex* He looked with scorn at the bad food.

scout [skɑwt] **1.** *n* someone sent to spy on the enemy. **2.** *n* a Boy Scout; a Girl Scout. **3.** *v* for someone to go ahead of the group and come back and tell what lies ahead. *Ex* Tommy scouted ahead of the rest of the hikers and found a river.

scowl [skɑwl] **1.** *v* to frown. **2.** *n* a frown.

scramble ['skræmbl] **1.** *v* to climb on rough ground, usually on the hands and feet and usually fast. **2.** *v* to mix up thoroughly. *Ex* John scrambled eggs in the frying pan.

scrap [skræp] **1.** *n* a small piece of something, like paper or cloth. **2.** *n* a fight; a quarrel. **3.** *v* to fight; to quarrel.

scrape [skreyp] *v* to rub against something with a rough or sharp edge.

scratch [skrætʃ] **1.** *n* a mark made with something sharp. **2.** *n* a long, narrow injury of the skin. *Ex* I got a bad scratch from the cat. **3.** *v* to scrape with fingernails or claws. *Ex* The cat scratched me.

scrawl [skrɑwl] *v* to write in a messy way that is not easy to read.

scream [skrim] **1.** *n* a very loud, high-pitched cry of surprise, pain, or fear. **2.** *v* to make a loud, high-pitched cry of surprise, pain, or fear.

screech [skritʃ] **1.** *n* a piercing scream. **2.** *v* to make a piercing scream.

screen [skrin] **1.** *n* a lightweight wall you can move about. **2.** *n* what a television or movie picture is shown on.

screw [skruw] *n* a special kind of thick nail with grooves. *Ex* Screws are used to hold pieces of wood or metal together.

screwdriver ['skruwdrɑyvɚ] *n* a tool used to turn a screw into a hole in wood or metal

scribble ['skrɪbl̩] *v* to write in a careless and messy way.

script [skrɪpt] *n* handwriting; printing that looks like handwriting.

scrub [skrəb] *v* to rub something, usually with a brush, to get it clean

sculpture ['skəlptʃɚ] *n* the art of carving stone or wood, or working clay or metal into statues and beautiful designs.

scurry ['skɚi] *v* to hurry along.

sea [si] *n* the salty water that covers part of the earth where there is no land.

seafood ['sifuwd] *n* fish and shellfish eaten as food.

sea gull ['si gəl] *n* a seabird, usually colored gray and white. *Ex* The sea gull makes a loud, screeching sound.

seal [sil] **1.** *n* a fish-eating animal that can also live on land. *Ex* Seals are mammals with beautiful, brown fur. **2.** *v* to close or fasten something so that it cannot be opened without breaking the fastening.

seam [sim] *n* a line where two pieces of material are joined together by sewing.

seaplane ['sipleyn] *n* an airplane that can take off from and land on the sea or the land.

search [sɚtʃ] **1.** v to look everywhere for something. **2.** n the act of looking everywhere for something.

searchlight ['sɚtʃlayt] n a very powerful beam of light that shows things clearly in the dark.

seashell ['siʃɛl] n the hard covering on some kinds of fish and sea animals. *Ex* Rachel collects seashells on the beach.

seashore ['siʃor] n a beach; a place by the sea where people take vacations. It is also called the seaside.

season ['sizn̩] **1.** v to add things, like salt and pepper, to food to improve its flavor. **2.** n a period of the year. *Ex* Spring, summer, fall, and winter are the four seasons of the year.

seat [sit] n a piece of furniture used for sitting.

seaweed ['siwid] n plants that grow in the sea.

second ['sɛkənd] **1.** adj next after first and before third. **2.** n a measurement of time. *Ex* There are 60 seconds in a minute.

secondary ['sɛkəndɛri] adj second in importance; next after primary.

secret ['sikrət] **1.** n something known only to a very few people. *Ex* I am going to tell you a secret that you must not tell anyone else. **2.** adj private; not public; known only to a few people.

secretary ['sɛkrətɛri] n someone who writes or types business letters in an office.

section ['sɛkʃn̩] n a part or a piece of something.

security [sə'kyuwrəti] n safeness.

security guard [sə'kyuwrəti gɑrd] n a person whose job is to guard people or places.

see [si] v to use the eyes to look at something. *pt* saw. *pp* seen.

seed [sid] *n* the part of a plant from which new plants grow. *Ex* Grains of corn are seeds that new corn plants will grow from.

seek [sik] *v* to look for. *pt* sought. *pp* sought.

seem [sim] *v* to look like; to appear to be like. *Ex* It seems like winter today.

seen [sin] *v* the past participle of see.

seesaw ['si'sɔ] *n* a strong board fastened in the middle to a heavy piece of wood or metal. *Ex* Two people can sit on a see-saw, one on each end, and go up and down in turn. It is also called a teeter-totter.

seize [siz] *v* to grasp and hold on to.

seldom ['sɛldəm] *adv* not often.

select [sə'lɛkt] *v* to choose.

self [sɛlf] *n* your own person.

selfish ['sɛlfɪʃ] *adj* thinking only of yourself, and not caring about other people's wishes; greedy.

sell [sɛl] *v* to give something in exchange for money. *pt* sold. *pp* sold.

semester [sə'mɛstɚ] *n* one half of the school year. *Ex* The first semester begins in the fall.

semicircle ['sɛmisɚkl̩] *n* a half circle.

semicolon ['sɛmikowlən] *n* a punctuation mark (;) sometimes used to separate major parts of a sentence.

Senate ['sɛnət] *n* one of the two groups of people elected to make laws in the U.S. *Ex* The U.S. Congress consists of the Senate and the House of Representatives.

senator ['sɛnətɚ] *n* a member of the Senate; a lawmaker who has been elected to the Senate.

send [sɛnd] *v* to make a person or thing go somewhere. *pt* sent. *pp* sent.

senior ['sinyɚ] **1.** *n* someone who is older and more important than others. **2.** *n* a person in the final year of high school. **3.** *adj* older and more important.

sensation [sɛn'seyʃn̩] **1.** *n* a feeling. *Ex* My hand is so cold that there is no sensation in my fingers. **2.** *n* an exciting happening; an exciting success. *Ex* The play was a sensation.

sense [sɛn(t)s] **1.** *n* good or right knowledge. **2.** *v* to be able to learn about something through taste, smell, touch, sight, or hearing.

senseless ['sɛn(t)sləs] **1.** *adj* foolish; stupid; without good sense. **2.** *adj* not conscious of what is going on.

sensible ['sɛn(t)səbl̩] *adj* wise; having good sense.

sent [sɛnt] *v* the past tense and past participle of send.

sentence ['sɛntən(t)s] **1.** *n* a number of words which make a complete thought when put together; a group of words put together according to the rules of grammar. **2.** *n* a punishment for breaking laws. *Ex* He received a sentence of ten days in jail.

sentry ['sɛntri] *n* a soldier who keeps guard.

separate 1. *adj* ['sɛprət] not joined together; divided. **2.** *v* ['sɛpɚeyt] to divide; to move apart.

sequin ['sikwɪn] *n* a small, round, shiny ornament sewn on clothing to make it sparkle.

sergeant ['sɑrdʒn̩t] *n* an officer in the military or the police.

serial ['sɪriəl] *n* a story or film that appears in parts and not all at one time.

series ['siriz] *n* a number of things or events following one another in regular order.

serious ['siriəs] **1.** *adj* not funny. *Ex* Stop laughing and start being serious. **2.** *adj* worrisome; severe. *Ex* Molly has a serious illness.

serpent ['sɚpənt] *n* a snake.

servant ['sɚvn̩t] *n* someone who is paid to work in someone else's house.

serve [sɚv] *v* to work for someone; to hand out food at meals; to sell things over the counter in a shop.

service ['sɚvəs] **1.** *n* the act of serving; the serving of customers in a restaurant or a cafe. **2.** *n* a religious ceremony.

session ['sɛʃn̩] *n* a period of time devoted to some activity.

set [sɛt] **1.** *v* to place something somewere. **2.** *v* to put dishes, glasses, and silverware on a table before a meal. *Ex* Why do I always have to set the table? *pt* set. *pp* set. **3.** *n* a number of things of the same type; a collection of individual items that make up a whole. *Ex* Grandfather has a new set of false teeth. Mrs. Wu just bought a complete set of dishes.

settle ['sɛtl̩] *v* to agree on something; to bring about agreement. *Ex* Let us settle this argument peacefully.

settler ['sɛtlɚ] *n* one of the people who move into a new region and make a new home.

several ['sɛvrəl] *adj* more than two of something; a few.

severe [sə'vir] *adj* very serious; not merciful; stern.

sew [sow] *v* to join cloth together with a needle and thread.

sewer ['suwɚ] *n* the underground pipes which carry wastes away from buildings.

sex [sɛks] *n* either of the two groups, male and female, that animals and humans are divided into.

shabby ['ʃæbi] *adj* nearly worn-out; almost ragged.

shade [ʃeyd] **1.** *v* to keep the light away from something. **2.** *n* a darker area which sunlight cannot reach. *Ex* There is lots of shade under those trees.

shadow ['ʃædow] *n* a dark area which appears on the ground when an object gets in the way of light.

shaggy ['ʃægi] *adj* covered with rough, long hair or fur, usually messy.

shake [ʃeyk] *v* to move something quickly up and down or from side to side. *Ex* Please don't shake the baby's bed. *pt* shook. *pp* shaken.

shaken ['ʃeykn̩] *v* the past participle of shake.

shall [ʃæl] *v* a word used to express a command. *Ex* You shall go. *pt* should.

shallow ['ʃælow] *adj* not very far to the bottom; the opposite of deep.

shame [ʃeym] *n* a feeling of unhappiness because you have hurt someone or done something you know is wrong.

shameful ['ʃeymfl̩] *adj* wrong; mean. *Ex* What a shameful thing to do!

shampoo [ʃæm'puw] **1.** *v* to wash the hair of the head. **2.** *n* a special liquid soap used to wash the hair of the head.

shamrock ['ʃæmrɑk] *n* a kind of clover plant with tiny leaves divided into three sections.

shape [ʃeyp] **1.** *v* to cause something to take a particular form; to give something a form. **2.** *n* the form of something.

share [ʃɛr] **1.** *v* to give part of something to someone else. **2.** *n* a part or section that is given to someone.

shark [ʃɑrk] *n* a large, dangerous sea fish which has very sharp teeth.

sharp [ʃɑrp] *adj* having an edge that can cut or a point that can make holes.

sharpener ['ʃɑrpənɚ] *n* a machine that sharpens a pencil when the crank is turned; a pencil sharpener.

shatter ['ʃætɚ] *v* to break something into many pieces.

shave [ʃeyv] *v* to cut off hair with a razor; to scrape the hair off a male face with a razor.

shawl [ʃɔl] *n* a square piece of cloth folded and worn around the head and shoulders, usually by girls and women.

she [ʃi] *pro* a female person or animal. *Ex* She put her coat in the closet.

shears [ʃirz] *n* large scissors used for cutting things like paper, cloth, or hedges.

shed [ʃɛd] **1.** *n* a hut used to keep tools, supplies, or animals in. **2.** *v* to lose hairs; to take off clothing. *Ex* The house is a mess because the dog is shedding. *pt* shed. *pp* shed.

she'd [ʃid] *cont* she would; she had.

sheep [ʃip] *n* an animal covered with thick hair called wool. The plural is sheep. *Ex* There are seven sheep in the field. There is only one black sheep.

sheet [ʃit] **1.** *n* a single piece of something such as glass, paper, or metal. **2.** *n* a large piece of cloth used on a bed.

shelf [ʃɛlf] *n* a board fastened to a wall. *Ex* Please put this book on the shelf. The plural is shelves.

shell [ʃɛl] *n* the hard covering on a nut or an egg. *Ex* Some fish, animals, and insects have shells.

she'll [ʃil] *cont* she will.

shelter ['ʃɛltɚ] *n* a place where there is safety from danger or from bad weather.

shepherd ['ʃɛpəˑd] *n* a person whose job is to look after sheep.

sheriff ['ʃɛrəf] *n* the chief police officer in a county.

she's [ʃiz] *cont* she is; she has.

shield [ʃild] **1.** *n* something that you hide behind or hold up to protect yourself from attack. **2.** *v* to protect by standing in front of or holding a shield in front of.

shift [ʃɪft] **1.** *v* to move something, usually something heavy. *Ex* She shifted her weight from one foot to the other. **2.** *n* a group of people working together for a number of hours; a period of time when a group of people work together. *Ex* Maria's and Carlos's fathers both work the night shift at the factory.

shimmer ['ʃɪməˑ] *v* to shine with a soft, trembling light.

shin [ʃɪn] *n* the front of the lower leg bone. *Ex* The horse kicked me in the shin.

shine [ʃɑyn] *v* to give out bright light.

shingle ['ʃɪŋgl] *n* one of the flat pieces of material used to cover a roof.

ship [ʃɪp] **1.** *n* a large boat. **2.** *v* to send something by train, truck, airplane, or boat. *Ex* They shipped us a new part for our washing machine.

shipwrecked ['ʃɪprɛkt] *adj* having to do with people or property which were on a ship which was destroyed by a storm.

shirt [ʃəˑt] *n* a piece of clothing worn on the upper part of the body.

shiver ['ʃɪvəˑ] *v* to shake because of the cold.

shock [ʃɑk] **1.** *n* an unpleasant surprise; a sudden jolt of electricity. **2.** *v* to frighten or surprise someone with something unpleasant; to give someone a sudden jolt of electricity.

shoe [ʃuw] *n* a covering for the foot, usually made of leather, canvas, or plastic.

shoemaker ['ʃuwmeykɚ] *n* a person who makes or repairs shoes.

shook [ʃʊk] *v* the past tense of shake.

shoot [ʃuwt] *v* to send a bullet from a gun; to send an arrow from a bow. *pt* shot. *pp* shot.

shop [ʃɑp] **1.** *n* a place where things can be bought. **2.** *v* to go to different places to buy things; to go to different places looking for the lowest price on something you want to buy.

shore [ʃor] *n* the land at the edge of a lake or an ocean.

short [ʃort] *adj* not very long; not very tall.

shortening ['ʃortnɪŋ] *n* fat used in baking bread and pastry.

shorthand ['ʃorthænd] *n* a quick way of writing down what is said. *Ex* Many secretaries use shorthand.

shorts [ʃorts] **1.** *n* short trousers. **2.** *n* a kind of underpants worn by men and boys.

shot [ʃɑt] **1.** *n* an act of shooting. **2.** *v* the past tense and past participle of shoot.

should [ʃʊd] *v* the past tense of shall.

shoulder ['ʃowldɚ] *n* the joint where the arm is attached to the body.

shouldn't ['ʃʊdn̩t] *cont* should not.

shout [ʃawt] **1.** *v* to speak or call out very loudly. **2.** *n* a loud call; words spoken very loudly.

shove [ʃəv] **1.** *v* to push roughly. **2.** *n* a push; a rough push.

shovel ['ʃəvl] **1.** *n* a tool for digging or moving material like soil or snow. **2.** *v* to dig or move material with a shovel.

show [ʃow] **1.** *v* to point out; to guide. *pt* showed. *pp* shown. **2.** *n* a spectacle; a film; a play.

shower ['ʃawɚ] **1.** *n* a sudden, brief fall of rain, sleet, or snow. **2.** *n* a bath in which you stand up and water sprays all over you.

shown [ʃown] *v* the past participle of show.

shrank [ʃræŋk] *v* the past tense of shrink.

shred [ʃrɛd] **1.** *n* a scrap or strip torn off of something; a bit. **2.** *v* to tear something into scraps or strips.

shriek [ʃrik] **1.** *v* to make a high-pitched scream. **2.** *n* a high-pitched scream.

shrill [ʃrɪl] *adj* high-pitched and piercing to the ears.

shrimp [ʃrɪmp] *n* a small shellfish that turns pink when it is cooked.

shrink [ʃrɪŋk] *v* to become less or smaller. *pt* shrank. *pp* shrunk. *Ex* Some kinds of cloth shrink when they have been washed.

shrivel ['ʃrɪvl] *v* to dry up and become smaller. *Ex* A raisin is a shriveled grape.

shrub [ʃrəb] *n* a small, woody plant that does not grow very tall; a bush.

shrunk [ʃrəŋk] *v* the past participle of shrink.

shudder ['ʃədɚ] *v* to tremble with fear or disgust.

shuffle ['ʃəfl̩] **1.** *v* to move along without lifting your feet. *Ex* When you shuffle, your feet make a rubbing sound. **2.** *v* to mix a pack of cards before playing a game.

shut [ʃət] **1.** *v* to close. *pt* shut. *pp* shut. **2.** *adj* closed; not open.

shutter ['ʃətɚ] *n* a wooden cover for a window used to keep heat and light out in the daytime and cold out in the winter.

shy [ʃay] *adj* not wanting to be with lots of people; timid.

sick [sɪk] *adj* ill; not well.

side [sayd] *n* the part between the back and the front of something. *Ex* We have a lovely tree near the side of the house. I have a pain on my right side.

sidewalk ['saydwɔk] *n* a hard area next to a street where people can walk.

siege [sidʒ] *n* an attempt to capture a town or fort by surrounding it, so that help cannot reach it.

sift [sɪft] *v* to separate grains or powder from larger lumps by shaking matter through a screen or a special device.

sigh [say] **1.** *v* to breathe out heavily when you are tired or sad. **2.** *n* a large puff of air breathed out when you are tired or sad.

sight [sayt] **1.** *n* the ability to see. **2.** *v* to locate something in your vision; to spot something with your eyes. *Ex* Elaine sighted a ship on the horizon.

sign [sayn] **1.** *n* a board with printing on it that tells you something, like a traffic sign. **2.** *n* a signal; a movement to show what you mean, like nodding your head to mean yes. **3.** *v* to write your name on an important paper such as a check, letter, or contract.

signal ['sɪgnəl] **1.** *n* a message sent by signs, colored lights, or hand movements. *Ex* We waited for the traffic signal to change. **2.** *v* to send a message by some kind of a sign. *Ex* The police officer signaled us to go on.

signature ['sɪgnətʃɚ] *n* the special way you have of writing your name. *Ex* Your signature should be exactly the same each time you write it.

silence ['sɑylən(t)s] *n* the absence of any sound.

silent ['sɑylənt] *adj* not making a sound.

silk [sɪlk] *n* a very fine, smooth cloth made from threads that silkworms spin.

silkworm ['sɪlkwɚm] *n* a caterpillar that spins silk threads.

sill [sɪl] *n* the wooden or stone ledge at the bottom of a door or window.

silly ['sɪli] *adj* not sensible; not thinking carefully.

silver ['sɪlvɚ] **1.** *n* a shiny, grayish-white metal. *Ex* Money, knives, forks, and spoons are sometimes made of silver. **2.** *n* the color of the metal silver. **3.** *adj* of a silver color.

silverfish ['sɪlvɚfɪʃ] *n* an insect pest which gets into drawers and closets.

silverware ['sɪlvɚwɛr] *n* knives, forks, and spoons made of silver or any other metal.

similar ['sɪmələr] *adj* like, or almost like, something else.

simple ['sɪmpl̩] *adj* easy; not difficult.

since [sɪn(t)s] *prep* from a time in the past. *Ex* I haven't eaten since yesterday.

sincere [sɪn'sir] *adj* honest; meaning what you say.

sing [sɪŋ] *v* to make music with the voice. *Ex* Birds, as well as people, can sing. *pt* sang. *pp* sung.

singe [sɪndʒ] *v* to burn slightly; to scorch.

singer ['sɪŋɚ] *n* a person who gets paid for singing; a musician who sings.

single ['sɪŋgl] **1.** *adj* only one. *Ex* I don't have a single dollar. **2.** *adj* not married. *Ex* My brother is married, and my sister is single.

singular ['sɪŋgyələ·] **1.** *adj* one only; not plural. *Ex Cow* is a singular noun. **2.** *n* the state of a noun when it is not plural; a noun referring to just one thing or person. *Ex* The word *cow* is in the singular.

sink [sɪŋk] **1.** *n* a place in the kitchen where there is running water for washing dishes and preparing food. **2.** *v* to go under the water. *pt* sank. *pp* sunk.

sinus ['saynəs] *n* one of the small cavities deep behind the nose. *Ex* Sometimes sinuses swell up and cause headaches or they can get infected.

sip [sɪp] **1.** *v* to drink something a little bit at a time. **2.** *n* a tiny drink of something.

siren ['sayrən] *n* something like a whistle or a horn that makes a loud, wailing noise.

sister ['sɪstə·] *n* a daughter of the same parents. *Ex* You and your sister have the same parents.

sit [sɪt] *v* to be on a chair or a seat; to bend down onto a chair or a seat. *pt* sat. *pp* sat.

site [sayt] *n* an area of ground where a building is, or will be built.

situation [sɪtʃə'weyʃn̩] **1.** *n* the place or position of something. **2.** *n* a state of affairs; the circumstances belonging to an event.

size [sayz] *n* the amount of space something occupies.

skate [skeyt] **1.** *n* a shoe with a metal blade or wheels attached. *Ex* Skates allow a skater to move quickly and smoothly on ice or a flat surface. **2.** *v* to move quickly and smoothly on ice or a flat surface while wearing skates.

skeleton ['skɛlətn̩] *n* all of the bones inside a body; the bones of a body remaining when the flesh has wasted away.

sketch [skɛtʃ] **1.** *n* a rough, quick drawing. **2.** *v* to make a rough, quick drawing.

ski [ski] **1.** *v* to move quickly over snow on two long pieces of wood called skis. **2.** *n* one of a pair of long pieces of wood attached to special boots for the sport of skiing.

skid [skɪd] *v* to slide sideways, as a car sometimes does on wet or icy roads.

skill [skɪl] *n* cleverness; the ability to do something well.

skillet ['skɪlət] *n* a frying pan; a heavy pan in which food is fried.

skillful ['skɪlfl̩] *adj* clever; able to do something well.

skim [skɪm] **1.** *v* to glide quickly over the surface of something. **2.** *v* to take the cream off the top of milk.

skin [skɪn] **1.** *n* the outside covering of the body. **2.** *v* to remove the skin from something. *Ex* You should skin a catfish before you cook it.

skip [skɪp] **1.** *v* to jump up and down on one leg at a time. **2.** *v* to leave out something. *Ex* Joel always skips the dull parts of the story.

skipper ['skɪpɚ] *n* the captain of a ship.

skirt [skɚt] *n* the part of a dress which hangs down from the waist; a garment covering the lower part of the body, worn by women and girls.

skit [skɪt] *n* a little play; a story acted out by people who are not real actors.

skull [skəl] *n* the bony part of a human or animal head.

skunk [skəŋk] *n* a small, black animal with white stripes and a bushy tail. A skunk gives off a horrible smell when it is in danger.

sky [skɑy] *n* the air above you that you see when you look up out-of-doors.

skyscraper ['skɑyskreypɚ] *n* a very tall building.

slab [slæb] *n* a thick slice. *Ex* Juan ate a huge slab of ice cream. The building is covered with slabs of stone.

slack [slæk] **1.** *adj* loose; not tightly stretched. **2.** *adj* having to do with a time when people are not busy. *Ex* Summer is always a slack time for our store.

slain [sleyn] *v* the past participle of slay.

slam [slæm] *v* to shut or bang something with a very loud noise.

slant [slænt] *v* to lean or slope; to be at an angle.

slap [slæp] **1.** *v* to hit with the palm of the hand. **2.** *n* a blow struck with the palm of the hand.

slash [slæʃ] **1.** *v* to make long cuts in something, sometimes violently. **2.** *n* a long cut in something.

slate [sleyt] *n* a kind of stone sometimes used for roofs and floors.

slaughter ['slɔtɚ] **1.** *v* to kill an animal for food; to kill one or more people without mercy. **2.** *n* the killing of animals for food; the killing of one or more people.

slave [sleyv] *n* someone who is owned by another person and who must work for that person.

slay [sley] *v* to kill. *pt* slew. *pp* slain.

sled [slɛd] *n* a vehicle with metal or wooden runners, that moves easily over snow-covered ground.

sleek [slik] *adj* smooth and shiny. *Ex* The coat of a well-fed horse is sleek.

sleep [slip] **1.** *n* the state of sleeping. **2.** *v* for the body to rest in a state where you are not aware of what is going on around you. *pt* slept. *pp* slept.

sleepy ['slipi] *adj* tired; in need of sleep.

sleet [slit] *n* rain mixed with snow or hail.

sleeve [sliv] *n* the part of clothing that covers the arm.

sleeveless ['slivləs] *adj* without sleeves.

sleigh [sley] *n* a large sled, usually pulled by horses. *Ex* They say that Santa Claus rides in a sleigh pulled by reindeer.

slender ['slɛndɚ] *adj* slim; narrow; thin.

slept [slɛpt] *v* the past tense and past participle of sleep.

slew [sluw] *v* the past tense of slay.

slice [slays] **1.** *v* to cut a piece or slab of something. **2.** *n* a flat piece cut from something, like a slice of bread or cake.

slid [slɪd] *v* the past tense and past participle of slide.

slide [slayd] **1.** *v* to move smoothly down or along on something. *pt* slid. *pp* slid. **2.** *n* a device on a playground which you can slide down. **3.** *n* a small frame containing a piece of film with a picture on it. *Ex* The slide is slid into a slide projector so that the picture can be seen, and then it is slid out again.

slide projector ['slayd prədʒɛktɚ] *n* an instrument which shows color pictures on a screen or the wall.

slide rule ['slayd ruwl] *n* a ruler used for calculating. *Ex* A slide rule has a central part which slides back and forth.

slight [slayt] *adj* small in quantity or importance; slim or slender.

slightly ['slaytli] *adv* by a small amount.

slim [slɪm] *adj* thin; slender.

slime [slaym] *n* thin, slippery mud or dirt.

sling [slɪŋ] **1.** *n* a piece of cloth tied around your neck and shoulder to hold up an injured arm. **2.** *v* to throw something; to throw something carelessly. *Ex* Please don't sling your clothing all over the place. *pt* slung. *pp* slung.

slink [slɪŋk] *v* to creep or prowl. *pt* slinked, slunk. *pp* slinked, slunk.

slip [slɪp] **1.** *v* to slide when you don't mean to. **2.** *v* to move away quickly and quietly. **3.** *n* a dress-like undergarment worn by girls and women.

slipper ['slɪpɚ] *n* a soft shoe that is worn indoors.

slippery ['slɪp(ə)ri] *adj* smooth on the surface so that you can slip easily. *Ex* There is ice on the sidewalk, and it is very slippery.

slit [slɪt] **1.** *v* to make a long, thin cut. *pt* slit. *pp* slit. **2.** *n* a long, thin cut.

slob [slab] *n* a very messy person.

slope [slowp] **1.** *v* to slant; to aim upward or downward. **2.** *n* a slant; a hill.

sloppy ['slapi] *adj* messy.

slot [slat] *n* a narrow opening, usually in a machine, for something like a coin to fit in.

slouch [slawtʃ] *v* to walk or move in a lazy, drooping way; not to hold yourself upright.

slow [slow] **1.** *adj* taking a long time; not fast. **2.** *v* to become slow; to make something more slow.

sludge [slədʒ] *n* nasty, soft mud.

slug [sləg] **1.** *n* a kind of snail which has no shell. **2.** *v* to hit something or someone with a fist. **3.** *n* a hard blow with the fist.

sluggish ['sləgɪʃ] *adj* very slow; as slow as a slug.

slung [sləŋ] *v* the past tense and past participle of sling.

slunk [sləŋk] *v* a past tense and a past participle of slink.

slush [sləʃ] *n* melting snow; soft mud.

sly [slɑy] *adj* cunning; clever; sneaky.

smack [smæk] *v* to hit with the open hand; to slap.

small [smɔl] *adj* little; the opposite of large.

smart [smɑrt] *adj* clever; quick to learn; well dressed and stylish.

smash [smæʃ] *v* to break something into pieces, usually with a crashing noise.

smear [smir] **1.** *v* to spread or rub something greasy or sticky so as to leave a dirty mark. **2.** *n* a dirty mark; a place where dirt has been rubbed around.

smell [smɛl] **1.** *n* what your nose tells you about something. **2.** *n* an odor. **3.** *v* to test something for its odor by sniffing the air near it; to sense an odor.

smile [smɑyl] **1.** *v* to put a happy look on your face, especially your mouth. **2.** *n* a happy look on your face, especially your mouth.

smock [smɑk] *n* a loose garment usually worn over other clothes to keep them clean.

smoke [smowk] **1.** *n* a cloud of tiny particles that comes from something burning. **2.** *v* to make smoke; to burn tobacco in a cigarette or a pipe.

smoke alarm ['smowk əlɑrm] *n* a device which sounds an alarm if there is smoke in the air.

smolder ['smowldɚ] *v* to burn slowly without much flame.

smooth [smuwð] *adj* without any bumps; the opposite of rough.

smother ['sməðɚ] *v* to cover completely; to put out a fire by covering it; to kill a living thing by covering it so that it cannot breathe.

smudge [smədʒ] *n* a stain; a smear of dirt.

smuggle ['sməgl̩] *v* to bring something into a country without paying tax; to bring something into a country illegally.

snack [snæk] **1.** *n* a small, quick meal, like a sandwich or a bowl of soup. **2.** *v* to eat a snack; to nibble bits of food between meals.

snail [sneyl] *n* a small animal with a shell on its back that moves very slowly.

snake [sneyk] *n* a crawling animal with a long body and no legs. *Ex* Some snakes are dangerous because they have a poisonous bite.

snap [snæp] **1.** *v* to break with a sudden, sharp noise. **2.** *v* to move the thumb and the longest finger in a way to produce a loud, sharp noise. **3.** *n* a loud, sharp noise.

snarl [snɑrl] **1.** *v* to make a growling noise with the teeth showing. **2.** *n* an angry, growling noise made with the teeth showing. **3.** *n* a knot or a tangle.

snatch [snætʃ] *v* to grab something quickly.

sneak [snik] *v* to creep along quietly.

sneakers ['snikɚz] *n* shoes made of canvas and rubber; gym shoes; tennis shoes.

sneer [snir] **1.** *v* to smile in a scornful or mocking way. **2.** *n* a scornful or mocking smile.

sneeze [sniz] **1.** *v* to make a sudden blowing noise through your nose because it tickles. **2.** *n* a sudden blowing noise through your nose.

sniff [snɪf] **1.** *v* to take a noisy breath through the nose. **2.** *n* a noisy breath taken through the nose.

snip [snɪp] *v* to cut a little piece off something, usually with scissors.

snore [snor] *v* to make a loud breathing noise through the nose while sleeping.

snorkle ['snorkl] *n* a tube with one end sticking out of the water so that swimmers can stay underwater and still breathe air.

snout [snɑwt] *n* the long nose of some animals which sticks out. *Ex* Pigs and porpoises have long snouts.

snow [snow] **1.** *n* drops of water that become frozen in the air in winter. *Ex* Snow makes the ground white. **2.** *v* for snow-flakes to drop out of the sky. *Ex* It is so cold that it is snowing.

snowball ['snowbɔl] *n* a ball of snow pressed together.

snow day ['snow 'dey] *n* an extra day at the end of the school year to make up for days missed when the school was closed because of too much snow.

snowman ['snowmæn] *n* a human figure made out of snow.

snowshoe ['snowʃuw] *n* a pair of frames strung with thin strips of leather. *Ex* People wear snowshoes to keep their feet from sinking into deep, soft snow.

snug [snəg] *adj* cozy and warm.

soak [sowk] *v* to make something or someone very wet.

soap [sowp] *n* something used with water to make things clean. *Ex* Please buy a cake of soap at the store.

soar [sor] *v* to fly high into the air.

sob [sɑb] **1.** *v* to weep; to weep noisily. **2.** *n* a loud, sad cry. *Ex* She was so sad that she could only answer with loud sobs.

soccer ['sɑkɚ] *n* a sport played on a field with a round ball that is kicked.

social ['sowʃl] *adj* having to do with people.

social studies ['sowʃl stədiz] *n* the study of groups of people and how they get along.

social worker ['sowʃl wɚkɚ] *n* a person whose job is to help people with their problems.

society [sə'sɑyəti] **1.** *n* human beings thought of as a group. **2.** *n* a group of human beings joined together for a purpose.

sock [sɑk] **1.** *n* something put on to cover the foot before a shoe is put on. **2.** *n* a hard blow. **3.** *v* to strike; to slug.

socket ['sɑkət] *n* a hollow place that something is fit into. *Ex* Please screw this light bulb into the socket.

sofa ['sowfə] *n* a couch.

soft [sɔft] *adj* not hard or rough; not loud.

soft drink ['sɔft 'drɪŋk] *n* a sweet, bubbly drink which comes in a can or bottle.

soggy ['sɑgi] *adj* damp and heavy; very wet.

soil [sɔyl] **1.** *n* loose earth; dirt. **2.** *v* to make something dirty.

solar ['sowlɚ] *adj* having to do with the sun.

solar system ['sowlɚ sɪstəm] *n* the sun and its planets.

sold [sowld] *v* the past tense and past participle of sell.

soldier ['sowldʒɚ] *n* a member of the army.

sole [sowl] **1.** *n* the bottom of the foot; the bottom of a shoe. **2.** *n* a kind of flat fish which is good to eat. **3.** *adj* only.

solemn ['sɑləm] *adj* serious; very earnest.

solid ['sɑlɪd] *adj* hard and firm; not hollow; not liquid.

solitary ['sɑlətɛri] *adj* alone; single.

solution [sə'luwʃn̩] **1.** *n* a liquid; a substance dissolved in a liquid. **2.** *n* the answer to a problem.

solve [sɑlv] *v* to find the answer to some problem; to find a solution.

some [səm] **1.** *adj* few; not all. **2.** *pro* a few; some people.

somebody ['səmbɑdi] *pro* a person whose name is not stated.

someone ['səmwən] *pro* a person whose name is not stated.

somersault ['səmɚsɔlt] *n* a kind of a rolling of the body where the head is on the ground and the rest of the body goes up and over.

something ['səm(p)θɪŋ] *pro* a thing whose name is not stated.

sometime ['səmtɑym] *adv* at an unknown time.

sometimes ['səmtɑymz] *adv* not all of the time; now and then.

somewhat ['səmhwət] *adj* a little; rather.

somewhere ['səmhwɛr] *adv* at an unknown place. Also someplace.

son [sən] *n* a male child of a father or a mother.

song [sɔŋ] *n* the musical sounds sung by birds; the musical words and notes sung by people.

sonic ['sɑnɪk] *adj* having to do with sound waves, as in sonic boom.

soon [suwn] *adv* in a short time.

soot [sʊt] *n* a black, powdery stuff which comes from burning wood or coal. *Ex* Soot sticks to the inside of the chimney.

soothe [suwð] *v* to calm someone down; to comfort.

sore [sor] *adj* painful when touched.

sorrow ['sɑrow] *n* unhappiness; sadness.

sorry ['sɑri] *adj* feeling unhappy about something you have done or something that has happened.

sort [sort] **1.** *v* to put things together that belong together. *Ex* Please sort these cards in alphabetical order. **2.** *n* kind; type; class.

sought [sɔt] *v* the past tense and past participle of seek.

soul [sowl] *n* the spirit or invisible part of a person which is thought to live on after death.

sound [sɑwnd] **1.** *n* anything which can be heard. **2.** *v* to use a musical instrument to make a sound. *Ex* They sounded the trumpets on time.

soup [suwp] *n* a liquid food made by boiling meat, vegetables, or other foods together in water.

sour ['sɑwɚ] *adj* not tasting sweet.

source [sors] *n* the starting place of something; the place where something comes from; the person information comes from.

south [sɑwθ] *n* the direction on your right as you face the rising sun; the opposite of north.

South Pole [ˈsɑwθ ˈpowl] *n* the south end of the earth's axis; the southernmost place on earth.

sow 1. *n* [sɑw] a female pig. **2.** *v* [sow] to scatter seeds over the ground; to plant seeds in the ground. *pt* sowed. *pp* sown, sowed.

sown [sown] *v* a past participle of sow.

space [speys] **1.** *n* a place with nothing in it. **2.** *n* the place occupied by the sun, stars, and other planets.

spacecraft [ˈspeyskræft] *n* a special machine moved by rockets that can go far up into space.

spaceship [ˈspeyʃɪp] *n* a spacecraft.

spade [speyd] *n* a tool used for digging in the ground; a kind of shovel.

spaghetti [spəˈgɛti] **1.** *n* long, thin sticks of dried wheat paste. **2.** *n* a meal made from cooked spaghetti with a tomato sauce.

span [spæn] *n* the length of something from end to end. *Ex* That bridge has a very long span.

spank [spæŋk] *v* to smack with your open hand; to punish a child by striking with an open hand.

spare [spɛr] **1.** *adj* extra. *Ex* I have a spare tire in my car. **2.** *v* to let something go. *Ex* The hunter spared the life of the smallest deer. **3.** *v* to part with something. *Ex* I can spare two cookies and no more.

spark [spɑrk] *n* a tiny bit of something burning that flies out of a fire.

sparkle [ˈspɑrkl] *v* to give off bright flashes of light; to glitter. *Ex* Snow sparkles in the sunlight.

sparkler [ˈspɑrklɚ] *n* a kind of fireworks which gives off sparks when it is lit.

spark plug ['spɑrk pləg] *n* a part inside a car engine which makes a spark to burn the gasoline.

sparrow ['spɛrow] *n* a small, brown and gray bird.

speak [spik] *v* to say something. *pt* spoke. *pp* spoken.

speaker ['spikɚ] **1.** *n* a person who is speaking; a person who is giving a speech. **2.** *n* the part of a radio or record player which the sound comes out of; a loudspeaker.

spear [spir] **1.** *n* a pole with a metal point on the end. *Ex* A spear is used as a weapon. **2.** *v* to stab at something.

special ['spɛʃl] *adj* not like anything else; made for one use only.

specimen ['spɛsəmən] *n* one of something; a sample.

speck [spɛk] *n* a small spot or dirty mark; a tiny piece.

speckled ['spɛkḷd] *adj* marked with lots of small spots.

spectacle ['spɛktɪkḷ] *n* something interesting which makes people want to look at it.

spectacles ['spɛktɪkḷz] *n* eyeglasses.

spectator ['spɛkteytɚ] *n* someone who watches other people do something; a person who watches a spectacle.

sped [spɛd] *v* the past tense and past participle of speed.

speech [spitʃ] **1.** *n* speaking; language; the act of speaking. **2.** *n* a talk; a lecture.

speed [spid] **1.** *n* quickness; swiftness. **2.** *v* to go fast; to drive faster than the law allows. *pt* sped. *pp* sped.

speedometer [spə'dɑmətɚ] *n* the instrument on a car that tells how fast the car is going.

spell [spɛl] **1.** *n* magic words which are supposed to make something happen. *Ex* The witch put an evil spell on the monkey. **2.** *v* to put letters together in the right order to make up a certain word.

spelling ['spɛlɪŋ] *n* the study of how to spell; a class in how to spell.

spend [spɛnd] *v* to pay out money. *pt* spent. *pp* spent.

spent [spɛnt] *v* the past tense and past participle of spend.

spice [spɑys] **1.** *n* a dried or powdered flavoring for food, usually strong tasting and smelling. **2.** *v* to put spices into food.

spider ['spɑydɚ] *n* a small animal with eight legs. *Ex* The spider spins a web to catch insects.

spike [spɑyk] *n* a long, sharp point; a pointed rod of metal.

spill [spɪl] *v* to let something, such as powder or liquid, accidentally run out of a container.

spin [spɪn] **1.** *v* to go around and around. **2.** *v* to make thread out of wool, cotton, or similar material. *pt* spun. *pp* spun.

spinach ['spɪnɪtʃ] *n* a dark green, leafy vegetable.

spine [spɑyn] **1.** *n* the backbone of a person or animal; the edge of a book where the pages are attached. **2.** *n* a thorn; one of the stiff, sharp prickles growing on some animals such as the porcupine.

spinster ['spɪn(t)stɚ] *n* an unmarried woman.

spiral ['spɑyrəl] *n* something that winds upward, going around and around like a spring.

spire [spɑyr] *n* the long, pointed top of a church steeple.

spirit ['spɪrət] *n* ghost; soul.

spit [spɪt] *v* to throw something out of your mouth.

spite [spayt] **1.** *n* hatred; dislike; feeling bad about someone. **2.** *v* to be cruel and hateful toward someone.

spiteful ['spaytfḷ] *adj* saying and doing cruel things to someone you do not like.

splash [splæʃ] **1.** *n* the noise of something heavy falling into liquid. **2.** *v* to throw liquid about; to make a splashing noise.

splashdown ['splæʃdawn] *n* the landing of a space capsule in the ocean.

splendid ['splɛndəd] *adj* wonderful; grand; good.

splinter ['splɪntɚ] *n* a tiny piece of wood, glass, or metal, which has broken off from a larger piece.

split [splɪt] **1.** *v* to break or cut something from end to end. *pt* split. *pp* split. **2.** *n* a break or a cut in something.

spoil [spoyl] **1.** *v* to damage something or make it of no use. **2.** *v* to give in to a child's demands too often.

spoke [spowk] **1.** *n* a wire or rod running from the center of a wheel to the outside edge of the wheel. *Ex* One of my bicycle spokes is broken. **2.** *v* the past tense of speak.

spoken ['spowkṇ] *v* the past participle of speak.

sponge [spəndʒ] **1.** *n* the soft, yellow skeleton of a sea animal, which becomes much softer when it soaks up water. **2.** *v* to use a sponge or a cloth to soak up a liquid.

spool [spuwl] *n* a short rod of wood or plastic on which sewing thread is wound. *Ex* Please buy me a spool of white thread while you are at the store.

spoon [spuwn] *n* a tool used in cooking or eating food.

sport [sport] *n* a game, often played outdoors. *Ex* Football, basketball, and baseball are sports.

spot [spat] **1.** *n* a small mark. **2.** *v* to look very carefully to see something; to catch sight of. *Ex* Jeff spotted his friend Sally in the crowd at the football game.

spouse [spaws] *n* a wife's husband; a husband's wife.

spout [spawt] *n* a small tube or pipe through which liquid is poured, like the spout of a teapot.

sprain [spreyn] **1.** *v* to twist a muscle of a joint so badly that it swells painfully. **2.** *n* a painful injury to a muscle or a joint caused by twisting.

sprang [spræŋ] *v* the past tense of spring.

sprawl [sprɔl] *v* to sit or lie in a relaxed position with the arms and legs spread out.

spray [sprey] **1.** *v* to send out fine drops of liquid. **2.** *n* a lot of fine drops of liquid.

spread [sprɛd] **1.** *v* to open something outwards. *Ex* The bird spread its wings. **2.** *v* to cover a surface with something. *Ex* Molly spread the peanut butter on a slice of bread. *pt* spread. *pp* spread. **3.** *n* something which is used to cover something. *Ex* Frank bought a new bedspread. Margarine is sometimes called a spread.

spring [spriŋ] **1.** *v* to jump; to hop. *pt* sprang. *pp* sprung. **2.** *n* a coil of wire used to make furniture soft and comfortable. *Ex* The mattress of my bed has many springs inside. **3.** *n* a place where water runs out of the ground. *Ex* The cattle went down to the spring to drink. **4.** *n* the season between winter and summer.

sprinkle ['spriŋkl] **1.** *v* to scatter small drops of water or bits of something like sugar or sawdust. **2.** *v* to rain tiny drops of water. *Ex* It's sprinkling, so you need an umbrella.

sprout [sprawt] *v* to begin to grow. *Ex* The seeds I planted never sprouted.

sprung [sprəŋ] **1.** *v* the past participle of spring. **2.** *adj* having to do with a spring which is stretched out and useless.

spun [spən] *v* the past tense and past participle of spin.

spurt [spɚt] **1.** *v* to squirt out suddenly. **2.** *n* a rush of liquid. **3.** *n* a sudden burst of speed.

spy [spɑy] **1.** *n* someone who secretly watches what other people are doing, especially during a war. **2.** *v* to secretly watch what other people are doing.

square [skwɛr] *n* a shape with four sides and four 90-degree angles. *Ex* A record album cover is usually square.

square root ['skwɛr 'rʊt, 'skwɛr 'ruwt] *n* a number which, when multiplied by itself, is equal to the number you are trying to find the square root of. *Ex* 10 is the square root of 100. 3 is the square root of 9.

squash [skwɑʃ] **1.** *v* to crush something out of shape. **2.** *n* a game played on an indoor court.

squeak [skwik] **1.** *n* a small, high-pitched sound. **2.** *v* to make a small, high-pitched sound. *Ex* That door squeaks badly.

squeal [skwil] **1.** *v* to make a long, high, piercing sound. *Ex* Some animals squeal when they are frightened. Babies sometimes squeal when they are happy. **2.** *n* a long, high, piercing sound.

squeeze [skwiz] **1.** *v* to press hard; to crush; to hug. **2.** *n* a pressing; a hug.

squirrel ['skwɚl] *n* a small, red or brown animal with a long, bushy tail.

squirt [skwɚt] *v* to force liquid out of an opening in a sudden stream.

stab [stæb] **1.** *v* to pierce or cut with a pointed weapon. **2.** *n* a stabbing; a cut from stabbing.

stable ['steybl̩] **1.** *n* a building where horses are kept. **2.** *adj* firm; sturdy.

stack [stæk] **1.** *n* a large heap; a pile of things laid on top of one another. **2.** *v* to lay things on top of one another to make a pile.

stadium ['steydiəm] *n* an open-air sports arena with seats around the outside.

staff [stæf] **1.** *n* a pole or stick. **2.** *n* a group of people in an office; teachers in a school.

stage [steydʒ] **1.** *n* a platform in a theater or a hall where people act, sing, or speak. **2.** *n* a position or phase; one of the steps in a project or program. *Ex* Children learn language at an early stage of development.

stagecoach ['steydʒkowtʃ] *n* a horse-drawn coach which traveled across the country in olden days, stopping at certain places to let people on or off.

stagger ['stægɚ] *v* to walk unsteadily, lurching and stumbling.

stain [steyn] **1.** *n* a dirty mark; a coloring from something like oil or fruit juices. **2.** *v* to cause or leave a stain. *Ex* The spilled grape juice stained my shirt.

staircase ['stɛrkeys] *n* a number of stairs, usually with a side rail to keep people from falling.

stairs [stɛrz] *n* a set of steps in a building, for walking up or down.

stairway ['stɛrwey] *n* the part of a building which contains stairs or a staircase.

stake [steyk] *n* a strong, pointed stick or post. *Ex* Tent stakes are hammered into the ground to hold the ropes that support the tent.

stale [steyl] *adj* not fresh; dry and without much taste because of being kept too long.

stalk [stɔk] **1.** *n* a stem; the part of a plant that holds up a flower. **2.** *v* to creep quietly after an animal that you are hunting.

stall [stɔl] **1.** *n* a small area at a fair or a market where a person can sell things; the little room inside a restroom where the toilet is contained. **2.** *n* a place for one animal in a cattle shed or a stable. **3.** *v* to delay; to stop or slow down. *Ex* I am late because my car stalled.

stallion ['stælyən] *n* a male horse.

stammer ['stæmɚ] *v* to repeat the beginning of a word several times before going on to say the whole word; to speak in jerks and pauses.

stamp [stæmp] **1.** *v* to hit the floor hard with the foot. *Ex* The little boy was very angry, and he stamped his feet. **2.** *n* a small rectangle of paper which you buy from a post office to stick on a letter or package you wish to mail. **3.** *n* a rubber stamp.

stamp pad ['stæmp pæd] *n* a flat, metal can holding thick material which has ink in it. *Ex* A rubber stamp is stamped first onto the stamp pad and then onto paper, where an image is made in ink.

stand [stænd] **1.** *v* to be on your feet; to get onto your feet. *pt* stood. *pp* stood. **2.** *n* a stall; a place where things, especially newspapers or fruits and vegetables, are sold.

standard ['stændɚd] **1.** *n* a grade or level. **2.** *n* a goal or principle. **3.** *adj* normal; average; regular.

stank [stæŋk] *v* the past tense of stink.

staple ['steypl] **1.** *n* a basic food such as flour, sugar, meat, and milk. **2.** *n* a small wire bent in a special way so that it will hold papers together when driven into them by a stapler. **3.** *v* to attach papers together with a staple.

staple puller ['steypl pulɚ] *n* a device which removes staples from paper. It is also called a staple remover.

stapler ['steyplɚ] *n* a machine which drives wire staples into sheets of paper to hold them together.

star [stɑr] **1.** *n* one of the billions of suns in the universe which appear as tiny lights in the sky at night. **2.** *n* someone who is famous and popular, like a film star.

stare [stɛr] **1.** *v* to look at someone or something for a long time without looking away. **2.** *n* a person's gaze; an act of staring.

start [stɑrt] **1.** *v* to begin; to move suddenly. **2.** *n* a beginning; the point in time when a race begins.

startle ['stɑrtḷ] *v* to make a person or animal jump with sudden fear or surprise.

starvation [stɑr'veyʃn̩] *n* suffering or death caused by lack of food.

starve [stɑrv] *v* to be in great need of food; to die of hunger; to cause a living thing to die of hunger.

state [steyt] **1.** *n* a condition; a way of being. *Ex* The house was in a messy state. **2.** *n* one of the fifty subdivisions of the United States. **3.** *v* to make a statement; to say something.

statement ['steytmənt] *n* something said or told.

station ['steyʃn̩] **1.** *n* the place where a train stops to let people on or off. **2.** *n* a building for policemen and firemen.

stationary ['steyʃənɛri] *adj* not moving; standing still.

stationery ['steyʃənɛri] *n* writing paper and envelopes.

statue ['stætʃuw] *n* the figure of a person or animal made from stone, wood, or metal.

statute ['stætʃuwt] *n* a law.

stay [stey] *v* to be in one place and not leave.

steadily ['stɛdḷi] *adv* in a steady, firm way; constantly.

steady ['stɛdi] **1.** *adj* constant; without stopping. *Ex* We had three days of steady rain. **2.** *adj* standing firm; moving without jerking or shaking; loyal and faithful.

steak [steyk] *n* a thick slice of meat or fish.

steal [stil] *v* to take something which belongs to someone else. *pt* stole. *pp* stolen.

steam [stim] **1.** *n* a cloud-like gas that water turns into when it boils. **2.** *v* to cook something through the use of steam.

steel [stil] *n* a very strong metal made from iron.

steep [stip] *adj* rising nearly straight up from the ground. *Ex* You will get tired from climbing a steep hill.

steeple ['stipḷ] *n* a high, pointed tower on a church.

steer [stir] **1.** *v* to guide a vehicle to the right or left. **2.** *n* a young bull.

steering wheel ['stirɪŋ hwil] *n* the circular thing which you hold on to and turn when you drive a car.

stellar ['stɛlɚ] *adj* having to do with the stars.

stem [stɛm] *n* the thin part of a plant that holds up the flowers and leaves.

stenographer [stə'nɑgrəfɚ] *n* a person whose job is to write down what someone says and type it afterwards.

stenography [stə'nɑgrəfi] *n* the art or skill of writing down rapidly what someone says.

step [stɛp] **1.** *v* to put one foot in front of the other when walking. **2.** *n* one stair in a staircase. **3.** *n* one of a number of stages in a project or program.

stereo ['stɛriow] *n* a record player which plays in stereophonic sound.

stern [stɚn] **1.** *adj* severe; strict; grim. **2.** *n* the back part of a ship or a boat.

stethoscope ['stɛθəskowp] *n* the instrument a doctor uses to listen to your heart and lungs.

stew [stuw] **1.** *v* to cook food, especially meat with vegetables, by boiling it slowly. **2.** *n* a food made of slowly boiled meat and vegetables.

stick [stɪk] **1.** *n* a long, thin piece of wood; anything shaped like a stick, such as a stick of wax or gum. **2.** *v* to poke or stab; to pierce. **3.** *v* to become fastened; to cause to become fastened. *pt* stuck. *pp* stuck.

sticky ['stɪki] *adj* clinging or holding on; sticking like glue or honey.

stiff [stɪf] *adj* firm; hard; not easily bent or moved.

still [stɪl] *adj* not moving; calm.

stilts [stɪlts] *n* a pair of tall poles with footrests. *Ex* Stilts can make you seem very, very tall.

sting [stɪŋ] **1.** *v* to cause pain by sticking something sharp into flesh. *pt* stung. *pp* stung. **2.** *n* the act of stinging; a tiny, painful injury caused by an insect like a wasp or a bee.

stink [stɪŋk] **1.** *v* to have a bad odor; to cause a bad odor. *pt* stank. *pp* stunk. **2.** *n* a very bad odor.

stir [stɚ] *v* to move; to shake up or mix; to mix with a spoon.

stirrup ['stɚəp] *n* a metal ring hanging down each side of a saddle. *Ex* A stirrup is flat at the bottom so that you can put your foot in it when you ride a horse.

stitch [stɪtʃ] **1.** *v* to sew. **2.** *n* a loop of thread that has been sewn.

stock [stɑk] **1.** *n* supplies of food or other goods stored by shopkeepers. **2.** *v* to build up supplies. *Ex* The grocery store stocks its shelves during the night.

stocking ['stɑkɪŋ] *n* a kind of sock that covers the whole leg. *Ex* Stockings are usually made of nylon or some other man-made fiber.

stole [stowl] *v* the past tense of steal.

stolen ['stowlən] *v* the past participle of steal.

stomach ['stəmək] **1.** *n* an organ in the body which holds food after it has been swallowed. **2.** *n* the central part of the human body which runs from the belt line up to the ribs.

stomachache ['stəməkeyk] *n* a dull pain in the stomach.

stone [stown] **1.** *n* a piece of rock. **2.** *n* the hard seed inside some fruits like peaches and plums.

stood [stʊd] *v* the past tense and past participle of stand.

stool [stuwl] *n* a little seat with no back or arms.

stoop [stuwp] *v* to bend the upper part of the body downwards.

stop [stɑp] **1.** *v* to end or leave off doing something; to bring to a halt; to come to a halt. **2.** *n* a halt; a stopping; a place where something, like a bus, usually stops.

stoplight ['stɑplɑyt] *n* a traffic light; the light at intersections with red, yellow, and green signals.

stopper ['stɑpɚ] *n* something that is put into the neck of a bottle to close the opening.

stop sign ['stɑp sɑyn] *n* an eight-sided, red sign with white letters saying STOP. *Ex* You must stop your car or bicycle and look both ways at a stop sign.

store [stor] **1.** *n* a shop; a place where things are sold. **2.** *v* to keep something until it is needed.

stork [stork] *n* a large bird with very long legs and a long beak.

storm [storm] **1.** *n* a sudden outburst of windy weather with rain, snow, or hail. **2.** *v* to rain, snow, or hail very hard.

story ['stori] *n* an adventure, told or written. *Ex* Stories can be true or invented, like a fairy tale.

stove [stowv] *n* something that makes heat to cook with or to warm rooms.

straight [streyt] *adj* not crooked or curved.

straighten ['streytn̩] *v* to make straight; to put things neat and tidy.

strain [streyn] *v* to make every effort; to put all of your strength into doing something.

strainer ['streynɚ] *n* a kind of bowl with holes in it. It is usually made of metal or plastic.

strange [streyndʒ] *adj* unusual; out of place.

stranger ['streyndʒɚ] *n* someone you do not know.

strangle ['stræŋgl] *v* to choke; to kill a living thing by squeezing its throat.

strap [stræp] *n* a long, thin piece of leather, usually with a buckle to fasten something.

straw [strɔ] **1.** *n* dry, stiff, yellow stalks that farm animals sleep on. **2.** *n* a paper or plastic tube for sucking up liquids; a drinking straw.

strawberry ['strɔbɛri] *n* a small, soft, red fruit with whisker-like hairs all over it.

stray [strey] *v* to wander away or go in the wrong direction by mistake.

streak [strik] *n* a stripe; a long, narrow mark.

stream [strim] *n* a small river.

streamer ['strimɚ] *n* a long, thin flag; a paper decoration for parties.

street [strit] *n* a road with houses or other buildings on both sides of it.

strength [strɛŋ(k)θ] *n* how strong and powerful something is.

stretch [strɛtʃ] *v* to make longer or wider by pulling.

stricken ['strɪkn̩] *v* a past participle of strike.

strict [strɪkt] *adj* severe; insisting on complete obedience.

stridden ['strɪdn̩] *v* the past participle of stride.

stride [strɑyd] *v* to walk with long steps. *pt* strode. *pp* stridden.

strike [strɑyk] **1.** *v* to hit very hard. **2.** *v* to stop work and demand more money or better working conditions. *pt* struck. *pp* struck, stricken. **3.** *n* a stopping of work by striking workers.

string [strɪŋ] **1.** *n* thick thread used for tying things up. **2.** *n* one of the parts of a musical instrument such as a violin or a guitar.

strip [strɪp] **1.** *n* a long, narrow piece of something. **2.** *v* to tear off a long, narrow piece of something. **3.** *v* to take off all of your clothes.

stripe [strɑyp] *n* a long, narrow line or mark of color. *Ex* Flags often have different colored stripes on them.

strive [strɑyv] *v* to try very hard. *pt* strove, strived. *pp* striven, strived.

striven ['strɪvn̩] *v* a past participle of strive.

strode [strowd] *v* the past tense of stride.

stroke [strowk] **1.** *v* to rub gently. **2.** *n* a blow; the sound of a clock striking.

stroll [strowl] **1.** *v* to walk slowly, in no hurry to get anywhere. **2.** *n* a slow walk to no place in particular.

stroller ['strowlɚ] *n* a small, four-wheeled carriage which carries an infant in an upright position.

strong [strɔŋ] *adj* not weak; not easily broken; able to lift heavy things.

strove [strowv] *v* a past tense of strive.

struck [strək] *v* the past tense and a past participle of strike.

structure ['strəktʃɚ] **1.** *n* something which has been constructed, like a dam or a building. **2.** *n* the way things are built up or arranged.

struggle ['strəgl] **1.** *v* to make a great effort; to fight to get free. **2.** *n* a battle; a fight or a big effort.

stubborn ['stəbɚn] *adj* not willing to give in to others; obstinate.

stuck [stək] *v* the past tense and past participle of stick.

student ['stuwdṇt] *n* someone who studies at a school or a university.

student body [stuwdṇt 'badi] *n* the group of students who attend the same school or university.

student council [stuwdṇt 'kawn(t)sl̩] *n* a group of students elected to represent the student body.

studio ['stuwdiow] *n* the workshop of an artist; a place where films are made; a room from which radio or television programs are broadcast.

study ['stədi] **1.** *v* to learn; to examine something closely. **2.** *n* a room, like an office, where a person can read and think.

study hall ['stədi hɔl] *n* a large schoolroom where students can read and do their homework.

stuff [stəf] **1.** *n* the material something is made of. **2.** *v* to pack tightly.

stuffy ['stəfi] *adj* without enough fresh air.

stumble ['stəmbḷ] *v* to trip over something or lose your footing.

stump [stəmp] *n* the part of the tree trunk that is left after the tree has been cut down.

stun [stən] *v* to knock someone senseless; to amaze or surprise greatly.

stung [stəŋ] *v* the past tense and past participle of sting.

stunk [stəŋk] *v* the past participle of stink.

stupid ['stuwpəd] *adj* foolish; silly; slow to think.

sturdy ['stɚdi] *adj* strong; healthy.

stutter ['stətɚ] *v* to speak with difficulty; to stammer.

sty [stɑy] **1.** *n* a place where pigs are kept. **2.** *n* a small swelling on the eyelids.

style [stɑyl] *n* the way something is done; fashion in clothing. *Ex* I don't like the new clothing styles. My writing style is very poor.

subdivision ['səbdəvɪʒn] **1.** *n* one of the parts of a whole. **2.** *n* an area of land which has been divided into smaller sections on which houses will be built.

subject ['səbdʒɪkt] *n* what is being talked or written about. *Ex* The subject of the speech was taxes.

submarine ['səbmɚin] *n* a special kind of ship that can go along under the water.

substance ['səbstən(t)s] *n* anything solid that you can handle or feel; the important part of something.

substitute ['səbstətuwt] **1.** *n* something which serves in the place of something else. **2.** *n* a teacher who teaches a class when the regular teacher is away.

subtract [səb'trækt] *v* to take away a number or a quantity from a larger number or quantity.

subtraction [səb'trækʃn̩] *n* an act of subtracting.

suburb ['səbɚb] *n* a small town or community near a large city.

suburban [sə'bɚbən] *adj* having to do with suburbs and life in the suburbs.

subway ['səbwey] *n* an underground electric train.

succeed [sək'sid] *v* to do what one sets out to do.

success [sək'sɛs] *n* a satisfactory ending to something you set out to do, like passing an examination or winning a race.

such [sətʃ] *adj* having the quality indicated. *Ex* This is such a dull day.

suck [sək] *v* to draw liquid into the mouth.

sudden ['sədn̩] *adj* happening all at once.

suddenly ['sədn̩li] *adv* unexpectedly; all at once.

suds [sədz] *n* soapy bubbles.

suede [sweyd] *n* a soft leather which does not shine.

suffer ['səfɚ] *v* to feel pain; to put up with.

sufficient [sə'fɪʃn̩t] *adj* enough.

suffix ['səfɪks] *n* a sound or syllable added to the end of a word to change its meaning. *Ex* The *ed* in the word *turned* is a suffix.

sugar ['ʃugɚ] *n* a white powder used in food and drinks to make them taste sweet.

sugarcane ['ʃugɚkeyn] *n* a plant with sweet-tasting stems from which sugar is made.

suggest [sə(g)'dʒɛst] *v* to tell others about an idea or plan that you think would be good.

suggestion [sə(g)'dʒɛstʃn̩] *n* an idea or plan; something which is suggested.

suit [suwt] *n* a set of clothes, such as a coat and trousers, which are meant to be worn together.

suitable ['suwtəbl̩] *adj* fitting in well; proper; right.

suitcase ['suwtkeys] *n* a flat case for carrying clothes on a trip; a piece of luggage.

suite [swit] **1.** *n* a set of rooms in a hotel or a large house. **2.** *n* a set of furniture for a room.

sulk [səlk] *v* to show anger and bad temper by not speaking and not being friendly.

sum [səm] *n* the total number when two or more things are added together.

summarize ['səmɚɑyz] *v* to go over the main points of what you have been saying or writing.

summary ['səmɚi] *n* a statement of the main points of something written, or of a speech.

summer ['səmɚ] *n* the season between spring and fall.

summer session ['səmɚ sɛʃn̩] *n* a session of school classes held during the summer months.

summit ['səmət] *n* the highest point of something, such as the summit of a mountain.

summon ['səmən] *v* to send for someone.

sun [sən] *n* the round, bright ball seen in the sky during the day. *Ex* The sun sends out light and heat.

sunburn ['sənbɚn] *n* burning or reddening of the skin from being out in the sun too long.

sunburned ['sənbɚnd] *adj* with burned skin from being in the sun too long.

sundial ['səndɑyl] *n* an instrument that shows the time of day by the position of the sun's shadow on a dial.

sung [səŋ] *v* the past participle of sing.

sunk [səŋk] *v* the past participle of sink.

sunny ['səni] *adj* full of sunshine.

sunrise ['sənrɑyz] *n* the time when the sun comes up; the actual rising of the sun.

sunset ['sənsɛt] *n* the time when the sun goes down; the actual setting of the sun.

sunshine ['sənʃɑyn] *n* the light from the sun.

suntan ['səntæn] *n* a tan or brownish color on the skin of a white person due to being in the sun a lot.

superintendent [suwpɚɪn'tɛndənt] *n* the person in charge of a building or a group of buildings; the person in charge of a group of schools; the person in charge of a factory.

superlative [sə'pɚlətɪv] **1.** *adj* of the highest degree; the best. **2.** *n* the form of an adjective expressing the highest degree. *Ex Biggest* is the superlative of *big*.

supermarket ['suwpɚmɑrkət] *n* a large store where you can buy all kinds of food and other things. *Ex* You help yourself in a supermarket and pay when you go out.

supersonic [suwpɚ'sɑnɪk] *adj* moving faster than sound travels in air.

supervisor ['suwpɚvayzɚ] *n* a person who oversees the work or play of other people.

supper ['səpɚ] *n* the last meal of the day.

supply [sə'plɑy] **1.** *v* to provide; to give something that is needed. **2.** *n* a stock or store; a needed amount of something.

support [sə'port] **1.** *v* to hold something up; to bear the weight of something. **2.** *n* something that holds something else up.

suppose [sə'powz] *v* to imagine; to pretend.

Supreme Court [sə'prim 'kort] *n* the highest court in the United States.

sure [ʃuwr] *adj* certain; knowing that one is right.

surely ['ʃuwrli] *adv* without question or doubt.

surface ['sɚfəs] **1.** *n* the outside of anything; the top of a lake, the sea, or the earth. **2.** *v* to come to the surface; to float to the surface.

surgeon ['sɚdʒn̩] *n* a doctor who treats patients by cutting out or repairing the diseased part.

surgery ['sɚdʒɚi] *n* the process of cutting out diseased parts of the body or repairing the inside of the body.

surly ['sɚli] *adj* bad-tempered; not friendly.

surname ['sɚneym] *n* the last name; the family name. *Ex* John Smith's surname is Smith.

surprise [sɚ'prɑyz] **1.** *n* something unexpected; something sudden and a little frightening. **2.** *v* to startle; to do something suddenly when it was not expected.

surrender [sə'rɛndɚ] *v* to give up.

surround [sə'rɑwnd] *v* to get or be on all sides of something or someone.

survey 1. *v* [sɚ'vey] to take a careful look over something or some place. **2.** *v* [sɚ'vey] to ask many people to give answers to the same questions so that you can find out what people in general think about something. **3.** *n* ['sɚvey] a set of questions to be asked of many people; the act of surveying public opinion.

suspect 1. *v* [sə'spɛkt] to have a feeling in your mind that something is wrong or that someone is not telling the truth. **2.** *n* ['səspɛkt] a person who is suspected of commiting a crime.

suspenders [sə'spɛndɚz] *n* special bands of a stretchy material that help hold a man's pants up.

swallow ['swɑlow] **1.** *v* to let food or drink go down the throat. **2.** *n* a bit of food or drink small enough to go down the throat; an act of swallowing. **3.** *n* a pretty bird with a forked tail.

swam [swæm] *v* the past tense of swim.

swamp [swɑmp] **1.** *n* wet, marshy ground. **2.** *v* to put too much water into something; to get too much water inside. *Ex* Sit still or you will swamp the boat.

swan [swɑn] *n* a large water bird, usually white, with a very long neck.

swap [swɑp] **1.** *v* to trade one thing for another. *Ex* I'll swap my red cap for your green one. **2.** *n* an act of swapping; something gotten by swapping.

swarm [sworm] **1.** *v* to gather together like bees in a hive. **2.** *n* a large number of people, animals, bees, or other insects gathered together.

sway [swey] *v* to swing or move from side to side.

swear [swɛr] **1.** *v* to make a very solemn promise. **2.** *v* to use very bad language. *pt* swore. *pp* sworn.

sweat [swɛt] **1.** *n* the moisture that comes from the skin when the body is hot. **2.** *v* for the skin to give off moisture when the body is hot.

sweater ['swɛtər] *n* a heavy, knitted shirt.

sweep [swip] *v* to use a brush or broom to clean the floor. *pt* swept. *pp* swept.

sweet [swit] *adj* not sour; tasting of sugar.

sweetheart ['swithɑrt] *n* someone you are very fond of; someone you love.

swell [swɛl] *v* to grow larger; to grow louder. *pt* swelled. *pp* swelled, swollen.

swept [swɛpt] *v* the past tense and past participle of sweep.

swerve [swɚv] *v* to turn aside quickly to keep from running into something.

swift [swɪft] *adj* fast; rapid; quick.

swim [swɪm] **1.** *v* to move along in the water using the arms and legs. *pt* swam. *pp* swum. **2.** *n* an act of swimming; a period of swimming.

swing [swɪŋ] **1.** *n* a seat hanging from ropes or chains. **2.** *v* to move in the air, back and forth, or from side to side; to ride in a hanging swing. *pt* swung. *pp* swung.

swipe [swɑyp] **1.** *v* to hit something or someone hard. **2.** *v* to steal something.

swirl [swɚl] *v* to move about quickly with a circling movement, as when dried leaves are blown about by the wind.

switch [swɪtʃ] *n* a lever which turns electricity on and off.

swollen ['swowlən] *v* a past participle of swell.

sword [sord] *n* a very long knife with a special handle. *Ex* Swords were used in battle long ago.

swore [swor] *v* the past tense of swear.

sworn [sworn] *v* the past participle of swear.

swum [swəm] *v* the past participle of swim.

swung [swəŋ] *v* the past tense and past participle of swing.

syllable ['sɪləbl̩] *n* a group of sounds that make a word or part of a word. *Ex* The words *boy* and *girl* each have one syllable. The words *women* and *children* each have two syllables.

symbol ['sɪmbl̩] *n* something like a sign that stands for something else. *Ex* The dove is a symbol of peace.

sympathy ['sɪmpəθi] *n* a feeling of kindness and pity towards someone who is sad or ill.

symphony ['sɪm(p)fəni] **1.** *n* a long piece of orchestra music with three or four main parts. **2.** *n* an orchestra which plays symphonies.

symptom ['sɪmptəm] *n* a sign of an illness. *Ex* Sneezing is a symptom of a cold or the flu.

synagogue ['sɪnəgɑg] *n* a group of Jews gathered together to worship; the place where Jews gather to worship God.

syrup ['sɪrəp] *n* a thick, sweet juice made by boiling sugar with water, fruit juice, or sap from a maple tree.

system ['sɪstəm] *n* a group of things working together.

T

tab [tæb] *n* a small flap or loop, usually on a piece of clothing.

table ['teybl̩] **1.** *n* a piece of furniture with legs and a flat top. **2.** *n* a set of facts or numbers arranged in columns. *Ex* Find the answer to the problem in the multiplication table.

tablecloth ['teybl̩klɔθ] *n* a large piece of cloth used to cover a table.

table of contents [teybl̩ əv 'kɑntɛnts] *n* a list at the beginning of a book showing the page numbers of the main parts of the book.

tablet ['tæblət] *n* a bit of powdered medicine pressed into a pellet. *Ex* I need an aspirin tablet for my headache.

tack [tæk] **1.** *n* a short nail with a flat head. **2.** *v* to sew something together with long, loose stitches.

tackle ['tækl̩] **1.** *v* to take on a job; to use much strength to try to do something; to pull down a player in the sport of football. *Ex* I'm too tired to tackle my homework now. **2.** *n* equipment for doing something, such as fishing tackle.

tadpole ['tædpowl] *n* a frog when it is very young, before its legs develop.

tag [tæg] **1.** *n* a label. *Ex* There is no price tag on this coat. **2.** *n* a children's game in which one person chases and tries to touch another.

tail [teyl] *n* the part that hangs out at the end of animals; the end of an airplane; the streamer of a kite. *Ex* A cat's tail is long and furry.

tailor ['teylɚ] **1.** *n* someone who makes or changes the fit of suits, coats, skirts, and trousers. **2.** *v* to make or change the fit of clothing.

take [teyk] *v* to get hold of; to carry away; to swallow medicine. *Ex* Please take the garbage out. Don't forget to take your pills. *pt* took. *pp* taken.

taken ['teykn̩] *v* the past participle of take.

talk [tɔk] *v* to speak; to say something.

talkative ['tɔkətɪv] *adj* fond of talking; talking too much. *Ex* Sammy is always getting into trouble because he is so talkative.

tall [tɔl] *adj* very high.

tame [teym] *adj* not wild; able to live with people as a pet. *Ex* A tame deer lives near our house.

tamper ['tæmpɚ] *v* to meddle or interfere with something. *Ex* Someone tampered with the lock on my door.

tan [tæn] **1.** *n* a light brown color. **2.** *adj* of a light brown color. **3.** *v* to make animal hide into leather.

tangerine [tændʒɚ'in] *n* a kind of small, sweet orange with a loose skin that comes off easily.

tangled ['tæŋgl̩d] *adj* twisted up in knots like hair that has not been combed.

tank [tæŋk] **1.** *n* a special heavy vehicle made of iron and steel, with big guns in it. **2.** *n* a large metal or glass container for water or other liquids.

tanker ['tæŋkɚ] *n* a ship that carries oil or other liquids.

tap [tæp] **1.** *v* to hit something lightly. *Ex* A tree branch is tapping at my window. **2.** *n* a light hit; the sound of a light hit. *Ex* I hear a tap at the door. **3.** *n* a kind of a handle used to turn the water on and off. *Ex* Turn off the tap so you won't waste water.

tape [teyp] **1.** *n* a narrow strip of something such as strong cloth, plastic, or sticky paper used to tie or fasten things together. **2.** *n* a special plastic ribbon used to record sound or pictures with sound. **3.** *v* to use tape to hold something closed. **4.** *v* to make a sound or picture recording on tape.

tape recorder ['teyp rɪkordɚ] *n* a machine that records and plays back sounds on a special kind of tape.

tar [tɑr] *n* a thick, sticky, black liquid which comes from wood and coal. Tar is used in making roads.

tardy ['tɑrdi] *adj* late; late for school.

target ['tɑrgət] *n* something you aim at when shooting. *Ex* She shot the arrow at the target.

task [tæsk] *n* a job; an amount of work which must be done.

taste [teyst] **1.** *n* the flavor of something. *Ex* This fruit has a sour taste. **2.** *v* to put a bit of food in your mouth or sip a drink to see if you like it or not. **3.** *v* to have a flavor. *Ex* The milk tastes sour.

taught [tɔt] *v* the past tense and past participle of teach.

tax [tæks] *n* money paid to the government to pay for things everyone uses, such as roads, bridges, schools, and hospitals. *Ex* We have both a sales tax and an income tax.

taxi ['tæksi] *n* a car that you pay to ride in. *Ex* Sarah took a taxi to the airport.

tea [ti] *n* a hot drink made by pouring boiling water onto the dried leaves of the tea plant.

teach [titʃ] *v* to give lessons; to instruct. *pt* taught. *pp* taught.

teacher ['titʃɚ] *n* a person who teaches in a school.

teacher's aide [titʃɚz 'eyd] *n* a person who helps a teacher in the classroom.

team [tim] *n* a group of people all helping each other in a job or a game.

teapot ['tipɑt] *n* a special pot to make tea in.

tear 1. *v* [tɛr] to pull apart; to rip. *pt* tore. *pp* torn. **2.** *n* [tir] one of the drops of water that comes from your eyes when you are sad or hurt. *Ex* Mark was crying, and the tears streamed down his face.

tease [tiz] *v* to annoy by making fun or mocking. *Ex* Stop teasing me!

teem [tim] *v* to be abundant; to be full to overflowing. *Ex* The river is teeming with fish!

teenage ['tineydʒ] *adj* between 13 and 19 years old.

teenager ['tineydʒɚ] *n* a person between 13 and 19 years old.

teeth [tiθ] *n* more than one tooth; the plural of tooth.

telegram ['tɛləgræm] *n* a short message sent by telegraph. *Ex* Sammy got a telegram from his brother in China.

telegraph ['tɛləgræf] *n* a device that allows messages to be sent very rapidly over electric wires.

telephone ['tɛləfown] *n* an instrument that carries sound through electric wires so that people far apart can talk to each other. *Ex* Please answer the telephone.

telescope ['tɛləskowp] *n* an instrument like a tube that you look through to see things that are far away, like the stars.

television ['tɛləvɪʒn] *n* an instrument that brings pictures and sound through the air from far away. *Ex* I had to stop watching television and do my homework.

tell [tɛl] *v* to give news or say what you know about something. *Ex* Tell me what you know about New York City. Please tell me another story. *pt* told. *pp* told.

teller ['tɛlɚ] *n* a person whose job is to take in or pay out money, usually in a bank. *Ex* The teller cashed the check for me.

temper ['tɛmpɚ] **1.** *n* a person's mood. **2.** *n* the ease with which a person gets angry.

temperature ['tɛmprətʃɚ] **1.** *n* how hot or cold something is. **2.** *n* a fever. *Ex* The sick baby had a temperature.

tempest ['tɛmpəst] *n* a violent storm with a very strong wind.

temple ['tɛmpl] *n* a building where people pray and worship; a building where Jews worship.

tempo ['tɛmpow] *n* how fast or slow a piece of music has to be played. *Ex* Fast music has a fast tempo.

temporary ['tɛmpərɛri] *adj* for the time being; not permanent.

tempt [tɛmpt] *v* to try to persuade someone to do something which ought not to be done. *Ex* The wonderful food tempted me to eat too much.

tenant ['tɛnənt] *n* a person who rents property from a landlord.

tennis ['tɛnəs] *n* a game played on a court with two or four people.

tennis shoes ['tɛnəs ʃuwz] *n* white, canvas shoes worn while playing tennis; gym shoes.

tense [tɛn(t)s] **1.** *adj* tight; strained; rigid. **2.** *n* a quality of a verb telling the time of the action of the verb. *Ex Went* is the past tense of the verb *go.*

tent [tɛnt] *n* a shelter made of a thick piece of cloth held up by sticks or poles.

tepee ['tipi] *n* a cone-shaped tent that some American Indians lived in.

tepid ['tɛpəd] *n* slightly warm; lukewarm.

term [tɚm] **1.** *n* a length of time. *Ex* The school year is divided into two or three terms. **2.** *n* the name of a thing.

terminal ['tɚmənl] **1.** *n* the place where buses, trains, or airplanes end their trips. **2.** *n* a screw or other piece of metal to which an electric wire is fastened. **3.** *n* a special electronic device with a keyboard that allows a person to communicate with a computer. *Ex* Andy's father works at a computer terminal all day.

termite ['tɚmɑyt] *n* an insect pest which eats the wood of houses and trees.

terrace ['tɛrəs] *n* a raised, flat area of earth; a lawn on a slant.

terrible ['tɛrəbl̩] *adj* awful; horrible.

terrier ['tɛriɚ] *n* a kind of small dog.

terrific [tə'rɪfɪk] *adj* very great; loud; wonderful. *Ex* Rachel's nephew makes a terrific noise.

terrify ['tɛrəfɑy] *v* to frighten someone very badly. *Ex* Mr. Long terrified Andy.

terror ['tɛrɚ] *n* very great fear.

test [tɛst] **1.** *v* to look at carefully; to give an examination; to quiz; to run a machine to see if it works properly. *Ex* We tested the radio, but it didn't work. **2.** *n* an examination; a quiz. *Ex* I failed a test yesterday.

testify ['tɛstəfɑy] *v* to give special knowledge about something in a court of law. *Ex* My father had to testify in court yesterday.

test tube ['tɛs tuwb] *n* a small, glass tube used to hold liquids. *Ex* Rachel is always breaking test tubes in chemistry class.

than [ðæn] **1.** *prep* compared to. *Ex* She is taller than me. **2.** *conj* compared to. *Ex* She is taller than I am.

thank [θæŋk] *v* to show gratitude to someone; to state your gratefulness to someone. *Ex* The old lady thanked me over and over.

thankful ['θæŋkfḷ] *adj* grateful; pleased. *Ex* The old lady was very thankful when I helped her.

thanks [θæŋks] *n* gratitude; words of gratitude. This noun is not used in the singular. *Ex* The old lady said many words of thanks when I helped her.

thank you ['θæŋk yuw] what you say to express gratitude; what you say when someone gives you something. *Ex* "Thank you for helping me," said the old lady.

that [ðæt] **1.** *adj* mentioned before; a particular one. *Ex* Where is that cake I baked yesterday? **2.** *adj* the one farther away; the opposite of this. *Ex* Please give me that cup. This one is broken. **3.** *pro* someone or something that you have been talking about; an idea or an opinion which has been expressed. *Ex* That is a horrible thing to say.

thatch [θætʃ] *n* a roof or covering of straw or reeds.

thaw [θɔ] *v* for something frozen to become unfrozen; to cause something frozen to become unfrozen.

the [ði, ðə] a word called an article which is used before a noun. *Ex* Where did you put the salt? The old man was very helpful.

theater ['θiətɚ] *n* a building where plays are performed; a building where films are shown.

theft [θɛft] *n* an act of stealing.

their [ðɛr] *pro* belonging to them. *Ex* They put their books on the floor.

them [ðɛm] *pro* the objective form of they. *Ex* Where did you put them? Give it to them.

theme [θim] *n* the subject of discussion; the main melody in a piece of music; the main idea in a piece of writing.

themselves [ðəm'sɛlvz] *pro* those people; they and no one else. *Ex* They did it themselves.

then [ðɛn] **1.** *adv* at that time; next. *Ex* Then he put the book on the desk. I will do it then. **2.** *n* that time. *Ex* She has been more careful since then.

there [ðɛr] *adv* to or at that place; not here. *Ex* Please put it there.

therefore ['ðɛrfor] *adv* for that reason.

thermometer [θɚ'mɑmətɚ] *n* an instrument for measuring how hot or cold something is. *Ex* The thermometer says it is below freezing.

thermostat ['θɚməstæt] *n* an instrument that measures hot and cold and turns heating or cooling equipment on or off. *Ex* Andy turned down the thermostat, and the house got colder.

these [ðiz] *adj* and *pro* the plural of this.

thesis ['θisəs] **1.** *n* a point of view; an opinion; a theme. **2.** *n* a long paper written for a high degree in a university.

they [ðey] *pro* those people or things. *Ex* They are quite happy now. They are too old to eat.

they'd [ðeyd] *cont* they would; they had

they'll [ðeyl] *cont* they will.

they're [ðɛr] *cont* they are.

they've [ðeyv] *cont* they have.

thick [θɪk] *adj* wide or deep; the opposite of thin.

thicket ['θɪkət] *n* shrubs and trees growing close together.

thief [θif] *n* someone who steals.

thigh [θay] *n* the part of your leg above the knee.

thimble ['θɪmbl]] *n* a metal or plastic cover for the end of the finger. *Ex* The thimble keeps the needle from hurting you when you sew.

thin [θɪn] *adj* not wide or fat; the opposite of thick.

thing [θɪŋ] *n* an object which is not named.

think [θɪŋk] *v* to use the mind; to have ideas. *pt* thought. *pp* thought.

third [θɚd] *adj* next after second; the last of three.

thirsty ['θɚsti] *adj* wanting to drink; needing to drink.

this [ðɪs] **1.** *adj* mentioned just now. *Ex* Where is this new hat you are so proud of? **2.** *adj* the one nearer; the opposite of that. *Ex* I want this one here, not that one there. **3.** *pro* a situation which you must deal with; an idea or an opinion which has been mentioned. *Ex* We have to do something about this.

thorn [θorn] *n* a sharp, woody spike on a bush or shrub. *Ex* There are lots of thorns on a rosebush.

thorough ['θɚow] *adj* careful; doing things completely. *Ex* They are very thorough house cleaners.

those [ðowz] *adj* and *pro* the plural of that.

though [ðow] *conj* although.

thought [θɔt] **1.** *n* an idea; thinking. **2.** *v* the past tense and past participle of think.

thoughtful ['θɔtfl] *adj* thinking deeply; thinking of what others would like. *Ex* Sally is a friendly and thoughtful person.

thousand ['θawzn̩d] *n* 10 times 100. One thousand is written 1,000.

thread [θrɛd] *n* a very long, thin piece of material used in sewing.

threaten ['θrɛtn̩] *v* to warn by frightening. *Ex* He threatened to send me home if I didn't stop talking.

threw [θruw] *v* the past tense of throw.

thrill [θrɪl] **1.** *n* a feeling of excitement. *Ex* The fast ride was a thrill. **2.** *v* to excite someone. *Ex* The wonderful present thrilled me.

throat [θrowt] *n* the inside of the front of the neck which contains the windpipe.

throb [θrɑb] *v* to quiver; for something, such as your heart, to beat very strongly. *Ex* Your heart may throb when you run.

throne [θrown] *n* a special chair for a king or a queen.

throttle ['θrɑtl̩] **1.** *n* the fuel control of a gasoline or diesel engine. **2.** *v* to choke or strangle.

through [θruw] **1.** *prep* from one end to the other. *Ex* Please walk quietly through the halls. **2.** *adj* finished. *Ex* Are you through with my pencil now?

throughout [θruw'awt] *prep* in every part of.

throw [θrow] *v* to release something like a ball or a stone out of your hand and into the air with force. *Ex* He threw the ball over the house. *pt* threw. *pp* thrown.

thrown [θrown] *v* the past participle of threw.

thrust [θrəst] *v* to push with great force; to throw. *Ex* She thrust the cat through the door.

thud [θəd] *n* a heavy, bumping sound when something falls to the ground. *Ex* His head hit the ground with a thud.

thumb [θəm] *n* the short, thick finger on a human hand.

thumbtack ['θəmtæk] *n* a short tack or nail with a very big, flat head, so that it can be pushed in by a thumb.

thump [θəmp] **1.** *v* to strike with the fist; to make a thudding sound. **2.** *n* a blow struck with the fist; a thudding sound.

thunder ['θəndɚ] **1.** *n* a loud noise which you hear during a storm after a flash of lightning. **2.** *v* to make a loud noise; to make the loud noise that comes after lightning.

thus [ðəs] *adv* therefore; for example.

tick [tɪk] **1.** *n* a soft, clicking noise such as a clock makes. **2.** *v* to make the sound of a clock.

ticket ['tɪkət] *n* a small piece of paper or cardboard which you get when you pay to ride a public vehicle, or go to a show.

tickle ['tɪkl̩] **1.** *n* a funny feeling on your skin which makes you want to scratch, or even laugh. **2.** *v* to touch or lightly scratch someone in a place so that the person laughs; to cause someone to laugh or be amused.

tide [tɑyd] *n* the coming in and going out of the sea.

tidy ['tɑydi] *adj* neat; in order; not in a mess.

tie [tɑy] **1.** *n* a narrow piece of cloth worn around the neck. **2.** *v* to make a knot; to make a bow.

tiger ['tɑygɚ] *n* a dangerous, wild animal like a very large cat. *Ex* The tiger has striped fur and lives mostly in India.

tight [tɑyt] *adj* closely fitting; closely packed; the opposite of loose.

tighten ['tɑytn̩] *v* to make tight; to make tighter.

tile [tɑyl] *n* a flat piece of baked clay used for floors or walls; flat or curved pieces of baked clay used for roofs.

till [tɪl] **1.** *prep* up to a certain time; until. **2.** *n* a cash drawer in a shop; a cash register. **3.** *v* to work or plow the soil.

tilt [tɪlt] *v* to lean to one side; to lean something to one side.

timber ['tɪmbɚ] *n* wood which is going to be made into something or used for building.

time [tɑym] *n* seconds, minutes, hours, days, weeks, months, and years.

times sign ['tɑymz sɑyn] *n* the multiplication sign: ×. *Ex* 2 × 2 = 4.

timid ['tɪməd] *adj* shy; easily frightened.

tin [tɪn] *n* a silvery metal.

tingle ['tɪŋgl̩] **1.** *n* a prickly feeling. **2.** *v* to have a prickly feeling.

tinker ['tɪŋkɚ] *v* to meddle with things; to work with something to try to fix it when you really do not know what you are doing.

tinkle ['tɪŋkl̩] **1.** *n* a soft, ringing sound. **2.** *v* to make a soft, ringing sound.

tinsel ['tɪn(t)sl̩] *n* long strips of silvery, sparkling material which are used to decorate Christmas trees.

tiny ['tɑyni] *adj* very small.

tip [tɪp] **1.** *n* the thin end of something; the pointed end of something. **2.** *v* to turn over; to tilt.

tiptoe ['tɪptow] *v* to walk on the tips of the toes very quietly.

tire [tɑyr] *v* to become tired; to bore someone; to make someone tired.

tired [tɑyrd] *adj* having the feeling that you need sleep or rest.

tissue ['tɪʃuw] **1.** *n* a very thin sheet of paper. **2.** *n* one of the different materials which a living body is made of.

title ['taytl̩] **1.** *n* the name of a book, a song, or a play. **2.** *n* a word, such as Doctor, Captain, or Sister, in front of someone's name.

title page ['taytl̩ peydʒ] *n* a page at the front of a book or paper which tells the title and the author.

to [tuw] *prep* toward; until; at.

toad [towd] *n* an animal that looks like a frog which has rough, lumpy skin.

toast [towst] **1.** *n* bread which is made brown and crisp by heating it. **2.** *v* to heat bread to make it brown and crisp.

toaster ['towstɚ] *n* an electric appliance which toasts bread.

tobacco [tə'bækow] *n* a plant with large leaves which are dried, cut up, and used for smoking in cigarettes, cigars, and pipes.

toboggan [tə'bagn̩] *n* a long, flat sled without runners.

today [tə'dey] *adv* on this day.

toe [tow] *n* one of the five things on the foot which are similar to fingers.

together [tə'gɛðɚ] **1.** *adv* in a group. **2.** *adv* with one another.

toil [toyl] **1.** *v* to work very hard. **2.** *n* hard work.

toilet ['toylət] *n* a bathroom; the basin for human wastes in the bathroom.

token ['towkn̩] **1.** *n* a symbol; an object which helps you remember something. **2.** *n* a piece of metal like a coin that can be used as fare on a bus or a subway.

told [towld] *v* the past tense and past participle of tell.

tolerance ['talɚ-ən(t)s] *n* the ability to put up with someone or something that you do not like.

tolerant ['talərənt] *adj* able to put up with someone or something you do not like.

tolerate ['taləreyt] *v* to put up with someone or something that you do not like.

tomato [tə'meytow] *n* a soft, round, red fruit, often used as a vegetable or in salads.

tomb [tuwm] *n* a place where someone is buried, either in the ground or in a stone box above the ground.

tomboy ['tamboy] *n* a girl who behaves like a boy and enjoys playing boy's games.

tomorrow [tə'marow] **1.** *adv* on the day after today. **2.** *n* the day after today; the future.

ton [tən] *n* a measurement of weight; one ton is equal to 2,000 pounds.

tone [town] **1.** *n* a sound, usually musical. **2.** *n* the quality of a person's voice, such as harsh or sweet.

tongs [tɔŋz] *n* a tool with two pieces of metal which can be squeezed together to hold things.

tongue [təŋ] *n* the thick, soft part inside your mouth that moves when you talk and with which you taste things.

tonight [tə'nayt] *adv* on this night.

too [tuw] *adv* also; as well.

took [tʊk] *v* the past tense of take.

tool [tuwl] *n* any instrument that people use to help them in their work. *Ex* Hammers and shovels are tools.

tooth [tuwθ] *n* one of the white bones in your mouth that you use to bite and chew with. The plural is teeth.

toothache ['tuwθeyk] *n* a pain in a tooth.

toothbrush ['tuwθbrəʃ] *n* a small, long-handled brush which you use to clean your teeth.

toothpaste ['tuwθpeyst] *n* a paste which you put on a toothbrush and use to clean your teeth.

top [tɑp] **1.** *n* the highest part of something. **2.** *n* a kind of spinning toy.

topic ['tɑpɪk] *n* a subject or theme.

torch [tortʃ] *n* a light which can be carried about, like a stick which is flaming at one end.

tore [tor] *v* the past tense of tear.

torn [torn] *v* the past participle of tear.

tornado [tor'neydow] *n* a violent, whirling wind that destroys whatever it gets near.

torpedo [tor'pidow] *n* a long, rounded bomb which is fired through or along the surface of the water.

torrent ['torənt] *n* a very fast-moving stream or river.

tortoise ['tortəs] *n* a very slow-moving animal with a very thick shell.

torture ['tortʃɚ] *v* to make someone suffer great pain in order to get a confession or an admission of something.

toss [tɔs] *v* to throw something carelessly into the air.

tot [tɑt] *n* a small child.

total ['towtḷ] **1.** *n* the sum of; the whole amount. **2.** *v* to add up figures.

totter ['tɑtɚ] *v* to walk unsteadily or shake.

touch [tətʃ] *v* to feel something with your fingers or with some part of your body.

tough [təf] *adj* hard; strong; not easily broken.

tour ['tuwɚ] **1.** *n* a visit to a place or a series of places; a vacation which takes you to one or more places. **2.** *v* to visit a place or a series of places.

tourist ['tuwɚɪst] *n* a person visiting a place as part of a vacation.

tournament ['tɚnəmənt] *n* a sports competition where several teams try to win to see which is the best.

tow [tow] *v* to pull something along by a rope.

toward [tord] *prep* in the direction of. Also towards.

towel ['tawəl] *n* a piece of thick cloth or paper that you use to dry things.

tower ['tawɚ] *n* a building or a part of a building that is very high and narrow.

town [tawn] *n* a group of houses and buildings together.

toy [toy] *n* an object that children play with.

trace [treys] *v* to copy a drawing by putting transparent paper over it and going over the lines with a pencil.

track [træk] **1.** *n* a footprint left by a person or an animal. **2.** *v* to follow an animal you are hunting by going along the trail it has made. **3.** *n* one of the iron bars that a railroad train travels on.

tractor ['træktɚ] *n* a powerful engine on wheels that pulls something along.

trade [treyd] **1.** *n* a particular kind of work, such as building things, hairdressing, or house painting. **2.** *v* to buy and sell; to exchange.

tradition [trə'dɪʃn̩] *n* a custom which has been practiced for many years.

traffic ['træfɪk] *n* cars, buses, and trucks moving along the street.

tragedy ['trædʒədi] *n* a disaster; a terribly sad happening.

trail [treyl] *n* footprints or other signs that have been left by someone or something; a path.

trailer ['treylɚ] *n* any wheeled vehicle pulled behind a car or truck.

train [treyn] **1.** *v* to teach. **2.** *n* a line of special cars pulled along railroad tracks by an engine.

trainer ['treynɚ] *n* someone who teaches a person or animal to do something well, like swimming or running a race.

traitor ['treytɚ] *n* someone who betrays his friends or country.

tramp [træmp] **1.** *v* to walk heavily. **2.** *n* a person who goes from place to place, often sleeping out-of-doors and begging for money from other people.

trample ['træmpḷ] *v* to tramp on.

trampoline ['træmpəlin] *n* a large piece of canvas fastened to a frame with springs. *Ex* You can bounce up and down and do somersaults on a trampoline.

transfer 1. *v* [træn(t)s'fɚ, 'træn(t)sfɚ] to carry or send something or someone from one place to another; to change from one bus, plane, or train to another. **2.** *n* ['træn(t)sfɚ] a slip of paper you can get when you ride a bus. It lets you complete your trip on another bus without paying another fare.

transform [træn(t)s'form] *v* to change the way something looks, as a caterpillar is transformed into a butterfly.

transistor [træn'zɪstɚ] **1.** *n* an electronic part which is found in radios, television sets, computers, and other devices. **2.** *n* a transistor radio; a portable radio using transistors.

translate ['træn(t)sleyt] *v* to express the meaning of words in one language in another language.

transparent [træn(t)s'pɛrənt] *adj* easily seen through. *Ex* Window glass is transparent.

transplant 1. *v* [træn(t)s'plænt] to remove a plant from the ground and plant it somewhere else. **2.** *n* ['træn(t)splænt] a kind of surgery in which a diseased part of the body is removed and a healthy part is put in its place.

transportation [træn(t)spɚ'teyʃn] **1.** *n* carrying from one place to another. **2.** *n* things that move people, like buses, trains, cars, planes, and ships.

trap [træp] **1.** *n* a device for catching animals or birds. **2.** *v* to catch something in a trap.

trapeze [træ'piz] *n* a kind of swing with only a thin bar for a seat.

trash [træʃ] *n* rubbish; garbage; useless material that is to be thrown away.

trash can ['træʃ kæn] *n* a bin or a large can for holding trash; a wastebasket.

travel ['trævl̩] **1.** *v* to make a journey; to go from place to place. **2.** *n* journeying; going from one place to another, like you do on a vacation.

tray [trey] *n* a flat piece of wood, metal, or plastic on which a person can carry things, such as cups, saucers, and food.

treacherous ['trɛtʃɚəs] *adj* not to be trusted; likely to betray.

tread [trɛd] *n* the thick, ridged pattern on a bicycle, car, or truck tire.

treasure ['trɛʒɚ] **1.** *n* a collection of money or jewels. **2.** *n* anything which is valuable or much loved.

treasurer ['trɛʒɚɚ] *n* a person who is in charge of the money of a business, government, or a club.

treat [trit] **1.** *v* to act in a certain way toward someone or something. *Ex* He always treats us kindly. **2.** *v* to give a gift of something to someone. *Ex* He treated us to a picnic. **3.** *n* a special outing or a present for which you do not have to pay. *Ex* His treat for us was a picnic. **4.** *n* a bit of candy, ice cream, or cake; something nice to eat.

tree [tri] *n* a very large plant with leaves and branches.

tremble ['trɛmbl̩] *v* to shake or quiver.

tremendous [trə'mɛndəs] *adj* very large; enormous; huge.

tremor ['trɛmɚ] *n* a shaking; a small earthquake.

trench [trɛntʃ] *n* a deep ditch.

trespass ['trɛspæs] *v* to go on someone else's land or property without permission.

trial ['trɑyl] *n* a test to see if something works well; the judging of a person or an issue in a court of law.

triangle ['trɑyæŋgl̩] *n* an area enclosed by three straight lines.

tribe [trɑyb] *n* a group of families who all live together, with one chief who rules them.

trick [trɪk] *n* something clever. *Ex* Some people can do magic tricks, and others can do tricks like walking on a wire.

trickle ['trɪkl̩] **1.** *v* to flow in a very thin stream. **2.** *n* a very thin stream.

tricycle ['trɑysɪkl̩] *n* a three-wheeled cycle.

trigger ['trɪgɚ] *n* the little lever which is pulled to fire a gun.

trigonometry [trɪgə'nɑmətri] *n* the mathematical study of triangles and the arcs and angles that relate to triangles.

trillion ['trɪlyən] *n* the number 1,000,000,000,000.

trim [trɪm] **1.** *v* to make something neat, often by cutting off the rough edges or loose threads. **2.** *v* to decorate a piece of clothing by adding something like lace or ribbon; to decorate a Christmas tree. **3.** *n* cloth, wood, or metal used to decorate something.

trip [trɪp] **1.** *n* a short journey. **2.** *v* to stumble or fall as a result of catching your foot on something.

tropics ['trɑpɪks] *n* the warm, humid parts of the earth. *Ex* I love to go to the tropics on vacation.

trot [trɑt] *v* to run, but not as fast as you can.

trouble ['trəbl] **1.** *n* anything which annoys or causes worry or unhappiness. *Ex* Please try to stay out of trouble. **2.** *v* to annoy or worry someone. *Ex* I am sorry to trouble you.

troublesome ['trəbḷsəm] *adj* causing trouble or difficulty. *Ex* Mr. Long can be very troublesome.

trousers ['trɑwzɚz] *n* a piece of clothing which covers you from your waist to your ankles, fitting around each leg separately; long pants.

trowel ['trɑwl] **1.** *n* a tiny shovel with a curved blade. *Ex* A trowel is used for gardening. **2.** *n* a flat, metal tool with a handle. *Ex* Bricklayers use a trowel to put mortar between bricks.

truce [truws] *n* a cease-fire; an armistice; a stopping of fighting. *Ex* A truce was called, and the fighting stopped.

truck [trək] *n* a strong vehicle used for carrying things from place to place.

trudge [trədʒ] *v* to walk along wearily, with heavy footsteps. *Ex* Joel had to trudge home through the snow.

true [truw] *adj* real; correct; accurate.

trumpet ['trəmpət] *n* a musical instrument which you blow into.

trunk [trəŋk] **1.** *n* the thick stem of a tree. **2.** *n* an elephant's nose. **3.** *n* a big box for sending clothes in.

trust [trəst] **1.** *v* to believe that someone is honest, or that you will not be tricked. **2.** *n* faith in someone or something.

truth [truwθ] *n* whatever is true.

try [trɑy] *v* to test to see if something works; to do the best you can.

trying ['trɑyɪŋ] *adj* annoying; frustrating.

T-shirt ['tiʃɚt] *n* a cotton, pullover shirt with short sleeves. *Ex* Many T-shirts have pictures or writing on them.

tub [təb] *n* an open container for washing in or for holding liquids; a bathtub.

tube [tuwb] **1.** *n* a long, thin, hollow piece of metal, wood, or other material. **2.** *n* a container from which you squeeze out the contents, such as a toothpaste tube.

tuck [tək] *v* to fold something into something else. *Ex* Be sure to tuck the edge of the sheet under the mattress.

tuft [təft] *n* a small bunch of grass, plants, hairs, or feathers growing together in a group.

tug [təg] *v* to pull hard at someone or something.

tugboat ['təgbowt] *n* a small but powerful boat which pulls or pushes large ships.

tug-of-war [təgə'wor] *n* a game in which a team pulls on each end of the same rope. Each team tries to pull the other team over a line.

tulip ['tuwləp] *n* a brightly colored flower with a few large leaves.

tumble ['təmbl̩] v to fall over suddenly.

tumbler ['təmblɚ] n a plain drinking glass.

tummy ['təmi] n stomach; belly.

tuna ['tuwnə] n a large fish which lives in the ocean.

tune [tuwn] **1.** n a melody; a lot of musical notes sounded one after the other to make a piece of music. **2.** v to make the different notes of a musical instrument match the musical scale. *Ex* Our piano needs to be tuned.

tuning fork ['tuwnɪŋ fork] n a metal instrument with two prongs that give out a musical sound when you strike it.

tunnel ['tənl̩] **1.** n a hole cut right through a hill or under the ground. **2.** v to make a tunnel; to burrow.

turbine ['tɚbən] n an engine that works by the force of moving water, steam, or gas.

turf [tɚf] n the top layer of earth with grass growing on it.

turkey ['tɚki] n a big bird with small wings and a fan-shaped tail. *Ex* Americans eat turkey at Thanksgiving.

turn [tɚn] **1.** v to move yourself or some object to the left or the right or all the way around. **2.** n a turning; a place to turn. **3.** n your chance or time to do something. *Ex* Hurry, or you will miss your turn.

turnstile ['tɚnstayl] n a device set in a passageway so that you can go through but you cannot come back out. *Ex* Turnstiles are found at football stadiums and subway stations.

turntable ['tɚnteybl̩] n a flat, circular panel which turns around; the part of a record player which carries a record around and around.

turpentine ['tɚpəntayn] n a kind of very thin oil used to thin paint.

turtle ['tɔtl] *n* a hard-shelled reptile which lives in and around water; a tortoise.

tusk [təsk] *n* one of the two very long teeth that stick out of the mouths of some animals such as elephants.

tutor ['tuwtɚ] *n* a person whose job is to help students learn a school subject by giving them private lessons.

tweed [twid] *n* a thick, wool cloth which is often used to make suits and overcoats.

tweezers ['twizɚz] *n* a very small set of tongs which can be used to take out splinters or pull out single hairs.

twice [twɑys] *adv* two times.

twig [twɪg] *n* a little branch on a tree or a bush.

twilight ['twɑylɑyt] *n* the fading, dim light just before the sun sets.

twin [twɪn] **1.** *n* one of a set of twins. **2.** *adj* paired; matched.

twine [twɑyn] *n* threads twisted together to make strong string.

twinkle ['twɪŋkl̩] *v* to shine and sparkle in flashes, like a star in the sky.

twins [twɪnz] *n* a pair of children or animals born at the same time to the same mother.

twirl [twɚl] *v* to turn around and around very quickly; to turn something around and around very quickly.

twist [twɪst] *v* to bend something; to wind one thing around another; to turn sharply.

type [tɑyp] **1.** *n* something that belongs to or stands for a group of things, like a person or kind of food. **2.** *v* to print words on paper by using a typewriter.

typewriter ['tɑyprɑytɚ] *n* a machine which prints words on paper. *Ex* A typewriter has keys with letters on them which you press.

tyrant ['tɑyrənt] *n* a person who rules over people in a cruel way.

U

ugly ['əgli] *adj* unpleasant to look at; the opposite of pretty.

ulcer ['əlsɚ] *n* an open sore on the skin or inside the body.

umbrella [əm'brɛlə] *n* a round piece of cloth stretched over thin sticks of metal. *Ex* An umbrella is held over a person to keep the rain off.

umpire ['əmpɑyr] *n* someone who decides whether players have broken the rules in baseball.

unable [ən'eybl̩] *adj* not able to do something.

uncle ['əŋkl̩] *n* the brother of your father or mother.

uncomfortable [ən'kəm(p)fɚtəbl̩, ən'kəm(p)ftɚbl̩] *adj* not at ease; feeling awkward.

under ['əndɚ] **1.** *prep* beneath. *Ex* Please put your books under your chair. **2.** *adv* to a lower place; in a lower direction. *Ex* Yes, put them under.

underground ['əndɚgrawnd] **1.** *adv* to a place beneath the surface of the earth. **2.** *adj* beneath the surface of the earth. **3.** *n* the world of criminals.

underline ['əndɚlɑyn] *v* to draw a line under a word.

underneath [əndɚ'niθ] **1.** *prep* under. **2.** *adv* under.

underpants ['əndɚpænts] *n* pants that are worn under regular clothing next to the skin.

understand [əndɚ'stænd] *v* to know what something means. *pt* understood. *pp* understood.

understood [əndɚ'stʊd] *v* the past tense and past participle of understand.

underwear ['əndɚwɛr] *n* clothing worn under regular clothing next to the skin.

undid [ən'dɪd] *v* the past tense of undo.

undo [ən'duw] *v* to unfasten, untie, or open something. *pt* undid. *pp* undone.

undone [ən'dən] *v* the past participle of undo.

undress [ən'drɛs] *v* to take clothing off.

unemployed [ənɪm'plɔyd] *adj* having no job.

unemployment [ənɪm'plɔymənt] *n* the state of not having a job; a state where many workers have no jobs because there are not enough jobs.

unexpected [ənɪk'spɛktəd] *adj* not expected; sudden.

unfortunate [ən'fortʃənət] *adj* unlucky; sad.

unhappy [ən'hæpi] *adj* sad; the opposite of happy.

unhealthy [ən'hɛlθi] *adj* sick; not well; not in good health.

uniform ['yuwnəform] **1.** *adj* similar; identical; same. **2.** *n* special clothes worn by those who belong to groups such as the police or the military.

unimportant [ənɪm'portənt] *adj* not important.

uninteresting [ən'ɪntrəstɪŋ] *adj* not interesting; dull; boring.

union ['yuwnyən] **1.** *n* a joining together; a uniting. **2.** *n* a group of workers who have joined together.

unit ['yuwnət] *n* a single thing; a group; a device or appliance.

unite [yə'nɑyt] *v* to join together; to join something together.

universal [yuwnə'vɚsl] *adj* having to do with everyone everywhere; having to do with the universe.

universe ['yuwnəvɚs] *n* all things existing on earth and in space.

university [yuwnə'vɚsəti] *n* a place where students who have finished high school can go for more education.

unkind [ən'kaynd] *adj* not kind; mean; cruel.

unknown [ən'nown] *adj* not known.

unless [ən'lɛs] *conj* except that.

unload [ən'lowd] *v* to take a load from.

unpleasant [ən'plɛzənt] *adj* not pleasant; nasty.

unsteady [ən'stɛdi] *adj* not steady; shaky.

unsuccessful [ənsək'sɛsfl̩] *adj* not successful; having failed.

untidy [ən'taydi] *adj* not neat; not well arranged.

until [ən'tɪl] **1.** *prep* up to a stated time. **2.** *conj* up to the time that.

unusual [ən'yuwʒəwəl] *adj* not usual; out of the ordinary.

unwell [ən'wɛl] *adj* ill; not healthy.

unwrap [ən'ræp] *v* to take the covering or wrapping off of something.

up [əp] **1.** *prep* toward a higher place. *Ex* Don't climb up the tree. **2.** *adv* toward a higher place. *Ex* Please move up. **3.** *adj* awake.

upon [ə'pɑn] *prep* on; on top of something.

upset [əp'sɛt] **1.** *v* to knock something over. **2.** *adj* worried; sick.

upside-down [əpsayd'dawn] *adj* turned over, with the top part underneath.

upstairs [əp'stɛrz] **1.** *adv* up the stairs; toward a higher floor of a building. **2.** *n* a floor above the ground floor of a building.

upstream [əp'strim] *adv* toward the upper part of a stream; toward the source of a stream.

upward ['əpwəd] *adv* going up; toward the sky.

urban ['ərbn̩] *adj* having to do with towns or cities and not the countryside.

urge [ərdʒ] *v* to try to get someone to do something; to try to persuade.

urinate ['yərəneyt] *v* to release waste fluid from the body.

us [əs] *pro* the objective form of we. *Ex* Please give them to us. Please do it for us.

use 1. *v* [yuwz] to do something with an object made for a special purpose. *Ex* Please use a knife to cut your meat. **2.** *n* [yuws] the using of something; what something is used for.

used [yuwzd] *adj* not new. *Ex* I do not wish to buy a used car.

used to ['yuwstuw] *v* a special phrase meaning *did often in the past. Ex* We used to go to the beach when I was young.

useful ['yuwsfl̩] *adj* helpful; handy and frequently used.

useless ['yuwsləs] *adj* of no use; of no worth or value.

usher ['əʃər] *n* a person who takes people to their seats in theaters or stadiums.

usual ['yuwʒəwəl] *adj* common; happening often or regularly.

usually ['yuwʒ(əw)əli] *adv* almost always; more often than not.

utilities [yuw'tɪlətiz] **1.** *n* the pipes and wires that come into a building, such as wires for the telephone and electricity and pipes for water, gas, and sewage. **2.** *n* the companies that supply water, gas, electricity, and telephone service.

V

vacant ['veykn̩t] *adj* empty; unused.

vacation [vey'keyʃn̩] *n* a period of time off from your job; a trip or a tour.

vaccinate ['væksəneyt] *v* to give an injection which will keep you from getting some diseases.

vaccination [væksə'neyʃn̩] *n* an injection which will prevent disease.

vacuum ['vækyuwm] **1.** *n* a space with no air in it. **2.** *n* a vacuum cleaner; an appliance which sucks dirt up from the floor.

vague [veyg] *adj* not very clear; not very certain.

vain [veyn] *adj* thinking how pretty or good-looking you are; having a very good opinion of yourself.

valentine ['væləntayn] *n* a card or greeting sent to someone special on Saint Valentine's Day, February 14th.

valley ['væli] *n* the low land between two hills or mountains.

valuable ['vælyuw(ə)bl̩] *adj* worth a lot of money; high-priced.

value ['vælyuw] *n* the worth of something; the price or cost of something.

van [væn] *n* a closed motor vehicle used for carrying things or people from place to place.

vanilla [və'nɪlə] *n* a food flavoring which comes from the dried seedpods of a climbing plant.

vanish ['vænɪʃ] *v* to go out of sight very quickly; to disappear.

vanity ['vænəti] *n* pride; vainness; too high an opinion of yourself.

vapor ['veypɚ] *n* mist, steam, or smoke floating in the air.

variety [və'rayəti] *n* a collection of many kinds of things; a show with different kinds of entertainment.

various ['vɛriəs] *adj* different; many; several.

varnish ['vɑrnɪʃ] *n* a clear liquid which is painted on wood to make it look shiny.

vase [veys] *n* a pretty container for putting flowers in.

vast [væst] *adj* huge; very big; immense.

veal [vil] *n* the meat from a calf.

vegetable ['vɛdʒ(ə)təbl̩] *n* any plant used for food.

vehicle ['viəkl̩] *n* anything with wheels used to carry people or things.

veil [veyl] *n* a thin piece of netting or material worn by women to hide their faces or to protect them from strong wind or sunshine.

vein [veyn] *n* one of the long, thin tubes that carries blood around in the body. *Ex* Arteries carry blood away from the heart and veins return blood to the heart.

velvet ['vɛlvət] *n* a soft material that looks and feels like fur with very short hairs.

vending machine ['vɛndɪŋ məʃin] *n* a kind of machine from which people can buy things like soft drinks, candy, and postage stamps.

venetian blinds [vəniʃn̩ 'blɑyndz] *n* a window covering made of wooden, metal, or plastic strips which can be tilted to let light in or keep it out.

vengeance ['vɛndʒn̩(t)s] *n* revenge.

vent [vɛnt] *n* an opening to let air in or out. Short for ventilator.

ventilator ['vɛntʃeytɚ] *n* a small opening in a wall to let stale air out or fresh air in.

veranda [vɚ'ændə] *n* an open porch with a roof, joined on to a house.

verb [vɚb] *n* a grammatical term for a word of doing or being.

verse [vɚs] *n* poetry; part of a poem.

very ['vɛri] **1.** *adj* absolute; exact. **2.** *adv* to a very high degree.

vessel ['vɛsl̩] **1.** *n* a ship. **2.** *n* a container, usually for liquid.

vest [vɛst] *n* a kind of jacket which has no sleeves; a waistcoat.

vet [vɛt] *n* a veterinarian.

veterinarian [vɛt(ə)rə'nɛriən] *n* a doctor for sick animals.

veto ['vitow] *n* the power to say no; a president's or a governor's power to say no to a law passed by a legislature.

viaduct ['vayədəkt] *n* a long bridge which carries a road or railway over a valley or low-lying area.

vice president [vays 'prɛzədənt] *n* the officer second in power to a president.

vicious ['vɪʃəs] *adj* wicked; fierce; very spiteful.

victim ['vɪktəm] *n* a person who is hurt or is killed by someone else's action.

victory ['vɪktɚi] *n* the winning of a battle, contest, or game.

video ['vɪdiow] **1.** *n* the part of a television broadcast which you see. **2.** *adj* pertaining to pictures broadcast or recorded on tape or video disk.

video disk ['vɪdiow dɪsk] *n* a disk like a phonograph record which has pictures and sounds recorded on it. *Ex* A video disk is played on a special player which is attached to a television set.

videotape ['vɪdiowteyp] **1.** *n* a special tape on which television pictures and sound are recorded with the help of a special machine. **2.** *v* to record pictures and sound on a videotape.

view [vyuw] **1.** *n* what you can see in front of you. **2.** *n* a special sight; a good image of something. **3.** *v* to watch something, like a film or television.

vigor ['vɪgɚ] *n* strength; energy.

village ['vɪlɪdʒ] *n* houses and buildings all together, like a town but smaller.

villain ['vɪlən] *n* a bad man; a rogue.

vine [vɑyn] *n* a plant that creeps up a pole, a fence, a wall, or along the ground.

vinegar ['vɪnəgɚ] *n* a sour liquid used in salads and pickles.

vinyl ['vɑynl̩] *n* a kind of plastic.

violent ['vɑy(ə)lənt] *adj* very rough; forceful.

violet ['vɑy(ə)lət] **1.** *n* a small plant with purple, pink, or white flowers. **2.** *n* a light purple color. **3.** *adj* of a light purple color.

violin [vɑyə'lɪn] *n* a musical instrument with four strings. A violin is held under the chin and played with a special stick called a bow.

virus ['vɑyrəs] **1.** *n* a very simple form of living matter which can cause disease. *Ex* A virus is too tiny to be seen. **2.** *n* a case of influenza; the flu or a bad cold.

visa ['vizə] *n* a note on your passport saying that it is all right to visit a certain country.

visibility [vizə'bıləti] *n* the clearness with which things can be seen. *Ex* It is foggy, and there is very low visibility.

visible ['vizəbl̩] *adj* able to be seen.

vision ['viʒn̩] *n* the ability to see; eyesight.

visit ['vizət] **1.** *v* to go somewhere and see what it is like there; to stop by the house of a friend; to call on someone. **2.** *n* an act of visiting. *Ex* We paid a visit to Joel's parents.

visitor ['vizətɚ] *n* a person who visits; a person who is visiting you.

vitamin ['vaytəmən] *n* a substance in foods that is good for you beause it keeps you healthy. *Ex* Milk and oranges have lots of vitamins.

vivid ['vivəd] *n* very bright; brilliant.

vocabulary [vow'kæbyələri] **1.** *n* all the words that a person uses or understands. **2.** *n* a list of words, usually in alphabetical order.

voice [voys] *n* the sound that comes from people's mouths when they speak or sing.

volcano [val'keynow] *n* a cone-shaped mountain that throws out hot ashes or liquid rock from an opening.

volleyball ['valibɔl] **1.** *n* a game played by two teams which hit a ball back and forth over a net. **2.** *n* the ball used in the game of volleyball.

volume ['valyuwm] **1.** *n* the amount, quantity, or bulk of something. **2.** *n* a book.

volunteer [vɑlən'tir] **1.** *v* to offer to do something that you do not have to do. **2.** *n* a person who volunteers.

vomit ['vɑmət] **1.** *n* food and liquid thrown up from the stomach when you are sick. **2.** *v* to throw up food and liquid from the stomach.

vote [vowt] *v* to cast a ballot in an election; to mark a piece of paper to show whom you wish to be elected.

vow [vɑw] *n* a solemn promise.

vowel ['vɑwl] *n* a speech sound which is not a consonant. *Ex* In English [i, ɪ, ɛ, ey, æ, ɑ, ɔ, ow, ʊ, uw, ə] are the vowel sounds. Vowels are often written with the letters *a, e, i, o, u.*

voyage ['voyɪdʒ] *n* a long journey by sea or in space.

vulgar ['vəlgɚ] *n* rude; not very polite.

vulture ['vəltʃɚ] *n* a large bird of prey that eats dead flesh.

W

wad [wɑd] *n* a bundle of paper, often used for packing.

waddle ['wɑdḷ] *v* to walk with short steps, rocking from side to side, as a duck does.

wade [weyd] *v* to walk in water.

wag [wæg] *v* to move something up and down or from side to side, as when a dog wags its tail.

wage [weydʒ] *n* payment for working at a regular job.

wagon ['wægņ] *n* an open vehicle with four wheels, used to carry heavy loads; a toy wagon.

wail [weyl] **1.** *v* to make a long, sad crying noise. **2.** *n* a long, sad crying noise.

waist [weyst] *n* the narrow, middle part of the body, above the hips.

wait [weyt] *v* to stay in place until someone comes or something happens.

waiter ['weytɚ] *n* a man who takes orders and serves food in a cafe or restaurant.

waitress ['weytrəs] *n* a woman who takes orders and serves food in a cafe or restaurant.

wake [weyk] **1.** *v* to become awake after being asleep; to wake up someone who is asleep. *pt* waked, woke. *pp* waked, woke, woken. **2.** *n* the trail left in water by a ship or boat. **3.** *n* a time of keeping watch over the body of a dead friend or relative.

walk [wɔk] **1.** *v* to move along on your feet, more slowly than running. **2.** *n* an act of walking.

walkie-talkie ['wɔki'tɔki] *n* a radio carried with you when you walk, used to send and receive messages.

wall [wɔl] *n* something built of wood, bricks, or other material, like the sides of a house or a building.

wallet ['wɑlət] *n* a small pocket case, usually of leather, for carrying paper money, tickets, stamps, and personal papers.

wallpaper ['wɔlpeypɚ] **1.** *n* a special kind of paper put on the inside walls of houses as decoration. **2.** *v* to glue wallpaper to the wall.

wand [wɑnd] *n* a magic stick used by fairies or by magicians when they do magic tricks.

wander ['wɑndɚ] *v* to roam about from place to place.

want [wɑnt] **1.** *v* to wish for, desire, or need something. **2.** *n* desire; need; lack.

war [wor] *n* a fight between two or more countries. *Ex* If two groups of people in the same country fight with each other, it is called civil war.

ward [word] *n* a large room in a hospital, where there are a number of beds for sick people.

warm [worm] **1.** *adj* more hot than cold. **2.** *v* to make something warm.

warm-blooded ['worm'blədəd] *adj* having a constant body temperature. *Ex* Humans and other mammals are warm-blooded.

warn [worn] *v* to tell someone to be careful because something dangerous might happen.

warp [worp] *v* to twist out of shape.

warrior ['wɔryɚ] *n* a man who fights for his country in time of war; an old-fashioned word for soldier.

warship ['wɔrʃɪp] *n* a ship that has guns and weapons for fighting in a war.

wart [wɔrt] *n* a small lump on the skin, usually on the hands or face.

was [wəz] *v* the past tense of the verb *be* which is used with *I, he, she,* and *it.*

wash [wɔʃ] *v* to make clean, using soap and water.

washroom ['wɔʃruwm] *n* a restroom.

wasn't ['wəznt] *cont* was not.

wasp [wɑsp] *n* a stinging insect something like a bee.

waste [weyst] **1.** *v* to use something up or spend money carelessly. **2.** *n* trash; rubbish; material defecated or urinated from a living body.

wastebasket ['weys(t)bæskət] *n* a small trash can in a room of a house or other building.

watch [watʃ] **1.** *v* to look at closely. **2.** *n* a small clock worn on the wrist or carried in a pocket.

watchful ['watʃfl] *adj* careful.

watchman ['watʃmən] *n* a man whose job is to keep watch over something, such as a building, usually at night.

water ['wɔtɚ] **1.** *n* the clear liquid in lakes, rivers, and oceans. **2.** *v* to put water on plants or lawns.

water closet ['wɔtɚ klɑzət] **1.** *n* a small room containing a bowl which has a rushing flow of water to carry away waste through a pipe; a bathroom; a restroom; a washroom. **2.** *n* a bowl which has a rushing flow of water to carry away waste through a pipe; a toilet. It is called the W.C. for short.

water cooler ['wɔtɚ kuwlɚ] *n* a machine which makes drinking water cool and makes it squirt in a stream when a button is pressed, usually found in the hallway of a public building.

waterfall ['wɔtɚfɔl] *n* a stream of water flowing down from a high place.

water fountain ['wɔtɚ fɑwntn̩] *n* a little sink where the water squirts out in a stream when turned on. It is sometimes called a fountain.

watermelon ['wɔtɚmɛlən] *n* a large melon, one or two feet long, filled with good-tasting, red material.

waterproof ['wɔtɚpruwf] *adj* able to keep water out. *Ex* My raincoat is waterproof.

wave [weyv] **1.** *n* a ridge of water moving on the surface of the sea or a lake. **2.** *v* to move something, like your hand or a flag, back and forth or up and down.

wavy ['weyvi] *adj* curving in and out.

wax [wæks] *n* a soft, yellowish material used in making candles. *Ex* Bees make wax to build the inside of their hives.

way [wey] **1.** *n* a road or path. **2.** *n* how to do something, like how to paint a picture.

we [wi] *pro* you and I; my group and I (but not you); you and I and others. *Ex* We are quite happy now. We are going to do it for you.

weak [wik] *adj* not strong.

weaken ['wikn̩] *v* to grow weak; to make something weak.

wealth [wɛlθ] *n* great riches; a lot of money.

wean [win] *v* to train a young child or young mammal to eat solid food rather than milk.

weapon ['wɛpṇ] *n* anything used to fight or hunt with, such as a gun, a heavy stick, or a bow and arrow.

wear [wɛr] *v* to be dressed in. *Ex* You wear thin clothes in summer and thick clothes in winter. *pt* wore. *pp* worn.

weary ['wɪri] *adj* very tired.

weather ['wɛðɚ] *n* the kind of day it is outside; the temperature of the air, the speed of the wind, and the amount of clouds in the sky.

weather vane ['wɛðɚ veyn] *n* a flat piece of metal, shaped like a rooster or a horse, that shows the direction of the wind.

weave [wiv] *v* to make cloth by twisting threads over and under each other. *pt* wove. *pp* woven.

web [wɛb] *n* the lacy net that spiders spin to trap insects.

we'd [wid] *cont* we would; we had.

wedding ['wɛdɪŋ] *n* a marriage ceremony where a man and a woman become husband and wife.

wedge [wɛdʒ] *n* a triangular piece of metal or wood, very thin at one end and thicker at the other. *Ex* A wedge is put between two things to hold them firm or to push them apart.

weed [wid] *n* one of many kinds of wild plants which grow where they are not wanted in gardens or among farm crops.

week [wik] *n* seven days; the seven days starting on Monday and ending on Sunday; the seven days starting on Sunday and ending on Saturday.

weekday ['wikdey] *n* any day of the week except Saturday or Sunday.

weekend ['wikɛnd] *n* Saturday and Sunday.

weekly ['wikli] *adv* every week; once every week.

weep [wip] *v* to cry tears. *pt* wept. *pp* wept.

weigh [wey] *v* to find out how heavy something is; to have a particular weight.

weight [weyt] *n* the amount that something weighs.

weird [wird] *adj* strange and frightening.

welcome ['wɛlkəm] *v* to greet someone with joy.

welfare ['wɛl'fɛr] **1.** *n* well-being; prosperity. **2.** *n* payments made to people to improve their well-being.

well [wɛl] **1.** *n* a deep hole in the ground from which oil or water is obtained. **2.** *adv* healthy; properly; skillfully.

we'll [wil] *cont* we will.

went [wɛnt] *v* the past tense of go.

wept [wɛpt] *v* the past tense and past participle of weep.

were [wɚ] *v* the past tense form of the verb *be* that is used with *you, we,* and *they.*

we're [wir] *cont* we are.

weren't [wɚnt] *cont* were not.

west [wɛst] *n* the direction in which the sun sets; the direction opposite to east.

wet [wɛt] **1.** *adj* not dry; covered or soaked with liquid. **2.** *v* to make something wet.

we've [wiv] *cont* we have.

whack [hwæk] *v* to strike something so hard that it makes a noise.

whale [hweyl] *n* a huge mammal found in the sea.

wharf [worf] *n* a landing place for loading and unloading ships.

what [hwət] **1.** *pro* which one; that which. **2.** *adj* which.

wheat [hwit] *n* a kind of grain from which flour is made.

wheel [hwil] *n* a large, flat circle made of wood or metal. *Ex* Cars, buses, and bicycles must have wheels to be able to move.

wheelbarrow ['hwilbɛrow] *n* a kind of small cart with only one wheel. *Ex* Wheelbarrows are used for carrying leaves, grass, or building materials.

when [hwɛn] *adv* at what time; at the time that.

whenever [hwɛn'ɛvɚ] *adv* at any time that; at every time that.

where [hwɛr] *adv* at what place.

wherever [hwɛr'ɛvɚ] *adv* at whatever place; to whatever place.

whether ['hwɛðɚ] *conj* if or if not.

which [hwɪtʃ] **1.** *pro* one of two or more people or things. *Ex* I don't know which to buy. **2.** *adj* having to do with one or another one. *Ex* I don't know which one to buy.

whiff [hwɪf] *n* a sudden puff of air, smoke, or scent.

while [hwɑyl] **1.** *n* time; a period of time. **2.** *conj* during the time that; as long as.

whimper ['hwɪmpɚ] *v* to cry in a low, whining voice.

whine [hwɑyn] *v* to make a sad, complaining, crying sound.

whip [hwɪp] **1.** *n* a piece of thin, strong cord or leather attached to a handle. **2.** *v* to beat something with a whip; to stir up eggs or cream very quickly.

whirl [hwɚl] *v* to turn around and around very quickly.

whisk [hwɪsk] **1.** *v* to move, sweep, or stir something very quickly. **2.** *n* a kitchen tool used for whipping eggs or cream.

whisker ['hwɪskɚ] *n* one of the stiff hairs on a man's face, or at the sides of the mouths of some animals such as cats, lions, and tigers.

whiskey ['hwɪski] *n* a very strong, alcoholic drink made from grain.

whisper ['hwɪspɚ] **1.** *v* to speak so softly that only someone very close to you can hear. **2.** *n* something spoken with a whispering voice.

whistle ['hwɪsl] **1.** *v* to make a high musical sound by blowing through your mouth with your lips nearly closed. **2.** *n* an act of whistling. **3.** *n* a small, tube-like instrument which makes a whistling sound when you blow it.

white [hwɑyt] **1.** *n* the color of snow. **2.** *adj* of a white color.

who [huw] *pro* what person or persons; which person or persons. *Ex* Who are you? I know who you are. He is the man who sold me the car.

whole [howl] **1.** *n* an entire thing, not part of it. **2.** *adj* entire; all, not a part.

whom [huwm] *pro* a form of *who* used with a preposition or as an object of a verb. *Ex* Whom did you see? To whom did you send the letter?

whoop [hwuwp] **1.** *n* a loud cry or shout. **2.** *v* to shout; to cry out.

why [hwɑy] **1.** *adv* for what reason. *Ex* Why did you come here? **2.** *conj* the reason for. *Ex* I don't know why you did that.

wick [wɪk] *n* the twisted threads of cotton in a candle or lamp, which you light.

wicked ['wɪkəd] *adj* evil; very bad.

wide [wɑyd] *adj* a long way from one side to the other; broad; the opposite of narrow.

widow ['wɪdow] *n* a woman whose husband is dead.

widower ['wɪdowɚ] *n* a man whose wife is dead.

width [wɪdθ] *n* how wide or broad something is.

wiener ['winɚ] *n* a sausage which is eaten in a long bun; a hot dog.

wife [wɑyf] *n* a married woman.

wig [wɪg] *n* false hair worn on the head.

wiggly ['wɪgli] *adj* moving back and forth; not able to sit still.

wild [wɑyld] **1.** *adj* not kept or looked after by people; untamed. **2.** *adj* acting like a wild animal. *Ex* Arthur, you are acting wild. Calm down!

wilderness ['wɪldɚnəs] *n* a wild area of land where no one lives.

wildflower ['wɑyldflawɚ] *n* a flower that grows without being planted by anyone.

will [wɪl] *v* a word that expresses the future. *Ex* I will do it tomorrow. *pt* would.

willful ['wɪlfl] **1.** *adj* always wanting your own way. **2.** *adj* intentional; on purpose.

willing ['wɪlɪŋ] *adj* pleased to do something you are asked to do.

willow ['wɪlow] *n* a tree with long, bending branches and narrow leaves.

win [wɪn] *v* to come first in something like a race or a game. *pt* won. *pp* won.

wind **1.** *n* [wɪnd] fast-moving air that blows things about. **2.** *v* [waynd] to turn or twist something around, like winding up a ball of string.

windmill ['wɪndmɪl] *n* a machine that is worked by the wind. *Ex* Windmills are used to pump water.

window ['wɪndow] *n* a glass-covered opening in the wall of a building, which lets light and air in.

windy ['wɪndi] *adj* having to do with a day when the wind is blowing hard.

wine [wayn] *n* a strong drink made from the juice of grapes.

wing [wɪŋ] *n* one of the two feathered parts of a bird's body with which it flies. Airplanes and insects also have wings.

wink [wɪŋk] **1.** *v* to shut and open one eye quickly; for a light to turn on and off quickly. **2.** *n* an act of winking.

winner ['wɪnɚ] *n* the team or person who wins a game or a contest.

winter ['wɪntɚ] *n* the coldest season of the year; the season between fall and spring.

wipe [wayp] *v* to clean or dry something by rubbing.

wire [wayr] *n* a long, thin piece of metal.

wise [wayz] *adj* knowing and understanding a lot of things.

wish [wɪʃ] **1.** *v* to want something very much. **2.** *n* a desire for something; a statement of hope that something will happen.

wit [wɪt] *n* understanding; cleverness.

witch [wɪtʃ] *n* a wicked, dangerous woman who is supposed to be able to do magic.

with [wɪθ] *prep* near to; alongside; against. *Ex* I can only play with kids my own age. Elaine is over there with Rachel. Please don't fight with each other.

withdraw [wɪθ'drɔ] *v* to leave; to remove yourself officially, as from a class or a school.

wither ['wɪðɚ] *v* to dry up; to shrivel.

within [wɪθ'ɪn] *prep* inside; in the inner part.

without [wɪθ'ɑwt] **1.** *prep* lacking. *Ex* I can't write without a pencil. **2.** *adv* not having. *Ex* You will have to do without. **3.** *n* outside. *Ex* There is enough trouble here, and we don't need any more from without.

witness ['wɪtnəs] *n* someone who has seen something happen; someone who has seen something happen and tells about it in a court of law.

witty ['wɪti] *adj* clever and amusing.

wizard ['wɪzɚd] *n* a man who is supposed to be able to do magic.

wobble ['wɑbl̩] *v* to rock unsteadily from side to side.

woke [wowk] *v* a past tense and past participle of wake.

woken ['wowkn̩] *v* a past participle of wake.

wolf [wʊlf] *n* a dangerous, wild animal that looks like a large dog.

woman ['wʊmən] *n* a grown-up female human being.

women ['wɪmən] *n* the plural of woman

won [wən] *v* the past tense and past participle of win.

wonder ['wəndɚ] **1.** *v* to question; to want to know. **2.** *v* to be surprised at something marvelous, unexpected, or strange. **3.** *n* a miracle; something that holds all of your attention.

wonderful ['wəndɚfḷ] *adj* marvelous; amazing.

wonderland ['wəndɚlænd] *n* an imaginary country where amazing and wonderful things happen.

won't [wownt] *cont* will not.

wood [wʊd] *n* the material that trees are made of. *Ex* Our furniture is made of wood.

wooden ['wʊdn̩] *adj* made of wood; hard and stiff like wood.

woodpecker ['wʊdpɛkɚ] *n* a wild bird that pecks holes in the bark of trees to find insects for food.

woodwork ['wʊdwɚk] *n* carpentry; the wooden part of a building or furniture.

wool [wʊl] *n* the thick, warm covering of hair on a sheep, which is made into such things as blankets and clothing.

woolen ['wʊlən] *adj* made of wool.

word [wɚd] *n* a spoken sound or group of letters that means something when you hear it or see it.

wore [wor] *v* the past tense of wear.

work [wɚk] **1.** *v* to do something useful; to do a job. **2.** *n* a person's job; activity; effort.

workbook ['wɚkbʊk] *n* an exercise book in which you can write the answers.

workman ['wɚkmən] *n* a man who works with his hands, often using tools or machinery.

world [wɚld] *n* the earth, the people and things on it, and the air around it.

worm [wɚm] *n* a small, snake-like animal which lives in the soil and makes tiny tunnels in the earth.

worn [worn] **1.** *adj* shabby or ragged. **2.** *v* the past participle of wear.

worry ['wɚi] **1.** *v* to be afraid that something is going to go wrong or that something bad may happen to someone. **2.** *n* a fear that something will go wrong.

worse [wɚs] *adj* not so good; more bad.

worship ['wɚʃəp] **1.** *v* to honor and praise someone or something; to honor and praise God. **2.** *n* the praising of God.

worst [wɚst] *adj* most bad.

worth [wɚθ] **1.** *n* the value of something. *Ex* That is a diamond of great worth. **2.** *prep* deserving of. *Ex* That book is worth reading.

worthless ['wɚθləs] *adj* not worth anything; no good.

would [wʊd] *v* the past of will.

wouldn't ['wʊdn̩t] *cont* would not.

wound 1. *v* [wɑwnd] the past tense and past participle of wind. **2.** *v* [wuwnd] to injure; to make a cut in flesh. **3.** *n* [wuwnd] a cut; an injury to the skin.

wove [wowv] *v* the past tense of weave.

woven ['wowvn̩] *v* the past participle of weave.

wrap [ræp] *v* to cover something by folding paper or cloth around it. *Ex* I wrapped my mother's birthday present in red paper.

wrath [ræθ] *n* great anger.

wreath [riθ] *n* a ring of flowers or leaves twisted together.

wreck [rɛk] **1.** *n* something that has been destroyed or made useless. *Ex* That old car looks like a wreck. **2.** *v* to destroy. *Ex* Mr. Franklin wrecked his new car.

wrench [rɛntʃ] *n* a tool used to tighten bolts.

wriggle ['rɪgl̩] *v* to move about by twisting and turning.

wring [rɪŋ] *v* to make water come out of something, like wet clothes, by twisting and squeezing. *pt* wrung. *pp* wrung.

wringer ['rɪŋɚ] *n* a machine with two rollers that wring the water out of wet laundry.

wrinkle ['rɪŋkl̩] *n* a small fold or crease in cloth, paper, or the skin of old people.

wrist [rɪst] *n* the part of your arm that joins on to your hand.

write [rɑyt] *v* to draw letters or words so that people can read them. *pt* wrote. *pp* written.

writhe [rɑyð] *v* to wriggle or twist about.

writing ['rɑytɪŋ] *n* something that has been written.

written ['rɪtn̩] *v* the past participle of write.

wrong [rɔŋ] *adj* not right; evil or wicked.

wrote [rowt] *v* the past tense of write.

wrung [rəŋ] *v* the past tense and past participle of wring.

X

X ray ['ɛks rey] **1.** *n* a special kind of photograph which shows doctors what the inside of your body looks like. **2.** *v* to take a photograph using X rays.

xylophone ['zɑyləfown] *n* a set of narrow pieces of wood that make musical sounds when they are hit with wooden hammers.

Y

yacht [yɑt] *n* a kind of boat, usually with sails, used for racing or for pleasure.

yard [yɑrd] **1.** *n* a space, usually closed in by buildings or a fence. **2.** *n* a measurement of 36 inches or 3 feet.

yarn [yɑrn] **1.** *n* thread made from wool, cotton, or some other fiber. **2.** *n* a story told by a traveler.

yawn [yɔn] **1.** *v* to open your mouth wide and breathe air slowly inward and then let it out. *Ex* The speech made me sleepy, and I yawned three times. **2.** *n* an act of yawning.

year [yir] *n* a length of time. 365 days, 52 weeks, or 12 months make a year.

yearly ['yɪrli] *adv* every year; once each year.

yell [yɛl] **1.** *v* to call out very loudly; to shout. **2.** *n* a shout; a very loud call.

yellow ['yɛlow] **1.** *n* the color of a lemon or an egg yolk. **2.** *adj* of a yellow color.

Yellow Pages ['yɛlow peydʒəz] *n* the yellow-colored pages at the end of the telephone book where the business numbers are listed.

yes [yɛs] **1.** *adv* a word you say when you agree. **2.** *n* a statement of agreement.

yesterday ['yɛstɚdey] **1.** *n* the day before today; the past. **2.** *adv* on the day before today.

yet [yɛt] **1.** *conj* but. *Ex* He hasn't done it, yet he could if he tried. **2.** *adv* even; still; by now. *Ex* Here it is noon, and he hasn't done it yet.

yield [yild] **1.** *v* to give up, as when the enemy surrenders. **2.** *v* to produce, as when a field of wheat produces a good crop.

yogurt ['yowgɚt] *n* slightly sour, thick milk, often mixed with a fruity flavoring.

yolk [yowk] *n* the yellow part of an egg.

yonder ['yɑndɚ] *adv* over there, beyond.

you [yuw] *pro* the person being talked to. *Ex* How are you? You look quite happy.

you'd [yuwd] *cont* you would; you had.

you'll [yuwl] *cont* you will.

young [yəŋ] *adj* not old; in the early part of life.

youngster ['yəŋ(k)stɚ] *n* a young person who is not yet grown up.

your [yɚ] *pro* belonging to you. *Ex* Please put your coat in the closet.

you're [yɚ] *cont* you are

yours [yɚz] *pro* that which belongs to you. *Ex* That coat is yours.

yourself [yɚ'sɛlf] *pro* you and no one else.

youth [yuwθ] **1.** *n* the time when you are young; the quality of being young. **2.** *n* a young man.

you've [yuwv] *cont* you have

yo-yo ['yowyow] *n* a toy in the shape of a reel, which spins up and down on a string.

Z

zebra ['zibrə] *n* a wild animal like a small horse with stripes.

zero ['zirow] *n* nothing; a number (0) indicating none or nothing.

zigzag ['zɪgzæg] *adj* moving from side to side; turning to the left and right, over and over, while moving forward.

zinc [zɪŋk] *n* a bluish-white metal.

zip [zɪp] **1.** *n* a zip code. **2.** *v* to close a zipper.

zip code ['zɪp kowd] *n* a long number which is the last part of an address in the U.S.

zipper ['zɪpɚ] *n* a long metal or plastic fastener used to close purses, bags, and clothing.

zone [zown] *n* an area or section; an area of the world which is different from other areas.

zoo [zuw] *n* a place where wild animals are kept and people can come to look at them. The word is short for zoological gardens.

Facts About the States

State & Abbreviation	Capital	Major City
Alabama AL	Montgomery	Birmingham
Alaska AK	Juneau	Anchorage
Arizona AZ	Phoenix	Phoenix
Arkansas AR	Little Rock	Little Rock
California CA	Sacramento	Los Angeles
Colorado CO	Denver	Denver
Connecticut CT	Hartford	Hartford
Delaware DE	Dover	Wilmington
District of Columbia DC		Washington
Florida FL	Tallahassee	Jacksonville
Georgia GA	Atlanta	Atlanta
Hawaii HI	Honolulu	Honolulu
Idaho ID	Boise	Boise
Illinois IL	Springfield	Chicago
Indiana IN	Indianapolis	Indianapolis
Iowa IA	Des Moines	Des Moines
Kansas KS	Topeka	Wichita
Kentucky KY	Frankfort	Louisville
Louisiana LA	Baton Rouge	New Orleans
Maine ME	Augusta	Portland
Maryland MD	Annapolis	Baltimore
Massachusetts MA	Boston	Boston
Michigan MI	Lansing	Detroit
Minnesota MN	St. Paul	Minneapolis
Mississippi MS	Jackson	Jackson
Missouri MO	Jefferson City	St. Louis
Montana MT	Helena	Billings
Nebraska NE	Lincoln	Omaha
Nevada NV	Carson City	Las Vegas
New Hampshire NH	Concord	Manchester
New Jersey NJ	Trenton	Newark
New Mexico NM	Santa Fe	Albuquerque
New York NY	Albany	New York City
North Carolina NC	Raleigh	Charlotte
North Dakota ND	Bismarck	Fargo

Ohio OH	Columbus	Cleveland
Oklahoma OK	Oklahoma City	Oklahoma C
Oregon OR	Salem	Portland
Pennsylvania PA	Harrisburg	Philadelphia
Rhode Island RI	Providence	Providence
South Carolina SC	Columbia	Columbia
South Dakota SD	Pierre	Sioux Falls
Tennessee TN	Nashville	Memphis
Texas TX	Austin	Houston
Utah UT	Salt Lake City	Salt Lake Cit
Vermont VT	Montpelier	Burlington
Virginia VA	Richmond	Norfolk
Washington WA	Olympia	Seattle
West Virginia WV	Charleston	Huntington
Wisconsin WI	Madison	Milwaukee
Wyoming WY	Cheyenne	Cheyenne
Guam GU	Agana	Agana
Puerto Rico PR	San Juan	San Juan
Virgin Islands VI	Charlotte Amalie	Charlotte Am

Presidents of the United States

No.	Name	Years in Office
1	George Washington	1789–97
2	John Adams	1797–1801
3	Thomas Jefferson	1801–09
4	James Madison	1809–17
5	James Monroe	1817–25
6	John Quincy Adams	1825–29
7	Andrew Jackson	1829–37
8	Martin Van Buren	1837–41
9	William Henry Harrison	1841
10	John Tyler	1841–45
11	James K. Polk	1845–49
12	Zachary Taylor	1849–50

13	Millard Fillmore	1850–53
14	Franklin Pierce	1853–57
15	James Buchanan	1857–61
16	Abraham Lincoln	1861–65
17	Andrew Johnson	1865–69
18	Ulysses S. Grant	1869–77
19	Rutherford B. Hayes	1877–81
20	James A. Garfield	1881
21	Chester A. Arthur	1881–85
22	Grover Cleveland	1885–89
23	Benjamin Harrison	1889–93
24	Grover Cleveland	1893–97
25	William McKinley	1897–1901
26	Theodore Roosevelt	1901–09
27	William Howard Taft	1909–13
28	Woodrow Wilson	1913–21
29	Warren G. Harding	1921–23
30	Calvin Coolidge	1923–29
31	Herbert Hoover	1929–33
32	Franklin D. Roosevelt	1933–45
33	Harry S. Truman	1945–53
34	Dwight D. Eisenhower	1953–61
35	John F. Kennedy	1961–63
36	Lyndon B. Johnson	1963–69
37	Richard M. Nixon	1969–74
38	Gerald R. Ford	1974–77
39	Jimmy Carter	1977–81
40	Ronald W. Reagan	1981–89
41	George H. W. Bush	1989–93
42	William J. Clinton	1993–

National Holidays
of the United States of America

New Year's Day	*January 1st*
Martin Luther King Day*†	*January 15th*
Abraham Lincoln's Birthday*	*February 12th*

George Washington's	
Birthday†	*February 22nd*
Memorial Day*†	*May 30th*
Fourth of July	
(Independence Day)	*July 4th*
Labor Day	*First Monday in September*
Columbus Day*†	*October 12th*
Election Day*	*First Tuesday in November*
Veterans Day†	*November 11th*
Thanksgiving Day	*Third Thursday in November*
Christmas Day	*December 25th*

*These are legal holidays (banks, schools, government offices close) only in some of the states.

†For all federal employees, and in some states, these holidays are celebrated on Mondays, regardless of their actual dates.

Numbers

Cardinals		*Ordinals*	
1	one	1st	first
2	two	2nd	second
3	three	3rd	third
4	four	4th	fourth
5	five	5th	fifth
6	six	6th	sixth
7	seven	7th	seventh
8	eight	8th	eighth
9	nine	9th	ninth
10	ten	10th	tenth
11	eleven	11th	eleventh
12	twelve	12th	twelfth
13	thirteen	13th	thirteenth
14	fourteen	14th	fourteenth
15	fifteen	15th	fifteenth
16	sixteen	16th	sixteenth

17	seventeen	17th	seventeenth
18	eighteen	18th	eighteenth
19	nineteen	19th	nineteenth
20	twenty	20th	twentieth
21	twenty-one	21st	twenty-first
30	thirty	30th	thirtieth
40	forty	40th	fortieth
50	fifty	50th	fiftieth
60	sixty	60th	sixtieth
70	seventy	70th	seventieth
80	eighty	80th	eightieth
90	ninety	90th	ninetieth
100	one hundred	100th	(one) hundredth
101	one hundred one	101st	(one) hundred first
200	two hundred	200th	two-hundredth
300	three hundred	300th	three-hundredth
400	four hundred	400th	four-hundredth
500	five hundred	500th	five-hundredth
600	six hundred	600th	six-hundredth
700	seven hundred	700th	seven-hundredth
800	eight hundred	800th	eight-hundredth
900	nine hundred	900th	nine-hundredth
1000	one thousand	1000th	(one) thousandth
100,000	one hundred thousand	100,000th	(one) hundred thousandth
1,000,000	one million	1,000,000th	(one) millionth

Most Common Fractions

½	one-half
⅓	one-third
¼	one-fourth or one quarter
⅕	one-fifth
⅗	three-fifths
⅛	one-eighth
⅝	five-eighths